Praise for *Reclain*

"An electrifying read that will entertain and enlighten. A real eye-opener and heart activator. Read it now!"

—Joe Vitale, bestselling author, *The Attractor Factor*

"Lee has done it again. This is a great book full of practical and easy-to-apply wisdom about how to manifest the life of your dreams. I highly recommend it."

—Jack Canfield, CEO of the Canfield Training Group,
author of *The Success Principles*

"Lee Milteer's down-to-earth book, *Reclaim the Magic*, is crammed full of stories and information to help you get from where you are to where you want to be. Her successful life is evidence that she follows her own advice. Good job, Lee."

—Raymon Grace, author and lecturer

"Lee Milteer's *Reclaim the Magic* is a profound book for spiritual development. Opening with a shocking personal story, Lee demonstrates how her tragedies propelled her to deeper self-awareness and self-knowledge. Here is a comprehensive guide to the best spiritual tools currently available for overcoming past disappointment, negativity, fear, shame, and guilt to claim the life you really desire. I highly recommend this book to new and seasoned students on the path of self-development. This book—and Ms. Milteer—are the "real deal."

—Baeth Davis, *http://YourPurpose.com*

RECLAIM *the* MAGIC

The Real Secrets to Manifesting Anything You Want

LEE MILTEER

RAINBOW RIDGE
BOOKS

Cover and interior design by Frame25 Productions
Cover photo © Igor Zh. c/o Shutterstock.com

Published by:
Rainbow Ridge Books, LLC
140 Rainbow Ridge Road
Faber, Virginia 22938
www.rainbowridgebooks.com
434-361-1723

If you are unable to order this book from your local bookseller, you may order directly from the distributor.

Square One Publishers, Inc.
115 Herricks Road
Garden City Park, NY 11040
Phone: (516) 535-2010
Fax: (516) 535-2014
Toll-free: 877-900-BOOK

Visit the author at:
www.milteer.com
www.leemilteerschoolofwisdom.com

Library of Congress Cataloging-in-Publication Data applied for.

ISBN 978-1-937907-33-4

10 9 8 7 6 5 4 3 2 1

Printed on acid-free recycled paper in the United States of America

This book is dedicated to my soul mate: Clifton Williams.

You are the Wind under my Wings.
I love you with all my heart.

Thank you for always being my biggest support system.

Table of Contents

Acknowledgments

One of the most important lessons of my life is that no one becomes successful alone. It takes a team of people to support you in all big endeavors. I want to acknowledge the wonderful team of people who have assisted to make this book a reality. First, I want to again thank my publisher, Robert Friedman. This is the third book of mine he has published. My first two books he published were *Success Is An Inside Job* and *Spiritual Power Tools for Successful Selling* with Hampton Roads Publishing. Now his new publishing company, Rainbow Ridge Books, which is distributed by Square One Publishers, of Garden City, New York has picked up *Reclaim the Magic*. Thank you Bob, I am deeply grateful you have had faith in me all these years.

I would also like to thank my team at Lee Milteer, Inc. who have supported me with their positive reinforcement and many hours of hard work of editing and assisting me to create this book. Many thanks to my creative director, Carly Jones O'Connor, personal assistant Birit Trematore, Pat Nama, and my other staff for their hard work to make my business run smoothly while I devoted so much time to this book.

A big thank you to dear friends and partners of the Lee Milteer School of Wisdom, Lily Noon, Jose Antonio Castillo and their staff, for all they do with promotion and support to get this material into the world.

Thank you to my dear friend Diane Roach for being a great support and spiritual advisor to me.

I want to acknowledge my dearest and best friend, treasured mentor, and my adopted family member, Dan Kennedy, for his untiring encouragement, wisdom, humor, and marketing assistance. Dan, thank you for the hours of humor we share about the insanity of the world.

A huge thank you to all my Peak Performers GKIC coaching members, Millionaire Smarts® sponsors, personal coaching clients, and the Lee Milteer's School of Wisdom Mystery School students and customers for their belief and trust in me.

A special appreciation to my soul mate Clifton Williams for his love and support. This book is dedicated to him for his tireless love and patience for all I do in the world. He is my cheerleader and I am deeply grateful to have a mate as devoted to me as he is daily.

Foreword

This book is for you if:

- You have been doing what you have been taught to do for success, love, health, and happiness, but things still are not working in your life the way you want them to.
- You feel there are answers but you're not getting them from the external world.
- Life has changed and what used to work is not really working anymore.
- Life has become a TO DO list and you're feeling exhausted from trying to do everything yourself.
- You feel you have no control and are living in fear, doubt, confusion, and frustration. You are disheartened and don't know what to do about the insanity of it all.

You are most likely feeling the exhaustion, overwhelm, and stress from all the mental, emotional, physical, spiritual, and financial challenges life is throwing at you daily. The human race is moving at a pace no one in our recorded history has ever experienced. The ever-changing world and its values, the relentless and negative fear-based media programming, and the intensity of our fast-paced lives all has a cumulative effect on the amount of energy we have left to proactively participate in making time and space for our own goals and dreams.

If you are feeling something is missing in your life, you are right—it is!

You're missing the magic you used to feel about the hope of a better future, the joy of living, and your true knowledge of your own divinity and ability to manifest in the world.

Right now most people are feeling that life has changed and what used to be fulfilling has lost its luster. What that means is that you are being called into a more authentic direction for your soul's growth.

Sadly, the world programs us to stop listening to our hearts, to disregard our feeling nature, and to only make our decisions and actions from our left brain's rational programmed mind. This has caused a huge imbalance in our natural instincts.

As a society, we have been beaten down from the relentless media who program us to feel and act like victims. Today is the day you can stop the insanity and *reclaim the magic* that is truly inside of you, wanting to come out. This information will change the way you view your life in the future because you will discover a new framework of what the real rules of the universe are for harmony, success, love, health, well-being and prosperity, and a connection to your Divine Source. You don't have to be stressed out, frustrated, overwhelmed, and depressed. You have simply forgotten that there is real magic in the world and that you can choose to tap into it. When I refer to magic, I'm referring to your natural connection to Infinite Intelligence and your inner knowing that you have the power to manifest all that you desire, which sparks an unparalleled passion and excitement for life. Instead, most people live their lives just trying to soldier through it. You do your best but inside there are doubts and questions: When is life going to be fun? When is it my turn to live well and be prosperous? Why do these bad things keep happening to me?

You're unhappy because your soul is craving the magic of being realigned with your spirit and purpose of living again. You are disconnected from your Spirit/Source/God/Infinite Intelligence energy and want to have a partnership with this divine energy again so you can experience the magic of love, joy, prosperity, health, fun, and hope for the future. Only you have the power to create for yourself. I am going to share what I know to be true about how you can recapture the magic you so richly deserve in your life.

We are being called *now* to shed our old skins of what is no longer important and open up to a new empowered life. Now is the time to unplug from the wrong things, beliefs, and behaviors that have gotten us into the mess of living an unfulfilled life and being victims who are programmed by other people with their own agendas.

Most people are experiencing an identity crisis because what used to work no longer works. We need new tools for a new reality. We must now claim our birthright to be the king or queen of our own reality.

Think of yourself as a powerful bright light. When you are plugged into the unlimited supply of Spirit/Source/the Universe/God, no matter what you call it, this Infinite Intelligence is always there and can be utilized to assist you, but only if you know the secrets of tapping into this powerful energy.

I am going to share with you how you can take your personal power back, plug into the unlimited source of true power, and design a life for yourself that truly makes your heart sing!

The intent of this book is to remind you who you are and how to claim your natural birthright as a manifestor, and help you become fully conscious of the abilities and powers you have within you. I am going to share concepts that are familiar and others that are completely new to you. I am going provide modern, practical techniques, energy tools, and spiritual mindset knowledge that I've collected over my many years of studying and that I personally know to be true for me.

It will be up to you to mold and shape the tools I provide into your own personality, your own skills, and where you are in life. I want you to be an artist and a scientist at the same time. If used in a conscious way, the information I will share with you will transform your life and help you find your purpose to live an effective, prosperous, rewarding, and meaningful life.

Thank you for joining me on this grand adventure of reinventing yourself so you can experience and use the true magic that is all around you! You must give yourself permission to believe that you have the power and ability to change your life and create a new life right now!

I ask you to start listening to that inner part of you that wants more. Listen to your own feeling nature about what is right for you right now! Today is the day to give yourself permission see the big picture of amazing possibility and new exciting and rewarding adventures that can open for you. The past is a locked door; the future will depend on what you do today. Your point of power is this very moment.

Enjoy this book!

Love, light, and blessings to you.

Lee Milteer

ONE

The Magic of Owning Your Own Divinity

Every single soul on the earth has a king or queen within them who wants to reign over their own life. The word majesty means greatness, bestowing the highest rank of sovereign power or dignity upon someone. Everyone has the ability to let their soul's greatness shine; it is our natural inheritance. It is your divine inheritance to be a powerful manifestor, and now is the time for you to wake up and claim the true nature of your powers. You have the ability to create and achieve anything you want in life if you are willing to go for it with all your heart and soul and dedicate the appropriate spiritual, mental, emotional, and physical actions to your desires.

Our real power in life is 99 percent spiritual and 1 percent physical, yet most people only use 1 percent of their true natural powers. Most people spend 99 percent of their energy trying to change their life or circumstances using only their physical, mental, emotional, or financial energy or power. They deplete their energy trying to do it all themselves instead of tapping into the assistance that is accessible when we ask for it. As the Bible says: *"Ask and it will be given to you."* If you ask and then allow yourself to listen to your inner guidance, you will know there is an invisible connection to assist you no matter what challenge you are faced with in the physical world. We all have what I call "spiritual helpers" and we must ask our helpers to assist us to make sure we are using all of our resources and making the best decisions possible. These helpers come to our aid with intuitive suggestions and other people, and information sources that help us solve our challenges, find resources, or be inspired with new ideas we could not have come up with on our own.

We're now living in a world that is shifting to a new level of consciousness which is why spiritual information has become so much more mainstream. Money and success are still super important to us, but we also want to live our lives with integrity, to achieve peace of mind, and to feel that life has a truly deep meaning and that we are contributing to it. We want our work to not only be profitable, but also to be rewarding and satisfying. We long to integrate our spiritual self with all parts of our life, including our business practices.

Sadly the majority of people have fallen off their true path in life and have stopped themselves from doing what their heart wants them to do. They allow their culturally programmed logical mind to step in and prevent them from using their own guidance and spiritual assistance.

Our present reality, our civilization, is dependent on you staying a victim of the past, other people, the media, and fear of the future. You were born with a great internal power to influence the universe around you to manifest the life you deeply want to experience. It is important that you accept your power and release all traces of victimhood. To release the old victimhood, you must develop an entirely new level of perception of your power to experience love, light, beauty, prosperity, joy, creativity, and grace. Your first job is to awaken to who you really are and accept this new view of yourself to be able to raise your own consciousness.

So Who Are You Really?

The true essence of who you are is divine energy that has temporarily projected itself into your existing physical body. The real you is the source of your majesty, greatness, and power. As a soul, you are always eternally evolving, expanding, and adding to your repertoire of spiritual tools to help you manifest the life purpose you came to the earth to experience. You have massive creative and manifesting powers built within you to achieve whatever your heart sincerely calls for in your life. All of your power is within you. To claim the ability to bring forth the king and queen within you, it is imperative that you give yourself permission to release your old programming and life, and put them behind you.

One of our lessons at this time is to realize our own Godhood, our connectedness with the Prime Creator and with all that exists. To reclaim the magic, you must realize that everything and everyone is connected, and that you are part of it. Your existence matters; you are an important aspect of the big picture of life. Once your mind opens to a new and deeper awareness, you can't go back to not knowing the truth about Infinite Intelligence. You understand that you are more than your physical body and that you're connected to spirit—to something that is so much more advanced than your human self. When you know this, you also know that you can let go of the drama, self-doubt, fear, and uncertainly about the future. When you're connected to your source, you have access to resources, knowledge, and assistance that only Infinite Intelligence can provide.

The truth is, you are a magnificent being and a member of the family of light. You came to the earth at this time to create a shift, to make a change, to assist in the transition of consciousness. Your purpose is to raise consciousness through love so the human race can evolve. We're at such a crucial time and you are one of the triggers and catalysts to help raise the earth's consciousness to a new place. The true key for you to do that is to understand that the universe is made up of love energy. Love is the basic building block. When you have love, all possibilities exist.

As the king or queen of your life, your real job is to love yourself enough to get into integrity with your soul's purpose. When you're able to live in this capacity you will become an inspiration to all those who encounter you. Light is knowledge and ignorance is darkness, so think of yourself as an ambassador of light—a light worker. There is a consciousness in all things and as a member of the family of light, you can implement and insert new probabilities in the chain of realities, which is how your personal transformation can occur.

No matter what situation you may find yourself in right now, it is the power of your thoughts that got you there. You must start to remember who you really are and fully understand that you can create your own reality. You must accept that you have the power to alter the frequency of your own life and future. Thought creates, and in that way you have the power to transform your experience.

Your frequency affects everyone and every place you go. Your real job is to be a conscious creator. You have to take responsibility for the fact that you are co-creating your own experience on earth. When you take it upon yourself to understand that you are the one creating your reality with your thoughts and beliefs, your entire life will change. Your ability to manifest will truly astonish you.

Our society gives power to external events and people and not to the natural source of power within each of us. There is a higher intelligence, a pure positive energy from the universe, a creative and loving force that is the source and substance of all reality.

You must direct your life with your inside power and internal knowledge not the external information you have been fed about how little is possible. You don't even know how powerful you are, which is your deepest soul lesson to learn. It is your job right now to remember that you are not like the unenlightened masses on this earth (*or you wouldn't be reading this book*). You are a member of the family of light. Your real life purpose is to awaken your spiritual consciousness so that you can direct your life from your internal knowledge versus external programming. Ralph Waldo Emerson stated: *"To be yourself in a world that is constantly trying to make you something else is the greatest accomplishment."*

As the king or queen of your life you have your own kingdom. Your task is to remember the importance of nurturing and treating yourself well, instead of putting others above you. You rule your life with benevolence and grace. You are confident that you have within you the connection to Infinite Intelligence, so you know what actions to take and when to take them. You are tapped into your source and access intuition as your true power.

To transform yourself you have to become your own authority. You must stop giving away your power and letting others control your decision-making process. Let's face it, most of the world doesn't get it. Most of the world lives in a much lower consciousness level. That means you have to take back your power from what society says. Well-meaning but often clueless people like teachers, parents, and professionals such as doctors, lawyers, and government officials have influenced you, but they don't understand real spiritual power. Instead, they operate from past beliefs and logical left-brain thinking.

Most people simply do not want to listen to their intuition and own common sense because they don't want to be responsible. They want someone else to tell them what to do and how to do it. They don't want to be the king or queen of their own lives and actually think, use discernment, and be 100 percent responsible for their life and results. It is easier to be a sheep and follow the herd. Sadly, they end up living a very unfulfilling life. We often let our logical minds rule us to the point of not hearing the wise inner voice that speaks and knows more about our future and long-term well-being than our logical, programmed mind.

To accept being the king or queen of your own life you have to have a sense of knowing and discernment that you are slightly different from average people. You do not follow the path of unconscious people. Your vibrational frequency is higher, and you are more intuitive, more aware, and more sensitive. You have love for the world.

Right now it is time for you to step into a new role in life and let go of the old paradigms and reality, and remember who you really are.

Let go of old fears and your programmed perception of yourself. Those limiting perceptions hold you back from becoming your authentic self and gaining your spiritual personal power. Too many people are afraid to pick up the pen to write their own story, so they let someone else take hold of it . . . then they lose control of their own destiny!

You can have complete control over your life; you have the power of love which gives you the power of manifesting. As Jesus said, *"You can do all that I do and more."* When you love and accept yourself as part of the all that there is, you realize you have resources far greater than you working on your behalf. You have spiritual helpers! There is an impeccable purpose to life and you are part of that. Your real work is to be your authentic self, so if you don't like your life story, rewrite it, re-label, or re-brand yourself. Claim it and it will come true. It is a spiritual law. As Albert Einstein said: *"The world as we have created it is a process of our thinking. It cannot be changed without changing our thinking."*

The world has changed and to be successful, you have to utilize every resource available to you. Now is the time for you to stop hiding who you really are and come out and be your authentic self.

This book is about you learning how to create a new upgraded version of you, what I refer to as a new "Inner Energetic Blueprint." As bestselling author Eckhart Tolle said: *"The world can only change from within."* You have to set up a new frequency for your vibration to set a new course. So your real work is to open up vibrational channels to fire up your inner codes to activate your true potential and self-direction.

You have amazing talents, potential, and skills that you have not allowed yourself to claim. You must now start to capitalize on these talents, skills, and experiences. You can navigate reality in a brand new way because the general population doesn't have these abilities. You have abilities and advantages that average people do not use. That is why you can be an incredible manifestor.

Reclaiming the magic is about recalibrating your energy and your vibrational frequency to a brand new level. There is a no more beautiful and compelling force in the world than a person who is awakening into their true self. That is what true enlightenment is about.

I do want to make a very important point—you are a self-fulfilling prophecy and what you believe about yourself is what comes to pass. What you think and feel about yourself comes true. If you don't become conscious of your thoughts, you are dooming yourself to be whatever society or old connections wanted you to think about your abilities. Accepting who your authentic self is can be a challenge because the outside world wants you to fit in and follow their rules of life. Life wants you to conform. When you conform you lower your consciousness energy and are less of an attractor of good.

When the movie and book *The Secret* came out many people thought it was new information, but this is not true. Centuries ago, people were writing about the Law of Attraction. Scholars in this century have written about the Law of the Attraction. Writers like Emerson, Blake, and Einstein, have all written about the Law of Attraction. In 1962, Catherine Ponder published a book called *The Dynamic Laws of Prosperity.* This book was all about Law of Attraction. Her main point was that you need to radiate out before you magnetize in. In other words, you can't get something for nothing. You have to give first.

Only when you are at the top of your game, and are energetically vibrating happiness, enthusiasm, positivity, and gratitude are you resourceful, creative, brilliant, effective, and prosperous. You are in the flow of Infinite Intelligence. Some people call this "the zone." You are at the right place at the right time; synchronicities happen for you that set you on the right course of action. Now is the time to give yourself permission to be who you are, not who the world wants you to be.

Know that your highest and best always comes to you with perfect, divine timing. You do not have to fight, manipulate, or struggle to get what you want in life. You simply have to recognize the gifts when they arrive, and then accept and act on them. You are connected to the Divine and when your heart is open . . . miracles happen.

Are You Still in Hiding?

A ship in a harbor is safe, but that is *not* why ships are built. So why is it so many people are *waiting* to live their lives, go for their dreams, and express their true authentic selves?

There is no better time than right now for you to come out and be your authentic self. What does it mean to be your "authentic" self? It means being your true self, who you *really* are, not who anyone thinks you should be or wants you to be. Being your authentic self means you do what makes you genuinely happy. You don't feel obligated to pay attention to what society is doing or saying, and you genuinely follow your own heart.

Part of being your authentic self is speaking your truth. If we aren't being true to ourselves, we can't be authentic. And when we aren't authentic, we aren't living the life we came here to live as the king or queen, and we are not following our soul's purpose.

When our words and actions align with what's in our hearts, that's when we live our truth and embrace our authentic selves. When we remain silent or do something that doesn't align with what we know to be true, we betray our authentic selves.

Some of the security that we've all sought after has become very fragile. Our personal identification has been challenged. What we used to believe in has been shaken. For many people, the future feels unknown and unsafe and, again, in this intense environment, it's actually hard to remember who you really are because most of your old programs have been running you. We fall into amnesia about our true power. We often let fear and doubt make us go towards what we consider security. We often make decisions from fear, which is not a good vibrational mode to be in when making any decision. When you focus on getting into alignment with your own spiritual source, you know when to listen to your inner truth. You have clarity about what is the highest and best direction to go towards. Integrity with self brings you into the highest connection to source energy.

When we speak our truth, it benefits us as individuals and on a societal level to help raise consciousness.

Sharing this consciousness material and coming out of the so-called metaphysical closet was challenging for me. I was concerned I would lose my business clients because they would view me as being "woo woo." Really, I am very seriously grounded in life and use universal wisdoms to manifest what I want, combined with my extensive business knowledge. When I started speaking my truth, just sharing things as I knew them to be true, I started feeling excited again, as if my life had been renewed. It has been incredibly liberating. I love working with people who want that edge, which is understanding the use of energy for success. Once I accepted my real purpose and allowed myself to be more authentic, that fresh new energy attracted much more joy, ease, and prosperity. I am living life more my way these days. Opportunities that I am a vibrational match with, flow easily into my life. I am blessed with more opportunities than I can accept. This allows me the inner confidence that all is well in my world. I can manifest whatever and whenever I want to.

This is what people are attracted to and the type of energy they want in their own lives. I encourage you to give yourself permission to let the real authentic you out in the world. You will be amazed at the new opportunities and people you attract into your world. Like does attract like. I will also disclose that as you raise your consciousness you will no longer attract some of the people from your old life and old story. You will *feel* different to them and often times that feeling is unconformable to them, so they fade out of your life. In the long run of your life, it is very positive to release people who don't support or respect you. When you change, your world will get an upgrade! Your

Inner Energetic Blueprint will start vibrating at higher frequencies bringing in more divine love and light.

It's time to come out of hiding. It's time for you to get very clear that you are a creator. You co-create with Infinite Intelligence. You must claim your personal authenticity because you are a multi-dimensional soul. You were born with the ability to create and it is yours to use in making the best life you can live.

Who Is Ruling Your Life?

Ask yourself these questions: When is it *my* turn in life to really take care of *myself*? When is it time to claim being the queen or king of *my* life?

The things you are most passionate about are not random; *they are your calling* to be your real self. The only way to be truly happy in life is to go towards the calling. Reclaim your own unique magic of loving and accepting yourself as you truly are. You do not have to be what others demand.

I suggest when making plans for your life—both long and short term—that you really take the time to consider the *cost of the life energy* you have to exert. To whom and to what have you given priority? Subconsciously, we often make other people the priority at our own expense. As with everything, there are times to put others first, but should you do this every time? I don't think so.

I want you to be aware that *you* are the one making the plans for your life. If you want serious transformation in your life, attitude, and energy levels then commit to a new spiritual well-being habit for yourself: For the next thirty days, put yourself and your needs first for a change. I promise you it will improve the quality of your life! The queen or king within will be very appreciative.

One of the greatest lessons I have ever learned is to *give myself permission* to love myself and put my needs first. By loving myself in this way, I can listen and acknowledge the wants and needs of other people while still being the queen of my own reality.

Interestingly, our world has taught us to sacrifice ourselves to make others happy . . . but we have to really review this belief. I used to sacrifice my time, money, and life energy in order to have others love me. I thought people would value me if I put them first. Sadly, that belief did not turn out to be true. The more I denied myself and took care of others, the more situations I created where I wound up unhappy and on the short end of the deal.

We teach people how to treat us, and I taught people that I would sacrifice *me* to make them happy . . . and they always wanted more of that treatment.

After much pain, I finally woke up to the fact that the *now* is all I have. I realized that I had to become conscious of exactly what I wanted in my life (including how I wanted to be treated by others) and it would not work to just sit and wait for others to give it to me. It became clear that my only real power was to give myself the life I wanted. The next chapter is a short version of my personal story, how I learned firsthand to value and love myself in spite of all the fear, trauma, drama, chaos, pain, betrayal, and grief.

The same is true for you. You can let the past go and reclaim the magic within you to create the life you truly desire. It's important you ask yourself what you can do right now to really claim and take back your own power. This book is going to assist you to change your life story by simply giving you the tools to change your mind right now about what is possible. It is never too late to claim the king or queen energy! Welcome to a new journey in life that will forever shift the trajectory of your future!

TWO

My Magical Story

"Magic is believing in yourself, if you can do that, you can make anything happen."
—Johann Wolfgang von Goethe

My deepest wish in writing this book is to give you back the magic that you may have lost due to the many challenges of life. I promise you *it is there and you will find it* . . . but you must first rediscover the magic to be able to enjoy it!

I want you to know that you are *not alone* in the obstacles and adversity that you may now face, no matter how bleak things may seem from time to time. I hope my personal stories, trials, and lessons that I have learned will assist you in overcoming whatever is standing in your way and that ultimately you will develop *your own personal power* . . . because it is there waiting for you now and always has been.

One of the jewels of information that is important in life is to know the legitimacy of the person offering the information. I have many stories in my long life and will share only a few of them with you to illustrate that *there is more to* a life than what you see, and that life is truly magical.

Early Life on the Farm

I was born a farmer-rancher's daughter in Chuckatuck, Virginia, a rural farming area with a population of sixty (at that time). That was the first strike against me—being born "a girl." My ancestors were all farmers from as far back as anyone can remember and everyone knows that farming families need *male offspring* to keep the farm going. I grew up in the house where my father was born and it was over 130 years old then and a mile and half from the nearest paved road. Daily life was not without its challenges and I suffered immensely growing up as a young girl there. Although I didn't know it at the time, the harsh reality of this early life would prepare me well for the roller coaster of life that lay ahead.

Perhaps the hardest metaphysical law that I have had to accept in life is the one that states that we choose our parents. When I was born, I had colic for six months and I screamed my head off, so clearly there was something amiss from the beginning of my life. I can imagine me thinking at the time. *"Oops! Why the hell have I landed here? Wrong bus stop. I didn't mean to get off here. Can I try another stop because I got the wrong parents? I did not sign up for this!"*

As I think back now, it seems the set of parents I was born to were "Muggles," which describes them to a tee if you have ever read or seen the Harry Potter book/movie series. They both had very difficult childhoods and they simply did not have the knowledge or resources for caring for a very sensitive child. As a result, my childhood was an extremely emotional, dysfunctional, physically violent, unhappy, and scary time. Sadly, my parents had a lot of personal baggage and no resources or knowledge of how to deal with their own demons. They just didn't know any better and had no role models to show them more rational behaviors. I honestly don't hold any ill feelings toward them—they were simply products of other people who were also brutal and unconscious, and victims of old beliefs and programming.

My mother never really bonded with me. She was twenty-one when she got married and got pregnant right away. She felt trapped and saddled with this baby girl and in her own unconscious way blamed me for being born. To be fair, I only added to her problems. She lived with an abusive man in the middle of nowhere, with no place to go, no money, and no other real options. My father had many good traits, but sadly he was severely scarred from his own childhood, having been deserted by his mother at his own father's funeral at seven years of age. He ended up being shuttled from one set of relatives to another, and no one really wanted him. He became an alcoholic, which presented many difficult challenges, considering he was a very large man, over six-feet-four inches tall, 280 pounds, and my mother was a tiny woman, just under five-feet tall, and well-trained to be a traditional farmer's wife.

Getting back to being "a girl," one of my first memories at about three years old was my mother with her friends talking about their kids and she said: *"We were so disappointed Lee was a girl. Her father really wanted a boy and he was just heartbroken when he got a girl."* I heard that story many times during my childhood and my mother was totally clueless about its devastating effect on me. I totally bought into the belief that I was cursed to be a girl. It started a pattern of feeling unloved and unwanted.

Then my brother was born and it was as if the Messiah had arrived! The family was so happy they had a boy! I became the invisible and unwanted child. My parents only valued male children because they grew up in that very old-fashioned mentality of ranch farmers. You had to have sons to keep the operation going, or so they mistakenly thought. So I became a bad-ass tomboy to make up for the deficiency of being born female.

My "Secret Skills" Begin To Emerge

The instinct to survive and protect myself from the massive dysfunction of my environment led to the realization that I *already* possessed certain keen intuitive abilities and I began to use this "secret skill" regularly to protect myself from my father's rage. It became important to know what kind of moods people were in. I could not depend on what people said, because it was often not at all what they meant. The physical cues and the meaning behind their words were often very different. My intuitive powers continued to grow and I learned to rely on them, as is the case with most children of abusive homes . . . just to survive the insanity of it all.

Paranormal Events & My Great-Grandmother

There were many other signs in my young experiences that there was more to life than what we have been taught to believe. When I was about four years old my baby brother, who was only one at the time, was sleeping in my mother's bed with her while my father was working at his second job. Life was hard and he had to work two jobs to support us: farming by day and a state job on the James River Bridge. He often worked the midnight to 8 a.m. shift, so he was out of the house a lot.

It was about 4 a.m. and still dark. Suddenly I woke up and realized that the bed was literally jumping up and down off the floor. My mother was screaming and could not get off the bed because it was moving so violently. This was not a dream because my mother spoke of it often with fear. I heard her tell her own mother once that she was positive *it was me* that was causing all the psychic disturbances. Clearly there was a massive amount of intense pent-up frustrated energy in the house. I certainly felt it and it expressed itself in this situation and many others.

These episodes of crazy furniture moving happened on more than one occasion and during these paranormal events I do not remember ever feeling afraid, not once. I never felt like there was something bad trying to "get us." When you live in the middle of nowhere and are not really connected with other people, things just seem normal because that is all you know. What else would a child think?

My great-grandmother, who raised my father after he was abandoned at seven years old, lived with us in our house. I often went to her for comfort and love. She was my champion. Unfortunately she passed away when I was five years old, and that occasioned yet another unusual story.

My parents took me and my brother to a nearby neighbor's house so we would not see the funeral hearse come to pick her up and take her away. Everyone in my family swears I was not in the house when the funeral people came. Yet as impossible as everyone said it was, I clearly remember the funeral home workers being in our house and putting my one and only protector in a green zippered bag. This sight upset me to no end because I thought she was sleeping. How could she breathe with that bag zipped up? I could actually see the men putting her in their vehicle and driving off down the lane, off the farm.

When I shared what I had seen, the family all told me it was a dream, but as a child of only five, I had never been exposed to that death scenario before. I had no mental references of this to dream of or to imagine. *I know I saw it.* Later in my life I even asked the neighbors if I was at their house during this time and they confirmed that I was there and that it was impossible for me to have "seen" what I described so vividly. Some may call this *remote viewing*, but I know a higher part of me saw them remove the person who I felt truly loved me.

After her death, my grandmother visited me in my bedroom at night just as she had done before. We would talk about my life and she never once mentioned she was dead or anything about the other side. There were some great asides to this story; my "ghost" great-grandmother hated to have loaded guns in the house and after her death my father would complain (on a regular basis) that someone had unloaded his guns and put the shells in the top drawer of a chest my great-grandmother owned. She used to do that when she was alive and apparently kept doing it after she left. There were many days, when I was alone in the house, that I could hear her walking around downstairs where her rooms were. Her ghost visits lasted a couple of years, but to me it was all very normal. I did not know at the time the true importance of my intuitive powers and the role they would play in my future.

The Alpha Lesson

My childhood environment was very isolated and lonely because my parents did not trust other people. Lacking human friendships, I turned to nature and my main companions were animals, with whom I developed very strong bonds. I learned on the farm what pure Alpha energy was. In every animal species, there is a leader or an Alpha of the group. On the ranch-farm we had herds of Black Angus cows, horses, pigs, chickens, peacocks, lots of big dogs, barn cats, and a few wild animals that had been hurt by hunters and were not able to live in the wild. There was a one-legged crow, some baby raccoons whose mother had been killed, and an assortment of abandoned stray dogs that we had rescued.

I observed that in each species there was a leader, an Alpha, and as I watched my father run his farm I clearly saw Alpha energy and how it worked with all the farm help. If the Alpha becomes weak, he or she will be challenged by the next strongest Alpha energy. This is the law of nature; there must be a leader. Most little girls don't get this bootcamp-to-reality childhood that I had, and the Alpha lesson was one that I would carry with me.

The Magic of Miss Samantha and the Thumb Wart

A very significant event happened that changed my life and made me totally believe there was an energy that I call "Magic." I was about eight years old and got this very bad wart on my thumb. It was getting progressively worse and it would not stop bleeding because I kept picking at it.

In Chuckatuck, Virginia there was this one little teeny tiny grocery store/post office. A few of the locals used to joke that it was "Glenda, the White Witch" who ran the store and lived above it, but everyone else called her Miss Samantha. People from surrounding areas came not only for supplies but also for physical healings for problems the local doctor couldn't solve. She was a bit of a challenge for the so-called "church folks," who were afraid of her and referred to her as a witch. What others said never seemed to bother her and she seemed to find this label funny.

Miss Samantha was this beautiful vibrant woman with very long blond hair who was actually a hands-on healer. She had this delicious sense of humor and an endearing infectious laugh. There was something that just made you feel good to be around her. She always paid attention to me and remembered my name and would give me candy when I was in the store. She somehow always made me feel special, so I loved going in to see her and would do so as often as I could.

One summer day when I was in her store, clearly picking at the thumb wart, she told me to follow her outside to the back of the store. There was no one else around at the time. As we were standing alone she put her hands over my infected hand and told the wart to go away. I remember how hot her hands were! Then she did something that seriously changed my view of reality forever. She looked at me in the eye and said: *"Lee, you will never think of this wart problem again. The Christ within you is now totally healing you and your hand is now perfect. You will never think of this on your hand again. You are whole, happy, and healthy. You will never think of this again."*

As I stood there listening to her and feeling these amazing hot hands on me I thought, *"How can I not think of this? It's bleeding. I'm picking at it. It hurts."* She repeated the entire thing a couple more times and then I remember going back in the store where she gave me an ice cream cone. Then I totally forgot the entire problem.

Later that fall I was on the bus going to school and suddenly remembered I once had a wart and I looked at my hand and it was gone. Whatever she did, it worked and the wart had vanished and never came back. I suddenly was awakened to the fact there was some kind of magical wisdom or knowledge to life that wasn't being shared in my reality. It changed my perception of what is possible. It opened up doors of curiosity that maybe life had more to offer than I had been previously led to believe . . . and yes, there is real magic in life!

I then spent as much time as possible with Miss Samantha "the healer." I would ride my pony up to the store and hang out with her. I would do little things to help her around the store and she would tell me important things about life, many of which I clearly did not understand at the time. She spoke almost a different language than anyone else around me. She talked about *energy* and how it affects us. Miss Samantha was truly my first important mentor and she urged me to journal my feelings daily and to write whatever I learned. Naturally I followed her advice.

The Life Lessons of Miss Samantha

Miss Samantha was an Earth Angel for me. Whenever I could, I would rush home after school to do my chores and saddle up my pony and head off to be in the store with her. If the store was not busy, she would sit and talk with me. I often told her of the unhappiness and stress of my home life. She was my confidante and comforter and always seemed to know the right thing to say to make me understand things better, or at least to feel better.

She opened my eyes to the fact that we are all connected to a higher great power and as humans we have simply been programmed not to use it. She warned me that if others knew of any of my out-of-the-ordinary beliefs, talents, or skills they would ostracize me for being different. She did her best to explain to me that the normal world likes things to be explainable and to conform to their comfortable worldview. Being different causes people to fear you or at least to mistrust you. She assumed that I was like her and it was okay if people did not understand us. Best keep my thoughts to myself.

She taught me that, for the most part, humans are afraid of their own natural powers. Besides my great-grandmother, she was the first person who validated that there was more mystical power in the world than was being shared—in education, society, or in church. I watched Miss Samantha heal people with her mind and hands, offer them suggestions on how to lead better lives, and think more positively about life. Those whom she had helped were her true supporters. With all the good she did, she was still shunned by some people because she was different. This, again, did not seem to faze her at all.

I will forever thank her for her insights in opening my mind to unlimited possibility. She allowed me to see life from the perspective that there is a great Cosmic Intelligence that I can tap into for creating what I need and want in life. She explained that we live in an energy field, which she called magical, and often told me people had lost their magic abilities because they forgot they had them! She said they were sleepwalking through life and she wanted to make sure I did not fall into the programmed trance that most people lived in their entire lives. Here is more of the wisdom she shared with me:

- Understand people are doing the best they can for the most part and forgive them. Do not hold anger or grudges because that energy will make you sick physically and poison your mind for the good in life.

- Honor your inner intuition first and not what others tell you is right. Should you feel in danger, get out of the situation immediately!

- You cannot control or change other people or how they treat you, but you can change and control how you react to it.

She was the first person who introduced me to my inner power and the inner trust of my own intuition. She also introduced me to the fact that no matter how bad things seemed to me at that time, life was preparing me for a much bigger role to play (which I did not really understand at all at the time). Her biggest teachings to me were:

1. What you think, you will become,

2. What you feel, you will attract, and . . .

3. What you imagine, you can create.

And Then One Afternoon It All Ended

One spring day about two years after I met Miss Samantha, I rode my pony to the store like I always did and found that she was packing to move. She had sold the store and was moving to another state. I realized I would never see her again. I was stunned and devastated to be losing my only real solace. I literally begged her to let me go with her. She said to me:

> *"You are never alone. You have a team of guides, helpers, and angels who will be with you if you call them. I have always spoken to you as if you were an adult because I am speaking to the Soul within you. I realize I share with you adult advice and that is because you are raising yourself. You may not always understand today what I am sharing but please try to remember you are loved deeply, not only by me but by your own spirit guides. You are never alone."*

Big concepts for a small kid!

The last time I saw her, as she was getting into her car to drive away to a new life, I stood there trying hard to be brave and not break down and cry. I wanted desperately to get in the car with her and disappear from my challenging childhood. Before she left, she kissed me goodbye and said:

> *"I have total faith in you, dear one, and you have a very big future, because God doesn't give you this many challenges*

unless you can handle them. They are meant to mold and shape you into something important. Never let circumstances determine your future or direction. Always remember that only you can decide your fate and destiny, and there are no limits if you believe in yourself."

She reminded me never to allow the outside world to determine my fate and to always listen first to the inner guidance within me. She held me tight and said:

"Remember me, dear child of God; I hope I have been of help to you and if you are ever afraid, think of me. If you do not know what to do, ask yourself what I would do or say, and then do that until you get your own sea legs and you know what to do from your inner guidance. I may not be here physically but I will always love you. I have known you before this life and I will know you in another life."

I was left alone now and clearly did not fully comprehend the meanings of all of her teachings. Since she had taught me to journal, I had written down most of her words of advice because they seemed so important and, frankly, it felt at the time like she was the only person giving me good advice. After she left, she sent me letters from time to time. She always had some motivational or inspirational messages or magazine tear-outs of pictures of horses, along with interesting articles she thought I would like. Sometimes she sent a notebook journal and she would write important things for me to remember. In one of them she wrote:

"Lee, you are always 100 percent responsible for your life. Everything you do is based on the choices you make. It's not your parents, where you live, your past, lack of money, the

weather, or your age that is to blame when things go wrong. You and only you are responsible for every decision and choice you make, so be careful of the decisions you make and listen to your heart and head before making them."

In another she wrote:

"Whatever you think—over time—is what you attract to yourself. Think Positive—Get Positive. Think Negative—Get Negative. Everything in the Universe is ENERGY."

One of the last things she ever sent me was a postcard that I kept up on my bathroom mirror until it literally fell apart: *"Forgive others, not because they deserve forgiveness, but because you deserve peace."* That's one of those wise sayings that are easier said than done. It can be a hard life lesson to learn.

Miss Samantha activated something inside me that helped me feel that I had a purpose in life. In many ways I have carried on her mission to be a "light worker" on earth. I always think of her with great love and appreciation. I even wear my hair like hers today. She was the mother I sincerely wanted but never had.

Fortunately, I did benefit from her life lessons later on, as I eventually took my career forward as a coach, speaker, and author. Whenever I found myself in a challenging situation, I would often think: What would Miss Samantha tell me to do here? It is a very comforting thought to connect with her energy. I was blessed to have had the opportunity to be influenced by her presence in life. She introduced to me the wonder and magic that life has to offer when you are open to seeing it.

But then, while I was still on the farm and missing her dreadfully I failed to remember some of her poignant lessons.

My Decision to Die

The brutality of my day-to-day life eventually took its toll and created within me the need to either die or physically escape. At twelve years old, there really wasn't a choice. I decided to commit suicide. We lived on the river and one early winter morning, feeling unwanted, unloved, and lost about how to keep going, I went down to the river to drown myself and end my suffering. I had truly forgotten the words of my beloved mentor, Miss Samantha, when she told me that I had *"a very big future."*

Thank goodness for all the dogs we had on the farm because they literally saved my life. Or maybe it was my spirit guides that Miss Samantha had spoken of. Some of the dogs loved to be in the water and some did not. On that fateful winter day with high winds howling, I jumped off the dock into the frigid cold water and *all of our dogs jumped right in after me.* The shock and surprise of this triggered something within me and I knew suddenly that they were in the water to save me and to change my mind. They all started trying to grab my clothes and pull me to shore, accompanied by some very high-pitched howling. I had *never* heard them do this before as a group. It was if they were all saying in unison to me, *"NO, you can't do this! We need you here. You can't leave us alone here. This is a tough place to live."*

So I let them pull me to shoreline and climbed out of the freezing water, clearly understanding that I was *not* supposed to kill myself. There was a reason for me to live! My deep connection to animals saved me more than once in my life. That old funny saying, *"Dogs are God's way of apologizing for your relatives"* certainly has been true for me!

A Paranormal Happening Saves Me from Rape

One of the most amazing life-altering paranormal experiences I had happened when I had just started to date, around sixteen years old. Someone had fixed me up on a first date with a guy whom I did not know well because he went to a different school. I lived eighteen miles from the nearest so-called civilization. We had gone to a movie and, on the way home, he decided to stop and park in a cornfield a few miles from my home. As soon as he stopped the car in spite of my protests, I realized I was in trouble and that his intention was to rape me. I was terrified.

Growing up a tomboy, I was not a pushover in any sense of the word and I had some skills in fighting and protecting myself. But he was considerably bigger and stronger than I and, even though I fought bravely, it was clear I was not winning. I was about 110 pounds and five-feet-five-inches tall and he was well over six-feet tall, close to 180 pounds, and a football player. We were in the middle of a field and there were no houses, cars, or anything for several miles around us. I was on my own. What would Miss Samantha do?

I remember clearly thinking, as I was doing my best to keep my pants on, *"God, please save me from this fate* now!" I remember distinctly thinking that if got pregnant from this attack, my father would murder me. I mean seriously, that was the brutal mentality of my family. It would not have mattered that I was raped. I would have suffered horrible consequences. I would have been harshly punished and most likely forced to leave my home, since, in the eyes of my family, my life and their own would be ruined and I would be an embarrassment to them. I was more afraid of that fate then the actual rape of my body. I clearly remember this beyond the panicky feeling that my life was in grave danger.

As the struggle continued between my attacker and me, suddenly everything started to feel as if it was happening in slow motion and I could see every detail vividly. All my senses became super-exaggerated and I clearly remember feeling the sensation you get outside in a storm when lightning is going to strike. The air felt electric and the hair on the back of my neck stood up.

At that very moment in the middle of the car, next to the dashboard, a bright light, a round gold-blue light appeared. It was a little larger than the size of a baseball and it felt alive with the gold and blue colors swirling in it. The appearance of this light immediately stopped my attacker. Frankly it was such a shocking experience that it scared us both badly. My first thought was, *"Thank God, someone heard me screaming and is here to save me."* I thought someone was shining a flashlight into the car. My attacker jumped out of the car and ran around the car looking for the person with the flashlight. He was furious that someone was interfering with his plans! I jumped out of the car to be free because I thought someone was there to protect me. To the shock of both of us, there was nothing but dark silence and emptiness outside the car. There was no one outside the car.

We both stood there staring into the car with both doors open, dumbfounded since this was a situation neither of us had ever experienced. There was no visible explanation of what and why this light was there. It seemed to have an energy source inside itself and was literally hovering in mid-air inside the car. I had so much adrenaline pumping that it was hard to think what to do. If I ran away from him I was still miles from home with no cell phones at the time. He also clearly had no idea what to do, but raping me was no longer on the agenda. Whatever this light was, I knew it had saved me from being raped and most likely saved my life.

I had no reference for what that gold-blue ball of light was, but it felt holy and fierce at the same time, like a powerful warrior angel. It did not seem to have human qualities. All I know is that it did not speak or make any sound at all but it did glow very brightly and seemed to be getting larger and brighter.

He finally screamed at me, *"Get in the car! I am taking you home."* Thankfully the light stayed in the car while he drove me home as fast as he could drive, cursing loudly the entire way for this light to get the hell out of the car. As soon as he slowed the car down at my house, I jumped out of the car and the light followed me out of the car. He could not have looked more relieved and drove off our land like a madman, never to be seen or heard from again!

Once I got out of that car, I suddenly knew that I had been saved and that I was protected. I had not been raped, I would not be pregnant and I was home safely. When I turned back to look for the light, it lingered in my sight for only a few seconds and then became smaller and smaller until it finally disappeared.

I stood there after the light left, my body in shock. This event had not been a dream; I had the torn clothes and bruises on my body from the fight against my attacker to prove it. Slowly it started to dawn on me: I had a brand new understanding about my life. Someone, something actually did love me and wanted to protect me. This something was not of this world.

Thankfully my family had gone to bed early and never saw me come in the house or saw the mess I was at the time. I cleaned myself up and hid the clothes. I never told my parents about this experience for fear they would never let me leave the farm again to date anyone. I thought of it often, though, and felt it may have been the spiritual guardians that Miss Samantha had spoken of who interceded on my behalf.

I did not date for a while after that and spent a great deal of time at the library trying to find any information that could explain what had happened to me and what that light was, to no avail. I was deeply afraid of telling anyone because I was sure they would think I was crazy.

Most everyone has had some type of experience of being saved, and most of the time attributed it to a regular person doing the saving! I have had those also. This light experience convinced me that there are also *invisible good forces* in this world and it changed what I believed about the possibilities of life. There clearly is a magical presence to this life!

My Intuitive Powers Expand

After that experience I started having intuitive flashes of insight and awareness that were highly accurate and clearly coming from a source wiser than myself. I started listening to my intuition and was much more careful about trusting others. I learned to be more aware of my own feelings and did not allow myself to be put in dangerous situations. If I had any feelings that someone or something was not safe, I simply removed myself from the situation as quickly as possible.

Every single day of your life, you have the ability to realize that you are more than your human body. You are part of the Cosmic Intelligence that we call many names: Source, God, Universe, and hundreds of other names. Miracles happen all the time and we have guidance from the Invisible. So why do we doubt that our own invisible spiritual connections are here to help us?

Looking back now, I can see the many ways my childhood set the tone and the meaning for my life. I received a strong foundation in moral values, farm work ethic, and a serious connection to nature and animals. I learned to be self-contained. I did not need to be entertained and was perfectly happy to be alone. I learned to have big picture thinking and understand how to envision what needs to be done and when. I understood the power of taking action and being proactive in challenging situations or environments. All these skills that I learned as I was growing up certainly contributed greatly to my success as an adult.

I Discover My True Talent!

By the time I was seventeen, I just knew there had to be more in store for me than life on the farm-ranch. Still in high school full-time, I applied for a real adult job at a radio station in the closest big city, which was Norfolk, Virginia. To my shock I actually got the job and began to work part-time on the weekends as a rock-and-roll disc jockey. I had already worked part-time jobs since I was twelve-years-old, so it was easy for me.

A few months after I started the position and after I had actually finished high school, the radio station's sales manager asked if I would like to try my hand at sales. He spent a few days explaining how the radio business worked and how advertising would improve clients' profits. He explained what the new job could mean for me—independence and more money. It sounded very exciting. What he didn't tell me was that the station had the lowest rating in the market and you couldn't give the advertising away! It was actually to my benefit that I did *not* know this or I might have become negatively influenced about the sales possibilities.

In my excitement I hit the ground running and on my very first day in the field I made a sale. On the second day, I made two sales. The radio station sales manager couldn't believe it. He immediately doubled my salary and formally installed me in the sales department. So my life as a wild and crazy D.J. had only lasted a few months until I found my real talent in life—sales! That entire summer after high school I broke every sales record the station had, and when it was time for me to leave for college in September everyone in management at the station begged me to stay. But there was no stopping me and I was off to an all girl's college in Washington, D.C.

What a massive disappointment college was for me! It felt so slow. The information I was studying seemed a huge let down, after having earned serious money doing what I loved and was talented at . . . sales. After about a year I knew I was wasting my time. I felt that I needed to go back to what I could do instinctively and with ease. Most people were in college trying to find what their talents and passions were and I already knew mine. As long as I believed in the product and the product had integrity, I was *very good* at sharing what I knew with others and letting them know how it would be of benefit to them.

Sometimes fate has a way of stepping in, and ironically the college was forced to close due to financial problems. I saw this as a way out of school and an opportunity for me to go back to work. I moved back home, only to find that my parents had given my room to my brother. The first thing my mother said to me, on my first day home was: *"We have no room for you and do not want you here. Why don't you marry your boyfriend and move in with him?"* Well, the challenge was that I did not love my boyfriend. However, after two weeks of being home and clearly not being welcome there, I felt cornered. No job, no car, and no money. No way of earning money without a car and no way to borrow money or get money from anyone. So in a moment of weakness and desperation to get out of the hell at home, I married my boyfriend, who happened to be a D. J at the same radio station where I wanted to go back to work.

An Untimely Marriage

I remember the day I got married. It was my birthday and I had just turned nineteen years old. I was wearing the only suit I had (a blue one), standing in front of the Justice of the Peace in Elizabeth City, North Carolina. As I was standing there, I thought I do not love this man but maybe I will learn to love him. After moving in with him, I cried for the next seven days. I desperately wanted to have the entire thing annulled, but I had no money or resources at the time to do anything but get married and escape the situation at home.

To say this was *not* a marriage made in heaven would be an understatement. He wanted a "traditional" woman like his mother, who would take care of him, and I was woefully underprepared to play the part. He *actually* wanted me to stay home all day in a tiny cramped apartment and be waiting happily with open arms when he came home from work. After a month of that hell, I went into the radio station (against his will) and got my old sales job back.

The marriage lasted only a few months. One day at the station, "Miss Virginia," a beauty queen, was a radio guest and it was clear she and my husband had a thing for each other. On my way home I happened to pass a motel and I saw his car in the parking lot alongside Miss Virginia's car. I drove into the lot and knocked on the motel door in front of where their cars were parked. The motel room had those small blinds on the door and suddenly I saw someone peek through. It was my husband's eyes. He quickly shut the blinds and there was silence. So I pounded on the door, yelling at him to come out and face me like a man. That produced no results and soon a motel guard arrived and told me that I must leave the motel's premises because I was causing a disturbance.

I immediately called a locksmith to come meet me at our apartment and then literally threw all his belongings out the door into the courtyard. When he finally got home that evening, trying to act as if he had no clue what I was talking about, I ended the marriage. At the same time, I was strangely calm and relieved that this marriage was over. I remember looking at our photo album for about thirty minutes and forcing myself to cry about it and then having this joyful feeling. I was free for the first time in my life. I had a job, an apartment and a car. I felt like my real life could start now. We were divorced within a short time and now at the tender age of twenty my life was about to start.

That was a magical time for me. I was free of the past and was earning an income far greater than I had ever dreamed possible. I was highly respected and rewarded just for using my *natural* talents. I continued to use my "secret skill" or intuitive powers that had manifested when I was young, and found I was drawn almost magnetically to the clients most suited to my products and likewise repelled by those who were not a fit. So my time was utilized in positive sales environments and I got results faster than the average sales person who was not using intuition.

Truth is, selling is nothing but good education. If you can find a match with product and buyer, then you are offering a good service. I never once regretted leaving college and my life flourished because I loved what I was doing. I was making a really good income and I was good at it. All those years of my father saying NO had forced me to learn to communicate in a way that was very persuasive and in retrospect, was fabulous training for my future.

Life is GOOD!

By the time I was twenty-two I had moved on from radio sales to become sales manager for a company called Background Music Service of Tidewater. This was a competitor to the national company who sold Muzak, the music that was piped into retail stores and doctor's offices. The company had been struggling. When I got there, I expanded their sales line to phone systems, intercoms, and paging systems, and we took music to shopping centers, airports, and office buildings all over the region. I was fortunate enough to acquire a reputation in sales as a hotshot, so other companies were always trying to hire me.

I spent a lot of time on construction sites, dealing with blueprints and writing proposals for new construction. One of my secrets to success was to always go after the "big" accounts and I never wasted my time with small accounts unless they called us. I found it was a better strategy to leverage my time with big payoffs instead of trying to sell a lot of small accounts, like the mom and pop stores that normally have financial challenges. And the small accounts were always harder sales to make. So I focused my time and energy on the big accounts, which meant multiple locations and faster profits.

I got married again and we bought a home. I had married someone that I really loved and had so much hope that my life was going to be a "happily ever after" story. Of course there were challenges; my husband was Jewish and twenty-two years older than me, with three teenaged kids who lived part-time with us and part-time with their mother. Suddenly I was a stepmother, with the oldest child only eight years younger than I was. The youngest was eleven at the time. This was a huge adjustment to reality.

His family was horrified that he had married a younger, non-Jewish girl and made it abundantly clear they were not happy with the union. They tried in vain to get me to convert to Judaism but I had no interest in conforming to any type of religious tradition. I had lost all interest in organized religion as a child and the last thing I wanted was more people forcing rules and restrictions on me. I could deal with the disapproval of not belonging; I grew up with that energy around me. It was familiar territory.

My new husband had graduated from Yale and was simply brilliant in book sense, but not so good with people or common sense. He and I had first worked together at a radio station and then had worked at an electronics company. Once we got married, we bought the background music company, and our life as self-employed people began. After reinventing the business and with the benefit of a couple of amazingly profitable years, we had the means and long periods of time to travel around the world as photographers, our passion and hobby at that time.

These travels gave me the greatest education of my life. Experiencing different cultures and becoming acquainted with various belief systems and traditions allowed me to appreciate and honor life from different perspectives. I developed a deeper awareness of a more spiritual part of myself, and my connection to all that is. I loved the freedom of travel and being a photographer. We had a great staff and our business ran for months at home without us. Life was amazingly promising, and for the first time it felt deliciously sweet and rewarding.

Murder! A Grisly Twist of Fate

Things were going my way! I was past the painful childhood trauma. I had a good life. But just before Christmas, something happened that would change my destiny forever.

One of my husband's life dreams had been to build and own a restaurant. He had been talking about it for as long as I had known him. Having been a building contractor, he had the plans, the partner investors, and the land to build his dream. The fly in the soup, however, was that building it would mean another restaurant in this very popular area of downtown would lose part of its leased parking areas to my husband's new restaurant.

The owner of this restaurant was furious about this new project and did everything humanly possible to stop it with the city planning office. That did not work for him and he was so upset about this loss of parking that he started threatening us in public, which frightened me to no end, since I felt he was dead serious. Even though he publicly threatened us several times and we reported it to the police every time, we were told that there was nothing they could do unless he actually brought physical harm to us.

Sadly, my husband, who was a very big guy and did not suffer fools lightly, did not take this man's threats of killing us and burning down our home seriously.

But the man *was* serious. He hired a professional hit man to kill my husband. On Christmas Eve, my love was shot in the face and died instantly at our front door. The police said that, had I been there at the time, I would also have been executed on the spot. The killer did not steal anything except the love of my life. Frankly, it was unbelievable that this type of thing could happen over parking spaces. Lacking enough evidence, the crazy restaurant owner who put the hit on us, was never charged with the crime. To everyone's shock, he committed suicide by shooting himself in the head a few months after the murder.

The irony of it all was that the crazy restaurant owner was buried less than fifty feet away from the grave of my husband. It was very difficult to go visit the love of my life's grave and leave flowers, only to see the headstone of the man who had him murdered. I was bitter that there had been no legal consequences, no way to make things right, or actions taken to punish him in any way. He had won in a way because our restaurant was never built. But as I have been reminded many times from many sources, he did punish himself through death for his despicable deeds. I will say this: Ending his life did not make up for the loss we all suffered due to his mental illness.

The Dark Night of My Soul

My life as I knew it and hoped it would be came to an end. It was a horrific experience and my world came crashing down on me in a way that I never could have dreamed possible. I lost all hope and totally forgot any of the magic life had to offer me. I hit an intense emotional bottom. Not only was the love of my life dead, I was now almost broke because of all the obligations that had to be honored.

There was no closure for me, no remedy for the fabric of my life that was torn apart. I barely existed in this heart-breaking reality and could not seem to move past what had happened. I numbed myself out with alcohol and prescription drugs. Doctors will give you all kinds of mind-numbing things when your spouse has been murdered.

Deeply disillusioned and depressed, there were days when I believed that I couldn't go on living. I began to question everything. How could this happen to me? What had I done to deserve such anguish? Is God really there? All of us, at some time in our life, seem to pass through this period of darkness and loss of hope. The mystics call it "the dark night of the soul." Frankly, I called it "being in living hell" at the time. The old saying about appreciating every moment of your life is very true. No one has any guarantees of what the future will bring or how it will turn out! In an instant life can dramatically flip and change the course of your future. It is a hard lesson and most of us are unprepared for it when it happens.

I did not do well at all with this new reality. I had no dogs to come jump into my life to save me. I was not close to my family for reasons I have explained. I barely got out of bed and hardly left the house for the first year unless I was absolutely forced to. I just could not pull myself out of the devastating grief and unrelenting anger. Life had lost all its magic for me. I could not find comfort or peace. I was seriously angry with God and everyone else for this turn of events and lost all faith that I had any guidance or protection. I became very self-destructive in my behaviors and had I not pulled myself out of this downward spiral, my life would have been wasted and ended badly.

This very difficult loss and dark time forced me into a time of serious soul-searching. Life challenged me to go within and ask myself who I was, why I was here, and what I was doing with my life. I had to find myself again because the person I had been was lost. I could not find myself, nor could I find the motivation to pick up where I had left off. What used to get me excited and motivated had vanished.

Fortunately, I had a few dear friends who were seriously concerned about me and came over with food, along with the "Come to Jesus" speech. I will admit they rattled me with evidence of how lost I was and the dark path I had chosen. One of their suggestions was for me to attend some seminars on healing grief that were being held in my area. Those were helpful. The real benefit from them was that I was able to the change my focus. In life, you get what you focus on, and I needed to change my mindset and stop *creating* more grief each day. The grief course was a great pattern interrupt and gave me the tools to start to move past the tragedy and start a new life.

Life Reshapes Itself As I Reclaim My Power

I began to believe again . . . and realized that life has to go on regardless of what happens. I came to the earth to be, so be! After difficult times it was up to me to remember that only I could take charge of the caliber of information that I fed my mind moment to moment. I literally had to stop the pity party and move on with life. This meant giving up being a victim. Certainly all of us have been programmed by society to feel sorry for victims and that it's not the victim's fault. We have learned that we don't have to face up to our own dysfunctional behaviors, thoughts, and beliefs so long as we can blame someone else. It was a hard lesson, but one I was forced to learn before I could find the real power to manifest great things in life.

Next, I signed up for some seminars on self-improvement. This information taught me to focus on the present and not the past, where I had felt like a victim. I got interested in how others had recovered from devastating events. I was forced to look at the inner me.

I learned to meditate and found that it opened up a whole new world—an inner world. I could receive guidance from something much wiser than myself. It is like the inner peace that you feel when you're out in nature or being around animals or people you love. It's the feeling of being one with the world. With all the life-changing drama, I had *forgotten* that I had the ability to tap into the magical energy flow of Source. I had forgotten all that Miss Samantha had taught me so long ago. I had neglected to take care of myself and my ability to always tap into the Source had faded.

As I became more aware of the spiritual part of myself again, my knowing that the physical world was not the ultimate reality returned. Deeply wanting to feel connected to something larger than myself, I started to read about many different religions. I revisited Christianity and went further into learning some of the Eastern philosophies like Buddhism. I went on to study Judaism and Native American traditions. I was impressed with different aspects of each belief system and the wisdom they had to offer. I found that I just couldn't buy into the dogma that most religions teach from some "long time ago" rules. I had to check with my own intuition to find what was right for me and what felt uncomfortable. I listened with my head and my heart. I needed checks and balances in all beliefs.

I did not feel the need to join churches or be part of groups, as I am more comfortable studying these things on my own. I love to read for my inspiration. So off to the library I went to immerse myself in new knowledge and wisdom that I hoped would change the course of my life. I had had enough bad luck and tragedy. I was determined to turn my life around and change my life story from one of a victim to one of success and fulfillment.

One day, on my way home from many hours at the library, I suddenly felt a spark of real hope for myself. It was something that I had not felt in a very long time. In high school, I had been a librarian's helper and worked during all my free time and breaks. Books are almost sacred to me and to this day I have a huge library of books in which I find wisdom and comfort. Just being around books makes me feel empowered. There is so much wisdom and knowledge right at your fingertips.

I read business success, spiritual, and metaphysical books like *Think and Grow Rich* and *You Can Work Your Own Miracles* by Napoleon Hill, and *The Magic of Believing* by Claude M. Bristol. The books that really stretched me were: *The Nature of Personal Reality* by Jane Roberts and then all of her channeled materials. I read the *Handbook to Higher Consciousness* by Ken Keyes, and *The Science of Mind* by Ernest Holmes. I devoured all of Florence Scovel Shinn's books: *The Game of Life, The Power of the Spoken Word, Your Word is Your Wand, The Secret of Success.* I read everything I could find from Dr. Wayne Dyer and *Psycho Cybernetics* by Dr. Maxwell Maltz. These were just a few of the literally dozens of books I absorbed during this time, as I tried to reinvent myself from victim to the new person I wanted to become. These authors introduced me to the concept that I had an inner consciousness that could help me to create my own reality.

This new awareness reminded me of what Miss Samantha had tried to instill in me as a young child and the way she lifted me up with personally empowering information. Sadly, if this knowledge is not reinforced daily, it is re-programmed by our focus on society's rational understanding of how life works. It takes practice to let the world's happenings go by as you focus on the concepts of creating your life with your own inner consciousness.

The more I learned, and the more I explored this new idea of creating my own reality, the more I came to believe in a higher intelligence, a pure positive energy from the universe, a creative and loving force that is the source and substance of all reality. I realized that the true creative power I was feeling was coming from some source other than me. We call this God, Love, Christ Consciousness, Cosmic Intelligence, Higher Power, The Pure Positive Universal Energy, Spirit, Higher Self, I Am, The Force, Source, Inner Guidance, and many other names. It became my passion to learn how to create a deeper connection with this Source in my own life. To me no matter what you called this force, it seems to have a magical quality to it, holy and mystical at the same time.

This very difficult time of my life forced me out of my comfort zone, out of what society, the church, and my parents had taught me about the reality of life and into a time of serious soul-searching. As the Bible says, *"Ask and you will receive."* I did not feel I had a choice. My safety net was gone, my previous belief system was blown to hell, and life was now demanding that I learn the lesson of recreating my own reality. Life was challenging me and forcing me to go within and question everything about my life, my beliefs, and my values.

What did I, Lee Milteer, want to do with my life? I had to find the truth and break away from the social programming and cultural demands forced upon me from my earliest recollections. I had to break away from what society said was possible and find out what my Cosmic Intelligence and God-Source knew was possible for me—my life purpose. There had to be more than what I had been taught—you live and die and go to heaven if you have been good. I knew there was more to life than that! We have a purpose for being on the earth. Our soul came here to do something!

A New Vision Emerges

With all this new awareness, reading these powerful books, and then studying different views of life, I was now discovering that my cultural programming and upbringing had led me to believe that life was something that would *happen to me* and all I could do was make the best of it. The power was outside of me, pressing in on my life. I realized that society programs us to believe that we are victims of the circumstances in our lives. Human societies give power to external events and people and *not to the natural source of power within each of us.* I was uncovering the truth that the power to create my destiny and all of life's details rested inside of me, my beliefs, and my actions and behaviors. I could choose to create my life and be the captain of my own destiny. I did not have to just let life happen to me; I could start to co-create my life using my thoughts, actions, and beliefs. This new view of life felt empowering and rewarding, and brought me to a place where I was I was beginning to feel connected to a higher source of power and not a victim of "reality."

I slowly pulled my act together and decided I was not going to try to go back to what I had done. My old life, my marriage, my home, and the old business were gone. I was pretty much broke and I had to do something to earn a living. I went to school and got my real estate license and found a position at a commercial real estate company, leasing shopping centers. I did not find it fulfilling, speeding around during the day showing people shopping centers or office building space. I did manage to sell a commercial building with great help from a serious long-time pro who co-brokered the sale. I sincerely disliked having to spend time at the city offices, looking up the sewer plots and plans and trying to get commercial buildings listed. I was not a match for this career.

I was at a critical point in my life. I could sell out and continue working in a job that did not bring me happiness, or I could begin to reevaluate and restructure my beliefs about what was really important—money or happiness? Why couldn't I have both?

Even with the pain and confusion I was feeling at that moment, I could still hear the small voice inside—the same voice that had, since the beginning, led me through the darkest of moments—telling me to pay attention and look at what in my life was not working. Then I would have to take the time to get clear on my new beliefs and allow them to motivate me toward my next level of success. After many long sleepless nights, I finally began to ask myself some of the most important questions of my life. What did I love to do? How did I want to live each day? What could I do that would allow me to wake up each morning excited about the day ahead? How could I earn a great living and love what I do?

Looking back, I realize it took a great deal of courage to face the reality that my life was not working and attempt to do something about it. I knew in my heart that, whatever I decided from that point forward, I would *have* to be independent. I had paid my dues making other people money. I was ready to do something that really excited and fulfilled me. I was ready to start my own business. I was ready to launch a new dream—this time, one that was closer to the "real authentic me."

A few weeks later, after a great deal of soul-searching, I created an opportunity at the real estate firm where I was working. The owners had been so wrapped up in their day-to-day problems that they were not training their employees to deal with the problems of the future. So, I proposed conducting a pilot training program that would empower their people to deal more effectively with the changes that were occurring due to the recession. To my surprise, they loved the idea and I set to work immediately! For the next three months, I worked nearly fourteen hours a day, researching and writing the program. The time went quickly because I enjoyed learning so much new information. On the big day, though ready to present the training program that I had written, I was terrified. Yet, after I began speaking, I felt as if I had been doing it my entire life. I was thrilled to have the opportunity to inspire people to make profound changes in their lives. In fact, I was so certain that this was what I wanted to do with my life that I took a leap of faith. Within a week, after the program was complete, I resigned from the firm to start my own training company—once again with the firm belief that I *must* go for my dreams.

I am a big believer in paying attention to the signposts the universe gives you. For years, people would say to me, you should be a professional speaker or an author, or be on TV. Those were nice complements but until you actually believe in yourself, you simply cannot see the signs the universe is giving you about your next adventure. Finally I got so fed up with my old life I sincerely felt I had nothing to lose. I figured I could not keep pretending I was wired like everyone else and could be happy to stay in a job for security. Deep down, I am a person who thrives with adventure and my own life certainly is my biggest adventure. With my new decision to be a professional speaker, I went to the printer and had cards made saying: *Lee Milteer, Professional Speaker and Trainer*. I was no longer going to wait for someone to inspire me. I was going for what I wanted.

As a speaker and author I would simply be selling ideas and concepts. I felt this was truly my calling in life. As confusing as my life had been in the past, what I was supposed to be doing now became crystal clear. I was to help others see their own potential and assist them with the techniques for finding their uniquely individual purpose. As I explored this new idea of creating my own reality, I began to realize more clearly that the true creative power I was feeling was coming from some source other than myself. I was not alone!

After a number of years speaking, I took notice that the salespeople attending my seminars were always searching for new ways to succeed in their work, yet they also seemed to want something more than just new techniques. They wanted their work to be rewarding. They wanted to have a sense of pride about their profession and to feel like they were making a contribution. These desires are spiritual in nature and I knew it would take spiritual techniques to bring about new results.

I too wanted more. After years of constant traveling and speaking and writing on human potential, I began to feel burned out. I was losing the passion for my work. This troubled me deeply, since I believed it was my soul's purpose to share information with people that would allow them to tap in to their own potential and talents.

The Magic Returns

So I went to one of my spiritual teachers for a counseling session. After listening to me describe my dismay at not feeling connected to my career and not being happy with my life, she said something that changed my life forever. I think of this teacher as an Earth Angel who gave me this profound gift of wisdom.

She said, *"You are a deeply spiritual woman and you have devoted over twenty years of your life to understanding universal spiritual truths. I have noticed that you live by day as a businesswoman in the mainstream world. You have created success in your field as well as being well respected. But in your private life you seem to be more interested in spiritual growth. I think part of your disillusionment with your career at this point is that your life is divided into two parts. Maybe it's time you merged. Marry your true spiritual passion with your profession. This is where you will find true happiness. Establish a new integrity between your personal and professional self."*

After that meeting, I felt as if a huge weight had been lifted from me. I gave myself permission to express my spiritual beliefs in my professional life. I didn't have to convince anyone to do anything. All I had to do was live and teach from a set of beliefs that honored who I was! Believing that my external world is a reflection of my internal world, I realized that I simply wanted to live from the truth as I knew it. No more masks. What you see is what you get. Merging these spiritual tools into my professional life affirmed and enhanced my integrity with myself and validated my feeling of being one with something bigger than myself.

So as you read these words please understand that sharing these materials has been a huge leap of faith for me. At one time, I was afraid to say the word God on stage. I had seen other business speakers talk about their religious beliefs and how this often turned people off in the business environment. My clients would write on my pre-program speakers' questionnaires that speakers should avoid speaking about religion. Early in my career I made a decision that I had to keep my spiritual beliefs and teachings separate from my business principles. Obviously, I have abandoned that thinking, and I now believe I must share these universal spiritual truths because these are truly the reason behind my success in business.

But let's be clear: I am not talking about *religion* here. I am sharing with you some simple tools that will allow you to honor your own personal spirituality, right where you are. These tools will help you use your inner power to fortify the life skills and resources you are already working with—and in every area of your life.

You have the power to create a joyful, happy, balanced, and prosperous life. You have the opportunity to use your life to make a difference in the world. Choose to use this book as a guide to help you create your own formula for success. Mold and shape this material into your own style and your own personality. Life is an adventure and your point of power to create whatever your heart desires is in this very moment!

What Did It All Mean?

Looking back on my life I can now see clearly the importance of all of these horrific life experiences. They instilled in me the need to access information *internally* versus the normal style of external programming. I now trust my inner knowledge far more than anything in the outside world and acquiring this skill has helped me become the successful businesswoman I am today. That was the purpose of it all.

But there was yet another important message that took me a while to understand: There are mystical energies everywhere in the world and there is an invisible presence that looks over you and guides you, *if you are open to it.* There is so much more to life than the eye can see. The BIG message is that we all have this magnificent purpose. We think we're insignificant, but the truth is we are all *very significant.* We're very important in life and life prepares us for our future. I often ponder that maybe the journey of our lives is not so much about becoming anything. Maybe it's about un-becoming everything that isn't really you, so you can be your authentic self—who you were meant to be in the first place.

THREE

The Magic of Your Mind

My main goal for this book is to share with you the magical tools that will help you stop just existing on the earth, feeling like a victim. I want to help you reclaim the magic that is within you, that you were born with but have not accepted or acknowledged before now.

Researchers report that 40,000 to 50,000 thoughts enter your mind every day. It has also been shown that as many as 80 percent of your thoughts are negative on an average day. That means you are reacting to external programming. Since our thoughts affect our emotions it is important that you recognize the numbing effect those negative thoughts have on your outlook, your attitude, your creativity, and your passion for life.

Most people believe that their personal thoughts have no power. Our thoughts have been described as harmless bits of consciousness that hold no substance or energy of their own. Neuroscientists, medical researchers, psychologists, and metaphysicians have proven that thoughts are electrical impulses that trigger chemical activity in the brain. When you think, you are giving your brain an electrical command and it responds by doing several things. Initially the brain reacts by releasing chemicals into the body and directing the central nervous system to take any required action. Your thoughts also trigger the brain to scan your memory and to record any necessary information about that thought that may be of future value. Your subconscious mind records every thought that goes through your conscious mind, as well as all the information automatically brought into the brain through all of your senses. These thoughts and information bits are then classified and recorded so they can be recalled when you need them.

First let's acknowledge that our brains are very sophisticated organs. We are made of more than just flesh and blood. In fact, we literally have four volts of electricity in our body. Every time we have a thought—right or wrong, true or false—some of that electric current travels from the conscious mind into the subconscious mind and creates an image or picture. We literally think in images, and the objective of the subconscious mind is to match the images in your mind with the reality of your life. All your future success must be envisioned in your mind before it can manifest in your life.

This is probably the opposite of what you have been taught to believe about your brain and about thinking. Since childhood, you've been taught to look for the evidence, the facts, and the proof *before* you believe something is possible. This limiting mindset certainly eliminates creative thoughts about what you believe is possible in your life. Your brain has been trained only to see and believe what the left-brain states are facts, thereby hampering your imagination and abilities to create a new reality with more personal power.

If you have unhealthy emotions of imagined fears, worry, resentment, or guilt, the body responds with a tense feeling of nervousness, stress-related illness, tiredness, and lack of energy and creativity. Your subconscious mind will produce whatever result you ask for. Shakespeare's statement from hundreds of years ago is still true: *"There is nothing good or bad, but thinking has made it so."*

You are made of energy and your self-image contains the imprinted energy patterns of who you are and what you believe. Think of this self-image as a blueprint from which your life is built. It is your Inner Energetic Blueprint.

The brain functions with precision, receiving, processing, storing, and then acting on the information it has stored. Remember that your brain, like the earth, does not discern what you plant. The earth works just as hard to grow weeds as it does beautiful flowers. The only difference is the seed that was sown. Like a seed, we are self-fulfilling prophecies because the mind, like the fertile soil of a garden, will produce what we have planted.

Many of your old self-limiting beliefs have no foundation of truth but they grow like weeds! Instead of empowering your authentic self and purpose, they hold you back from success. If you think or believe that you are destined to be poor, unlucky in love, clumsy, overweight, or average, which are all weed seeds, you will take unconscious actions that make these thoughts become reality. None of these thoughts are actually true, but continuing to think them creates beliefs and images in your mind, a sort of blueprint, which reinforces these negative and limiting statements until they actually become true for you.

The subconscious mind does not know the difference between factual reality and imagined reality. You know, your subconscious mind doesn't even know right from wrong. It doesn't know current events from past events or even imaginary events. It simply receives and files the thoughts. This powerful subconscious mind has the ability to hold and process massive amounts of data. The mind works upon the information and data you feed into it every day and creates the reality of your life from that information. That's why it's so important to carefully consider the kind of information you feed your mind. Everything that you think—true or false, good or bad——is processed by the conscious mind and imprinted on the subconscious. So, whatever information you repeatedly program into your subconscious about your abilities, your potential, and your worth is what you believe to be true about yourself and about what you will be able to manifest in your life.

The average person is so busy reinforcing their own existing limiting mental programs that they cannot connect with their authentic self's real talents and natural skills. Your current self-image, whether real or illusion, is the foundation upon which your entire life and future is built. You will simply act out the type of person you conceive yourself to be, based upon your beliefs about yourself. You will not know any better if you do not become conscious that you, and you alone, have the ability to re-direct the focus of your life by changing the thoughts you think about yourself.

Yet, the majority of our thoughts about our own abilities hold us back from achieving the quality of life that is available to us. It is human nature to follow the path of least resistance. Your mind also follows the habit of thoughts that create the least resistance. That is why the old thought patterns embedded in your mind (those "weed seed" thoughts) seem to have power to crowd out the new thought patterns or habits of mind that you would like to establish. By becoming truly conscious of this patterning effect and deliberately feeding your mind with thoughts that empower change, you magically create that new Inner Energetic Blueprint for your mind to operate from in the future.

Buddha said, *"All that we are is the result of what we have thought."* Your life is the sum total of the information you have programmed yourself to be by your thinking patterns—and for now, you believe it. You are influenced and programmed by the caliber of information that has been recorded in your own self-image, your Inner Energetic Blueprint.

Your Inner Energetic Blueprint is formed by your daily thoughts, and is the core of your being. It determines everything about you from how much money you make, your weight, how fast you age, the success of your relationships, and your risk ability, to how good you are at sports or math. This magical blueprint influences your brain about how to see the world. Are you an optimist, realist, or pessimist? Are you open-minded and curious about life or are you narrow-minded and not interested in learning anything new?

Every day, your Inner Energetic Blueprint sends you millions of messages about who you are. Most of us believe that we can't change our potential or our capabilities beyond whatever has been programmed into our Inner Energetic Blueprint by the many external influences we receive each day.

I have great news for you: You're not stuck with the old blueprint. You were born with a purpose and a reason for living and the truth is, for most people, that "purpose blueprint" got pushed into the back of your mental operations to make space for your survival-in-the-modern-world blueprint! As soon as you embrace these concepts and do the work to repair your blueprint, you will know that you have the choice to either reinforce old programs and beliefs about yourself (letting the weeds grow!) or to plant the seeds of power in your life with positive images.

So how did your self-image develop? Who told you who you would become? How are these images reinforced in your life? Let's look back at how it all began.

Without realizing it was happening, your brain was fed outdated, obsolete, one-sided information that hinders your motivation and distorts your beliefs about your capacity to create a more fulfilling and prosperous life. Most of our educational systems don't teach accurate information about how our minds operate. We are taught to follow the leaders, to do as we are told, and to behave. This type of thinking will not afford you an original life nor will it allow you to break free from the limitations of indoctrination by the world you were brought up in. You must start to question which of the beliefs you hold that serve you and which ones sabotage you.

Think for a moment of the untold hours of negative fear-based programming you have been subjected to over the course of your life. Just for fun, let's talk about those insane studies we are subjected to in all news, magazines, and newspapers. For example: The list of foods and components of foods that are bad for you is too long to master and changes almost daily. Salt is beneficial; no, salt will kill you. Ditto, red meat, cheese, carbohydrates, wine, and just about everything else you eat. Recently *Time Magazine* put butter on its cover for a redemptive article after decades of media telling everyone that butter is not good for your heart. I am not saying these things are good or bad, but the point here is that you are always being programmed by mind-numbing repetition of negative news from the media. Watch out for negative information that keeps you in a state of anxiety, doubt, fear, and lack of confidence.

This may be hard to swallow, but the truth is, we have been victims of our own societies' programming. We are indoctrinated by the beliefs of those who raised us, the schools and religions we learned from, and the culture of the times we live in. I will admit most of that programming is from people who have no ill intent but who were also programmed with faulty information. And yes, there are some people programming you who have nothing in mind but their own agendas, who are power and money hungry and operate purely from greed. It is your job to discern who is who. That is why you have free will.

Here is an important piece of the puzzle you need so you can take your personal power back: Your subconscious mind and your Inner Energetic Blueprint are tied together.

You were not born with negative information about yourself. You came into this world without any limiting beliefs at all. Any limiting information in your brain came from external sources from the environment that you were raised in, and the worldview of those who raised you. You cannot fully utilize your potential until you decide to take responsibility for the caliber of information you put into your mind and literally redesign your own personal Inner Energetic Blueprint.

For example, if as a child someone whom you considered an authority figure told you repeatedly something negative about yourself over a period of time, your subconscious mind would have kept recording that negative message until you consistently thought of it as a true fact for your self-image. The truth is that it was only someone's opinion, yet you have been solidly programmed that the message was, indeed, a fact. This may have caused you to believe that you don't have the potential, talent, or abilities that you needed to excel at the subject you were programmed by an outside source to fail.

So if, as a kid, you were told repeatedly that you were not good at math, when you have to perform a math calculation without a calculator now, you most likely experience mental and physical stress. Your brain freezes up because there is a conflict between your task and your beliefs about your ability. Because you were labeled as not good at math, you now doubt yourself, which inhibits your ability to use your potential in math. Most likely you will not choose a career that would need math or you would find ways to avoid it. The bottom line is, that "label" affected your life choices. We are truly self-filling prophecies based on the reinforced ideas that have been ingrained in our brains—the weed seeds sown by others, often family and teachers, in our fertile minds.

Sadly, we are not aware of the damage all this outside mental training does for our peace of mind. It affects our ability to take risks in the future because of the "be-afraid" scripts running in our brains. Further, we are rarely aware that we are asking others to put limiting ideas into their brains. But we do it daily.

You can change all this negative brain training by first simply being aware of it, and then having a clear intention every day to upgrade your mental scripts. Become aware that you have the power to change your life. Then practice becoming aware of your inner thoughts and self-talk so you can change it. Your subconscious mind is under the command of your conscious mind and it will store the positive scripts that you command it to store.

Remember that every day your subconscious mind is recording how your senses experience the external world and the thoughts you have about it all. This means that as you involuntarily or intentionally absorb daily news, TV shows, movies, newspapers, magazines, books, Internet sites, social media sites, your emails, texts, video-conferencing, and all conversations and all highly-charged emotions, every single bit of it is being recorded in your Inner Energetic Blueprint. Garbage In-Garbage Out is a phrase to remember when considering these ideas, because it is so true. When you allow garbage information into your mind, you are going to get faulty data back with which to make decisions! You cannot think thoughts of victimhood or lack and reap success and prosperity. Weed seeds cannot produce the lovely flowers you seek.

It's no wonder that some of us fail or give up at new ventures before we even start. Unless we take charge of the caliber of information that goes into our mind and change our inner pictures, we will be saddled with an outdated self-image and a comfort zone that will not allow us to become motivated to make our dreams come true. In the words of the late Dr. Maxwell Maltz, in his famous book *Psycho-Cybernetics, "The self-image sets the boundaries of individual accomplishment. It defines what you can and cannot do. Expand the self-image and you expand the areas of the possible."*

Famous writer Ralph Waldo Emerson declared that, *"The ancestor of every action is thought."* Your point of power is this very second in time and you can claim your personal power to decide today to no longer be a victim of the past or a victim of the outside world's programming. You can do that by maintaining constant awareness about your daily thoughts because thoughts have energy and a specific vibration rate. When you shift your inner vibration frequencies, you change what you attract into your life. You literally have the ability now to start upgrading and updating the information you believe about yourself and what is possible. When you start upgrading your belief systems, it will imbue your life with new capabilities and talents that literally create new patterns of energy in your Inner Energetic Blueprint.

Awaken to the knowledge that your big power in life—maybe your only power—is to take control of your inner thoughts, because they control your life. Life would not be so challenging if we humans were exposed to more truth about how life actually operates. Instead we are spoon-fed disempowering fear-based information daily by the media, schools, governments, and other power-based organizations that have their own agendas to promote. These completely ordinary functions of society tend to keep people in the prescribed neat little-box thinking mentality. Today is the day to break free from that external control over your life and future.

As success Author Napoleon Hill wrote, *"You have absolute control over but one thing—your thoughts. This divine prerogative of thought is the sole means by which you may control your destiny."* Hill continues, emphasizing that if you don't control your mind, you won't be able to control anything else, either. He calls your mind your "spiritual estate" and points out that whatever you think today will determine what you experience tomorrow.

To reclaim the magic you have within you, the magic to create the life you want, you must take charge of your thoughts. You must be aware of the caliber of information to which you are exposed daily. You must wake up and stop the insanity of letting this negative information be fed to your brain.

If you want more on this topic to assist you to reclaim your mental magic, you may want to invest in my audio program: *Reinventing Your Life: Success Self-Programming,* which has sold over a million copies and has assisted people to understand their ability to change their life. This informative and entertaining program can be found as a download at my website, *www.leemilteer.com.*

You have the power to upgrade your thoughts and train your mind to choose what you think instead of allowing random thoughts to hold you hostage. Your goal is to become inner-directed and focused, so that you decide what you want to think, rather than having your thoughts and emotions determined by the world around you.

To create this new Inner Energetic Blueprint, you have to gift your brain with new positive scripts that are stronger and more powerfully aimed at the life you want to live. Your subconscious mind will immediately start to act on the new stronger mental images. Then it becomes a matter of your subconscious mind trying to decide which program offers the path of least resistance. Your mind will simply pursue the program that has the most energy, the more specific direction, and the most power. You get that power with repetition of the new statements, which will build your new self-image.

The subconscious mind is a neutral machine which responds to information without subjective regard for its value in truth or accuracy. Your personal subconscious mind will accept and attempt to act on any information you give it, if you tell it often enough and strongly enough what you want. Frequent repetition of the new information that you desire to have your brain act upon is the powerful magical secret to eliminating unwanted scripts. The simple fact is that the more often you present your subconscious mind with the new preferred information, the more opportunities your subconscious mind will have to accept it and integrate it into your life.

Ultimately, you have to accept 100 percent responsibility for yourself and your future by controlling the caliber of information that you feed your magic mind. It is futile to believe that other people or outside circumstances will take care of you. If you search deeply in your heart, you know that only you will really take care of you. Taking full responsibility for your thoughts and actions is the true dividing line between successful and unsuccessful people. It is at the core of your success as an individual.

Schedule Reprogramming Times

The current brain research shows that it takes your magical brain at least twenty-one to thirty days to imprint a new electrical current that will form new bridges in the brain. It would be highly beneficial for you to set up a thirty-day regimen to reboot your Inner Energetic Blueprint. You can help it create a totally positive self-image that you personally decide on for your future. Your brain likes rhythms, so it is beneficial to begin at the same time each day. For example, first thing in the morning just before you get up and become active is one of the most powerful times of the day, so make the most of it. Remember, what your mind focuses on expands and sets the tone for your day. Setting your tone for the day is important to prevent you from allowing the external sources of negative information to determine your attitude for your day.

About 85 percent or more of the daily news you digest is negative or fearful information. The really bad thing about this is that you don't consciously realize how your feelings and emotions are being impacted—your subconscious mind will absorb everything to which it is exposed! Instead of allowing your moods, emotions, and mindset to be determined by the headlines, doesn't it seem like a more appropriate strategy to have planned methods to deliberately and consistently insert new positive ideas that empower you and enrich your day?

The second time of day which you will find to be very powerful for retraining your mind is just before you go to sleep. As you get comfortable and prepare yourself for sleep, begin repeating selected positive statements, which I call declarations or affirmations, to yourself until you naturally fall asleep. You will sleep better and awaken in a better mood because you have installed information in your subconscious mind that is healing and soothing.

When I started using these nurturing declarations, I felt more enthusiastic and creative in my life. That in turn created better quality days for me, as I felt freed up to be the authentic me. Miracles happened for me as my mind flowed with new creative thinking for solutions to old problems. I found myself less encumbered by old mental demons or the internal dialogue that had sabotaged me and my potential in the past.

Have you ever noticed that when you go to bed angry or frustrated, you tend to wake up with that same anger, or in a bad mood? This is your classic example of "garbage in-garbage out." The trick is to take charge of the quality of information your brain gets exposed to before you go to sleep. I suggest that as you are going to sleep at night you do something that has worked wonders for me personally. I simply tell myself that I love myself several times before I go to sleep. I find it has healed a part of me that truly needed to feel loved.

Another good place to use dead time to program yourself is in the shower. Start a wonderful ritual of saying your new empowered statements out loud with great enthusiasm while enjoying your morning shower. You can even sing them! It is a safe place and no one can hear you.

Another ideal time and place to insert better mental programming is while driving in your car. The average person spends more than seven hours per week in a car. This presents a prime opportunity for saying your new positive affirmations about yourself as if they were already true. Whether you say them out loud or silently to yourself, by speaking in a deliberate and measured manner, the words you utter become symbols of your power. You will start to view yourself as a directed person in control of your life.

Put your declarations on a digital recording. This gives your subconscious the opportunity to listen to your own voice. Your voice is the most powerful voice to your subconscious mind. I call these recordings "My Self-Programming Commercials."

Write your declarations. Whenever you have any dead time, as in waiting for an appointment, write out a powerful Declaration eight to sixteen consecutive times. Focus your attention on the meaning of the words and the feeling you get while writing them.

Post your most powerful and important declarations in places where you will see them frequently. Even though your conscious mind will start to ignore them, your subconscious mind always sees and records them. I personally have mine at my desk, refrigerator, bathroom mirror, and inside of my closet. I put these in personal places because they are not for public viewing.

Using these techniques will divest you of the encumbrance of others' beliefs, allowing you to become free to create the quality of life you deserve. Your personal declarations will help you gain the confidence to step out on your own. Creating and repeatedly stating your personal desires for your life will help you find the discipline, motivation, and energy to manifest a brand new reality and life for yourself. You have absolutely nothing to lose by trying these techniques and everything to gain.

Whether we acknowledge it or not, we are influencing people around us on a daily basis. Since it is proven that our self-image is created by our environment, why not benefit others by looking for, finding, and reaffirming what they do right? In this manner, instead of reinforcing negative programs to those around us, we can hopefully add some positive reinforcement. Your motto should be: Find the good in people and yourself and praise it.

If you have kids, I also suggest that you share these simple instructions with them so they will have the skills to create their own beautiful futures. Also, I sincerely hope you are taking this information to heart and upgrading the way you teach and speak to your children. We are all products of our environment and you can break the chain of pain if you become aware!

Magical Brain Retraining Statements

Here some personal examples I use almost daily, plus some other ideas to help you get started. Please take time to create your own personal declarations. *(It is important to insert your name in your declaration when possible.)*

- I (Your Name) NOW take full responsibility for my life and my thoughts.
- I am a perfect child of the universe.
- I love and appreciate myself and the journey that has led me to become the person I am today. I am open to new improvements daily.
- I am filled with creative energy and enthusiasm for life.
- I am blessed with wonderful health, happiness, joy, and blessings daily.
- Everything I need and want flows to me easily.
- Infinite Cosmic Intelligence supplies me with the inspiration to allow my authentic self to come out and prosper.
- Daily life is more joyful and rewarding. It has been worth the journey to become empowered.
- I am feeling healthier and more vitality daily.
- I am listening to and taking action on my intuition more every day, making my life flow easily.
- I am easily and effortlessly attracting wonderful personal and business opportunities to myself that utilize my natural talents and experience.
- I am attracting wonderful new people in my life who are supportive and energizing to be around.
- I am co-creating with Infinite Cosmic Intelligence the most perfect life.

- I am feeling more confident and successful daily.
- I am an actor to life.
- I am now honoring and appreciating myself and my personal gifts more and more daily.
- I am giving myself permission to release other people's drama and trauma and see the good in all people and all things.
- I am now forgiving all souls including myself for anything that hurt me in the past.
- I am accepting that I am a work in progress and I am getting better every day in every way.

Homework:

Create as many new magical brain retraining statements as you can to match your life right now. Write declarations to empower you to move past old, limiting views of who you are and what you can manifest in this life.

These statements are also known as affirmations or auto-suggestions. These terms came about because the word affirmation means to make firm. I prefer the term declarations because I am declaring who and what I am becoming to myself, my subconscious, and to the world. Wishful thinking has no effect or power other than to serve as a source of frustration for you at not getting what you want. When you declare you are going to do something you are creating a new program in your mind and, with repetition and action, this clear intention allows you to manifest new outcomes in your life.

Simple Formulas for Making & Using Declarations and Affirmations to Upgrade Your Inner Energetic Blueprint for New Results

Act as if your new declarations are true. It is important to *give yourself permission* to believe your declarations are *true right now.* By allowing yourself to capture the feeling you'd experience with this new picture, you allow your mind to imprint a new and stronger picture in your subconscious mind. This tool allows you to imprint your Inner Energetic Blueprint, which in turn creates a new pattern for achieving your goals.

- Create statements that picture yourself to be exactly what you want to be versus what others have told you is possible.
- When using your declarations, make sure that these new phrases have emotional force behind them. Emotion harnesses the extra energy you need to fund this magical shift. The words are not as important as your feelings.
- Always use the present tense. Example: *"I am now a published author"* rather than *"I want to be a published author."* Or if it is your weight you want to change: *"I am now a perfect size __ and weigh __ lbs."*
- State your declarations in the positive, rather than affirming what you don't want. Example: *"I now awaken on time, bright and fresh,"* instead of *"I no longer oversleep."*
- Keep your declarations short and simple to make a greater impact on your subconscious and to make them easier to remember. Example: *"I am now easily and effortlessly on time."*

- Use declarations that feel positive, expanding, and supportive. Only use declarations that *feel* right to you. If you use statements that feel incongruent, you will not believe yourself.
- Create declarations that focus on the "new you." Embrace a spirit of creating something new, rather than changing or resisting current reality. Example: *"I love being productive and finishing projects."*
- Use your name in your declaration whenever possible. This helps your subconscious mind accept a new picture of who you are becoming. Example: *"I, [Your Name], am now filled with creative, exciting energy."*

Negative Programming Pattern Interrupts

What do you say to yourself when you have made a mistake or reinforced a belief that holds you back? The sad news is that most of us actually make things worse for ourselves by browbeating ourselves about how dumb or stupid we are, destroying our self-esteem in the process. Everyone has off days and we all are human and make mistakes. We certainly don't berate babies trying to learn to walk by telling them how uncoordinated they are. What good is that? We reassure them, telling them it's okay and encourage them to do better next time. So why are you so hard on yourself? In some ways you are a baby right now, learning to retrain your magical mind from all the negative messages from yourself and others. The bottom line is this: you must be nurturing and loving to yourself if you want to improve your future and imprint an updated Inner Energetic Blueprint with the new you!

I have been teaching and using a life-changing technique called a pattern interrupt. In a pattern interrupt, you simply stop yourself from putting yourself down and belittling yourself with negative self-talk. By doing this you can prevent yourself from reinforcing the old unproductive mental pattern.

Example: How many times have you caught yourself saying, *"I am always late?"* Now think about what you are programming yourself to be—late! You now have a better strategy: instead of reinforcing the negative habit, say to yourself: *"Cancel, that is not like me. Next time I will leave earlier and be on time."* The purpose of the pattern interrupt is to follow up negative verbal or mental programming with statements to your subconscious mind to imprint a new thought. In this case, *"That's not like me to be late. I always leave early and I am always on time."*

I personally wish I could just catch myself once and suddenly have my mental patterns cleaned up—but this is not the case at all. As I have said earlier, it takes at least twenty-one to thirty days for your brain to program a change and for it to actually stick with you to become your new mental pattern.

When you use this technique, you are literally taking the four volts of electrical energy in your brain and creating a new program and your brain needs time to digest and absorb the new concept.

Your Past is Not Your Future—Unless You Want It to Be!

We can either dwell on the past or *move beyond it and focus on the future.* We all have negative past stories and, since we are self-fulfilling in our predictions about ourselves, it is time to stop dredging up and replaying the old bad luck stories, failed relationships, physical ailments, and all the negative times in our past. When we take the time to rehash these "stories," we are contributing to the Inner Energetic Blueprints that will determine our future. Enough with being the *victim*! Get over it now!

Dwelling on these past failures and injustices uses your electrochemical mental energy and *recreates the same bad experience* in your subconscious mind! This in turn gives it more power to make you feel bad or unworthy.

All energy has effects. What you focus on expands. Focusing on past painful events has a profound effect on what your future will be. Any time you dwell on your past failures or inadequacies, you only create more fear about your opportunities in the future. When you do this, you are literally rehearsing for future failure!

What your future will look like is totally dependent on the information and direction you give your brain with your self-talk. It is a practiced skill to learn to be able to choose what thoughts come into your mind, rather than be ruled by the thoughts that flow at random. You must recognize that you have the power of control to master your inner dialogue to make your mind *obey* you rather than *control* you. Realize that the past is a locked door. No matter how hard you may try, you cannot go back and change it. Your point of power is in the present—it is what you do with your present time and energy. Your future is created by the thoughts and energy you use today. It is up to you to give yourself the motivation, direction, and permission to stop talking about and thinking about what happened in the past. Focus your mental, physical, spiritual, and emotional life energy on what you are going to create in the future.

There are many probable futures that you have the power to create . . . so which one do you want? Only you can write your life's script. Your destiny and future is not preordained. Nor is it set in stone, nor are you destined to do anything other than the path you choose to take! Be smart and take the time to program the information, knowledge, and skills into your daily repertoire so that you are not a victim of life. Your thoughts create your reality. Your future is up to you!

Magical Essences . . .

- All of your future success must be envisioned in your mind before it can manifest in your life.
- You are made of energy and your self-image contains the imprinted energy patterns of who you are and what you believe. Think of this self-image as a blueprint from which your life is built. It is your Inner Energetic Blueprint.
- Whatever information you repeatedly program into your subconscious about your abilities, your potential, and your worth is what you believe to be true about yourself and about what you will be able to manifest in your life.
- By becoming truly conscious of this patterning effect and deliberately feeding your mind with thoughts that empower change, you magically create a new Inner Energetic Blueprint for your mind to operate from in the future.
- Your subconscious mind and your Inner Energetic Blueprint are tied together.
- Awaken to the knowledge that your big power in life—maybe your only power—is to take control of your inner thoughts, because they control your life.
- Whether you say affirmations out loud or silently to yourself, by speaking in a deliberate and measured manner, the words you utter become symbols of your power.

- Use a pattern interrupt. In a pattern interrupt, you simply stop yourself from putting yourself down and belittling yourself with negative self-talk. By doing this you can prevent yourself from reinforcing the old unproductive mental pattern.

- Focusing on past painful events has a profound effect on what your future will be. Any time you dwell on your past failures or inadequacies, you only create more fear about your opportunities in the future.

FOUR

The Magic of Your Energy

Every person has five kinds of energy: physical, mental, emotional, spiritual, and financial. When you view these energies as part of your life currency, it naturally follows that the way you spend, save, and budget them on a daily, weekly, and monthly basis becomes extremely important; as important as the way you manage your money. Most people never think about how they spend their energy, and at the end of the day they haven't managed their energy and have run out. They don't have any left to do the extra things they want to do. One of the most important things you can do every day is make sure you guard your life currency as you do your money. Your control and/or lack of control of these energies will determine your success and happiness and what you're able to manifest in your business and life.

I have learned how to tap into Infinite Intelligence to manifest magic in my life in very short time spans and you can too. I became successful and wealthy in spite of circumstances, massive competition, and all of the odds that confronted me—and you can too. I succeeded where others failed because I had the serious advantage of using Universal Principles and managing my energy fields. You may never have paid attention to the thoughts, feelings, and behaviors that have drained your time and energy, but feelings of anxiety or unnecessary worry, fears, doubts, and old grudges take up *energy*. Since you only have so much mental, physical, emotional, spiritual, and financial energy, you certainly don't want to waste it in directions that don't serve you or your intentions for your life.

You see, only when you are at the top of your game energetically are you resourceful, creative, brilliant, and effective. We all know this, but before we know it, we sometimes allow "stuff" to get us off balance. These leaks and vampires cause us to get out of integrity with our intentions, and throw us into a tailspin feeling overwhelmed, frustrated, angry, and dissatisfied in life and business.

On the other hand, when you're effectively managing your energy, you are in the flow of Infinite Intelligence. You are at the right place at the right time; synchronicities happen for you that set you on the right course of action. These are magical moments when things just go perfectly, as if divinely guided by invisible forces. You are aligned with your Source energy. You are in vibrational harmony with your higher self's purpose for you and it feels as if heaven's door opens. Your reality will unfold to bless your life in ways that feel almost magical.

The secret is to be aware and conscious of when you start to experience any self-defeating thoughts or behaviors that are out of integrity with your real purpose in life. I've found the best ways to help balance and get the most from the five types of energy, and I'm going to share those secrets with you in this chapter so that instead of letting the world control you, you can decide how you will use your life energy.

1. Physical Energy Currency

"A wise man should consider that health is the greatest of human blessings."
—Hippocrates

Let's look first at your physical energy and the importance of how you use your body—the vehicle that gets you around earth! It is the good health of your body that allows you to live a successful and happy life—yet sadly, so many people miss this. Are you treating your body well? Are you getting the recommended amount of exercise each week? Are you eating fresh, unprocessed foods and not over-eating? Are you getting enough quality rest?

It's time to be honest and have some personal integrity with your physical energy currency. If you are going on peak capacity and burning the candle at both ends, watch out. You will run out of physical energy if you continue on this spending spree, just as you would with money. Then you will be left with nothing.

We all talk about the need for good health, but we don't follow the rules ourselves, and we deplete our bodies of this vital energy source. You only have twenty-four hours in a day and it is up to you to figure out how to utilize your energy within the allotted timeframe in order to harness your maximum creativity. Are you worn out at day's end, or is your energy level still relatively high? How are you really using your physical energy each day? Where is it going? Are you using your energy to create valuable work in the world or in your home, or is it expended mostly by busy work and useless unproductive activities?

Please remember that your physical body and energy tie directly to your happiness and success in life. Think for a minute how, when your energy gets depleted, things begin to break down and decisions become hard. Your creativity and your motivation wane. You find yourself procrastinating, and being indecisive, frustrated, and confused.

One of the goals you must have is to allow your body to heal itself with sleep. Poor sleep quality will lead to impaired thinking and memory loss. When you improve your sleep, you will become healthy and more productive. Improve your sleep by cutting off electronics and the TV an hour before you go to bed. Instead, establish a soothing pre-sleep routine like reading or taking a hot bath. Use relaxing herbs and essential oils like lavender and chamomile to help you calm down to go to sleep, and avoid caffeine for four to six hours before you go to bed.

Another physical challenge we face is dealing with the daily stress we encounter—though some people don't even feel it physically until it is too late to repair easily. While civilization has evolved, our prehistoric response to stress has not. Our stress response developed through our ancestors back when they were running and/or fighting for their lives. Enter the Fight or Flight Response. Fight or flight is a physiological reaction that happens in response to a perceived threat to survival—whether it is real or imagined. There's no thinking involved, your blood pressure automatically elevates, stress hormones get released, and everything *not* important to survival shuts down, including non-essential survival systems like digestion, reproduction, and cell growth. This response to stress also stores in your body's chemical memory so that the next time you encounter whatever it is, you automatically perceive it as a bad thing and recreate the stress response you had last time—unless you interrupt that pattern.

In today's world, rather than saber-tooth tigers, our stressors include work-related issues, home issues, negative people, noise, information overload, and our perceived need to respond to everything right away. Life threatening or not, our bodies still respond the same way and if we don't do anything about it, a state of chronic stress builds into the body and mind. This depletes our ability to make good decisions, which clearly affects life on all levels.

If you do not pay attention to the implications of daily stress you will have to deal with the possible consequences including:

- Premature aging: The more stress you have, the more your cells look and act older
- Impaired thinking and memory loss
- Compromised immune system
- Infertility
- Weight gain and "stress" fat around the middle of your body

The good news is, there are many possible strategies to reduce your physical stress on a daily basis. Make sure you get enough exercise, maintain a nutrition program focused on removing the processed foods from your diet, and drink more water. Try yoga or tai chi, mediation, time in nature, playing with your animal companions, or enjoying a hobby that enlivens you. In addition, separating yourself from negative people will also assist you in lowering your physical experience of stress.

If you truly want to reclaim the magic in your life, first make your physical energy a big priority. When you do, you will notice right away that you have more available energy to take action on the ideas and dreams you want to manifest. The real message here is that your physical health is actually one of your greatest gifts in life. Most people squander their physical energy by mis-treating their bodies, their temple and vehicle to navigate this earth. You have to respect and cherish your body in order to have the magic energy to manifest your goals.

2. Mental Energy Currency

Your mental energy is crucial. There's an old saying which suggests that we are the sum total of the five people we most often associate with—hence the need to pay attention to who and what influences you. You must make a conscious decision to remove yourself from energy "vampires." Just say *no* to them in your head.

Speaking of secondhand negativity, it is important to be aware of your environment and how it affects you. Negative news and negative people deplete your energy. They suck the life and enthusiasm out of you and erode your ability to view the landscape of your own reality in a positive way. As a result, you miss the pockets of opportunity available to you to act positively in your daily life.

When you hear others say crazy stuff, immediately mentally repeat, "No, no, no, I don't believe that. That's not true." Never let your unconscious mind be influenced by secondhand negativity, especially from sources that have an agenda, like the news media.

And here's something interesting: If your body doesn't feel good, it's often because you're not thinking great thoughts. Please be honest with yourself about who and what is influencing you. Make a list of the people who make you feel good and enliven your spirit. Make another list of those who drag you down and leave you feeling negative and bitter. It's critical that you release the things and people that drag you down. You must begin now to change your inner beliefs. Once you do, the outer conditions will follow suit and change accordingly.

You must always nurture and feed your mind positivity. This means you should surround yourself with other smart, like-minded people who are visionary thinkers and who will challenge you and tell you the truth. We all need knowledgeable associates and friends who are honest—to help keep us on course. We need this kind of positive investment of mental energy. You need people of substance to tell you when your plans and goals are good and when they're not so good, because it's easy to lose perspective when you become emotionally attached to your ideas.

Remember this about your mental energy: When you're thinking positive thoughts you usually continue to think about positive things. When you think negative thoughts, you will tend to continue down the road of negativity. When you find yourself getting into an unhealthy state of mind, when you're in a bad mood and everything is going downhill quickly, you have to interrupt the pattern of your thoughts. Go play with your kids or your pets. Go take a walk outside in nature if possible. Go do something fun for five minutes. Do anything that is a pattern interrupt. Remember that the body follows the mind so your stress will ease as the joy you focus on expands into the rest of your day!

There's a quote by Gordon Hinckley that I love: *"Stop seeking out the storms and enjoy more fully the sunlight."* Right now, it's important to evaluate your mindset. Have you fallen into bad thinking habits, always looking for what is wrong in life? It's easy to fall into this mode when you allow other people to be negative when around you.

I would also like to remind you to stop using your energy to try to change other people. Your job is to release the things that drag you down. The truth is, there is little sense in attempting to change other people or external conditions. You must first change your inner beliefs and then outer conditions will change accordingly. It's not your job in life to fix others, but to nurture yourself so that you can offer appropriate assistance.

3. Emotional Energy Currency

So, how's your emotional energy management? Our emotions seem to come and go as they will, but they are actually triggered by our thoughts, and we have thousands of thoughts each day. Due to the fact that what we focus on expands, our emotional states follow our thought patterns.

When we get upset, we tend to digress into old childhood patterns, thoughts, and fears, and to lose control of our emotional energy. To really be in charge of our emotions, we must control the caliber of information that goes into our minds. We must be selective, because the body will follow the mind. If you start thinking about mistakes you've made, your body reverts to anxiety and feelings of failure, even if the mistake was twenty-five years ago. Your body cannot tell the difference between an imaginary and a real thing.

Notice that often, when you're upset with someone, you become a "reactor" rather than a "responder," which limits the value of what you offer in a tense situation. A first response based on an emotional reaction will usually get you in trouble and you may say something you will later regret. Try asking yourself: "What is my second and/or third response to this situation?" A second (or third) response usually comes from a more calm and reasonable place than the highly emotionally-charged first response. After all, people may forgive you, but they will not forget.

It's a good idea to create a twenty-four-hour rule so you don't respond to insane or angry people for twenty-four to forty-eight hours. Ask yourself: "Does this need to be answered? Does it need to be answered now? Does it need to be answered by me?" The benefit the twenty-four-hour rule is two-fold: one, so you don't pick up the insane or angry energy of the other person, and two, so you don't say something you'll later regret.

When we're in a good-feeling state, we're able to be much more in tune with our goals and desires. We attract situations, people, and events that help us attain the goals we've set for ourselves. We have the skill of awareness to see solutions to old problems, and hold lightly any challenges that may cross our paths.

Start paying attention to how you're feeling on a daily basis. When you catch yourself starting to feel bad, stop and reach for the next best-feeling thought. Like with your mental energy, doing a simple pattern interrupt can determine the quality of the whole rest of your day.

4. Spiritual Energy Currency

Integrating spiritual principles into your life both personally and professionally adds a new dimension to your success. Most people think that success only comes from using physical and mental energy when, in truth, that is only about 1 percent of their power. Consciously partnering with your highest nature—with your God Source—allows you to use the 99 percent of the power that is yours if you start to open your mind to its unlimited power.

Spirituality does not refer to any particular religion or religious belief. Whatever religion you practice that helps you connect to the Source is good. It *is* entirely your choice and of course, it's a very personal choice. In my own journey towards spiritual awareness, one quote from the book *The Road Less Traveled* by M. Scott Peck comes to mind:

"Spiritually evolved people by virtue of their discipline, mastery and love are people of extraordinary competence, and in their competence, they are called on to serve the world. In their love, they answer the call. They are inevitably, therefore, people of great power, although the world may generally behold them as a quiet ordinary person, since more often than not, they will exercise their power in quiet or hidden ways."

Once you begin to understand spirituality, you will know that there is more to life than what we access daily through our five senses. Our souls are not defined by birth and death on earth, nor controlled only by the rules governing the physical world. Life is more multi-dimensional in nature. As you add the spiritual energy component, you become more consciously aware of both the physical and the invisible dimensions that surround us.

Spiritual people in general tend to be more focused on their internal power and personal growth. They understand and appreciate their ability to decide how to interact with the physical world, how to mentally frame their experiences, and they are comfortable with the concept of inner guidance and intuition. They believe there's an invisible eternal part of themselves that is available for assistance whenever they need it.

When you feel connected to Source, you can definitely be a provider of goodwill to all. You can make a difference if you decide to see yourself as a person of service, and invest your spiritual energy in others. No matter what you do in life, you have the power and ability to allow your activities to uplift and help other people get what they want and need. By focusing on achieving a balanced, spiritually integrated life, you will have peace of mind. You will be amazed at how quickly this happens. I urge you to lift your spiritual energy level and embrace an inner mindset that will connect your spirituality with all areas of your life.

If you would like to read more about spirituality in life and the workplace, I invite you to read my book, *Spiritual Power Tools for Successful Selling*, that outlines how to harness the power of your mind through intuition, vision, and self-discipline.

5. Financial Energy Currency

In the area of your financial energy, you must take great care. Because they represent the investment of your mind and body, money and wealth have energy about them. An old saying goes like this: Respect money or be deserted by it. You are respecting yourself when you are careful and attentive to the finances in your life. How might you do that?

- Pay attention and know exactly what you have in your accounts.
- Hold every investment accountable, fully monetizing all assets and opportunities.
- Prudently develop cash reserves so you always feel secure.
- Make a habit of generous monthly giving to carefully selected worthwhile organizations or people.
- Focus on growing your money and investing wisely for the long run. Don't spend your interest money but reinvest it to grow money.
- Be aware of and actively remove waste and sloth, which are disrespectful to financial energy.

Treat your money with the true respect it deserves. Everyone in the world operates from a money-type system so devote attention to how you think about money and how much you respect it.

Personally, I've always believed in living below my means and the importance of creating a nice big nest egg. With each paycheck, I always "pay myself first," making sure that a portion goes into an appropriate savings or investment vehicle that I refuse to touch. I suggest that this be at least 10 percent of your salary. Once you make the commitment to begin saving like this, you must not stop. You should also determine a reasonable amount of your wealth that you gift to others—to the charities of your choice. You must become aware of the power of your financial energy and learn to be smart about it.

I always make sure that my office knows how important money is and that time is also a form of currency—just like money. Time should be spent doing effective money-making, profitable things. In business, your energy needs to go towards making sure your customers, clients, or patients are being taken care of since, in reality, they are the ones paying your salaries.

I urge you to *think big* and really *go for life*! Don't play it so safe financially that you miss out on success and prosperity. Allow a little risk-taking when budgeting your financial energy. Begin today to give yourself permission to *think big*. You are the only person who can give yourself the go-ahead to leap to the next level of income, success, and achievement.

Love, Nurture, and Protect Your Energy

You must be the captain of your own ship! If you truly want to be a massive success, you can't allow yourself to be controlled by the outside world and the needs and wants of others. You have to take care of yourself before you can take care of others. This takes some courage to do, but you can't give what you don't have. If you aren't willing to love, nurture, and protect yourself from the crisis demands of others, you will get sucked into the mud (the problem) with them. Yes, I am asking you to be selfish, but it certainly is time someone gave you the message that in today's world of needy people and their problems, you have to have the discernment to see how you're spending your life energy. Don't let others suck the life out of you. You must take care of you first.

I want to give you some advice, which I encourage you to use on your employees, neighbors, friends, and people who want *you* to solve their problems. If you allow yourself to get into a crisis mindset with another person, you can't help! To find creative, valuable avenues of action, you must be grounded, clear, and in a mindset that enables you to look for solutions. You won't be able to see appropriate solutions while you are upset, freaked out, or frustrated, so don't go there! Have discernment about how you spend your emotions. The truth is, you need your energy to handle your own problems. Why do you think you can fix anyone else's problems? Heads up—stop it! It's not your job to be the rescuer of the world. Stop wasting your time and energy on things and people you can't control.

I am challenging you to awaken the magic energies within yourself. You can learn to live without struggle and worry. Living your life by happenstance often leads to fruitless, powerless situations. Practicing the art of deliberate creation will bring you a conscious awareness of personal control and help you to optimize your choices.

Remember, your present reality is the sum of all of your thoughts. If your life seems small, it's probably because your dominant visual self-image is small. If you think big, you'll get big results and attract new resources and options. Learning to manage your five energies-physical, mental, emotional, spiritual, and financial as a vital part of your "life currency" will bring you a wealth of happiness and prosperity now and in the years ahead. I invite you to learn more about the 5 Types of Energy in my video series, which you can find at *www.fivetypesofenergy.com/book*. In these videos, I share how to use your life energies in more effective and profitable ways.

Magical Essences . . .

- Every person has five kinds of energy: physical, mental, emotional, spiritual, and financial.
- Your control and/or lack of control of these energies will determine your success and happiness and what you're able to manifest in your business and life.
- Please remember that your physical body and energy tie directly to your happiness and success in life.
- Your physical health is one of your greatest gifts in life.
- You must always nurture and feed your mind positivity.
- Remember this about your mental energy: When you're thinking positive thoughts you usually continue to think about positive things.
- Due to the fact that what we focus on expands, our emotional states follow our thought patterns.
- When we're in a good-feeling state, we're able to be much more in tune with our goals and desires.

- Integrating spiritual principles into your life both personally and professionally adds a new dimension to your success.
- Because they represent the investment of your mind and body, money and wealth have energy about them.
- You have to take care of yourself before you can take care of others.
- Practicing the art of deliberate creation will bring you a conscious awareness of personal control and help you to optimize your choices.

FIVE

The Magic of Releasing

As we have discussed, everything is made of energy. Every object you own has energy. The more physical objects you own, the more energy is used by you to maintain them. We all own unwanted, unneeded material objects that are taking up space in our living areas and in our brains. Furthermore, all this stuff around you has to be cleaned, stored, and insured. I bring this to your attention because if you really want to reclaim the magic and manifest the lifestyle you desire, it is time to have some discernment about what you keep—both in your physical and your mental space. Sometimes keeping track of all the clutter and unorganized stuff prevents you from having major breakthroughs and from creating solutions or new concepts for you, your business, or your life. All the unnecessary stuff you have is draining time, talent, and creative thoughts from you!

Material things tend to start accumulating without you really being aware of it. Our childhood background has a massive effect on who we are today. We must examine and review why we have certain tendencies to collect stuff. I'd like to share with you that I'm not just giving advice here. I've truly lived this challenge! In this short version of my own personal story, I am sure you will find points that relate to your life.

When you grow up on a farm, you learn to keep anything that could be used in the future. We kept stuff simply because when you're poor, you have to find ways to repair, remake, or reinvent things. Do you remember the old MacGyver TV show, where he would save himself and others by making useful gadgets from the parts of things he found in his surroundings? That was us, and most farmers and ranchers, who have huge barns in which to store this stuff.

Plus, my mother was a serious pack rat. She wasn't a hoarder, but she might have had some tendencies of that mental disease. I remember drawers you could hardly open because they were so filled. We opened a closet door very gently for fear of what might fall out. As a kid, I remember swearing I would never become a pack rat.

Because I grew up very poor, I had a huge desire to make something of myself. I had big aspirations to have a really nice home, a new car, and expensive clothes. I imprinted on myself the mindset that more is better. The more I had the more successful I thought I would feel.

As a child I wore hand-me-down clothes and I hated them. I never seemed to have the right things I needed to wear for special events. When I started making money and became successful I way over-compensated! I went out and got everything I would ever need for any kind of occasion ever. I was trying to make up for that poor childhood, for being embarrassed by my dreadful wardrobe.

Yet as an adult I found myself having way too many material things that were bought just to make me feel good. Now all these material things, which really for the most part had no meaning to me, had become stressful and were taking up way too much energy in my life to maintain them.

Finally, I got my first beach house in Virginia Beach, Virginia. The house was great at first, when I lived alone. I actually had my office on the first floor and life was grand. Then, I fell in love and got married. Suddenly, my husband's stuff had to come into the house. Things got a little complicated, as they say. I moved my office out of the house, so he could have his space that we call the "man cave." Over the years we have collected things from trips we wanted to remember. We've gotten a bazillion gifts from people, some of the gifts we love, and some we don't. So, the bottom line is, stuff kept coming in and coming in. I thought stuff was going out at a good rate because we always donate, but it's never going out at the same rate as it arrives.

My husband's mother and father passed away and we inherited some of their things, those life treasures that you feel obligated to keep for tradition's sake. So now there's more crystal, more china, more silver, a few antiques here and there, and the important memories of their life—photos. Some of my family passed away . . . same story, more stuff arriving at a house that was already maxed out.

Over time, I became more and more dissatisfied with my home. The closets, drawers, attic, garage, and even the outside storage unit, were completely filled. I expanded my business, bought a small office building and hired more staff, so more stuff was needed.

Now I had a house, an office, and a storage unit, all filled to bursting. Something had to give! I found myself waking up exhausted, annoyed, and frustrated, and at first I didn't really understand why. Keeping up with all this stuff was taking a huge toll on me. My dreams had come true; I was super-prosperous and living the American dream, yet I found myself stressed out instead of happy. Slowly I started to realize that I had way too much stuff.

Maybe I got more and more stuff trying to fill my life to avoid feeling something I didn't want to feel. There are tons of reasons why we all end up with too many material things, which sooner or later may become a burden, physically, financially, emotionally, and mentally. I can honestly admit to you that I bought many of the things because I didn't feel good enough about myself at the time. I felt like some of those labels would make me seem more worthy. I can look back and see that I have purchased a lot of material things in my life because I was simply stressed out or bored and desired the "high" that buying something new gives you . . . all those great but short-term endorphins.

We all have a story about why we are burdening ourselves with too many material things. Each of us has some kind of story about how we woke up one day and realized that all this accumulating stuff was sucking the life out of us. I can look back on my life and realize that I've over-compensated. I've created so much prosperity that I then had to face the reality of trying to judge what things in my life had true value for me.

Finally, I admitted that I was really at the stage of my life where I wanted less stress, and I had to find a way to do that. Perhaps you've been or are in the same place, though you may have arrived at the conclusion through your own story.

My personal spiritual advisor suggested that I have my home reviewed by a Feng Shui practitioner, who could give me suggestions on how to free up the energy in the house and those who lived there! She also suggested that I do a serious purge of everything in my life to assist me with these feelings of overwhelm.

I took my advisor's suggestion and hired a Feng Shui expert. He reviewed my home and office and gave me very clear "cures" on how to enliven the energy in my home and office again. He also gave the prescriptive advice to purge my life of anything that bound me to the unpleasant memories of the past. So I got rid of photos, books, files, and all of the other things that brought me down. I released gifts and clothes that were no longer congruent with my style. Gone was any and all clutter and stuff that simply was causing me stress to have to dust or clean, which I was not enjoying.

One of the hard questions I had to ask myself was this: Am I holding on tightly to disappointing purchases or investments that I should have released long ago?

The first thing that came to mind was the king-sized brass bed in my master bedroom. Every touch caused a fingerprint. When polished, this bed was a showstopper but polishing it was a stress to me. It cost over a $100 to have people come in to polish; or I had to spend several hours cleaning it. At one time that bed must have meant something to me but now it only represented work. Frankly, I had enough to do in my life without having objects in my life that took this kind of maintenance. I am happy to say I released that bed and almost everything in my home that required polishing.

I was stunned at the results of how my environments now felt to me. I personally felt so much better after the big purge and the Feng Shui treatments to my home and office. The shocker was how it opened a floodgate of new business. What was the secret? I was feeling better! I was thriving, not stressing, both at home and at work. My creative energies were flowing more, I was more enthusiastic, and those vibrational energies attracted more prosperity in my life. My marriage bloomed into more romance and fun! I was honestly taken aback at the amazing results I was experiencing by simply taking charge of the material stuff in my life. Our society simply doesn't understand or respect the power of the energy of the things in our lives, nor how to manage it.

I had a new motto now: *If it doesn't serve a purpose, have meaning or monetary value, out it must go!*

If you are not familiar with Feng Shui, here it is in the simplest terms: the ancient study and practice of how people are affected good or ill, by their surroundings, layout, and orientation of workplaces and homes. The purpose of Feng Shui practices is to change and harmonize your environment to improve your well-being in your inner and outer life. If you buy into the mindset that metaphysics operates similarly to modern physics, linking all matter and all minds into one Unified Theory, you can understand how our environment affects our mind and body. Carl Jung wrote, *"The ancient Chinese mind contemplates the cosmos in a way comparable to that of the modern physicist, who cannot deny that his model of the world is a decidedly psychophysical structure."*

Feng Shui is an environmental science, not a cult or a religion. You can't deny a practice that is thirty centuries old. It is not magic, voodoo, or witchcraft as some have called it. It is a tool that you can use to bring balance and harmony into your life. It connects your mental intentions to your surroundings and your source energy, so that you feel connected to the universe. It is about purifying the space in your house or office as a representation of your soul's connection. Feng Shui is about focusing intentions, rather than just coasting through your life on autopilot. Using this ancient art simply allows you to get back into the driver's seat of your life and accept responsibility for yourself and your thoughts and actions. It is so essential to take responsibility for our own lives by clearing away the debris of negativity in our environments. Only then can our spirits soar with true energy and vitality.

My personal favorite Feng Shui practitioner is famous author and speaker Lillian Too, who has written over eighty books on the subject, which have been translated into more than thirty languages. She is from Malaysia and speaks all over the world. You can find her at: *www.lillian-too.com*.

Since my goal is to give you the tools to reclaim the magic within, here are some hints and processes that I have been using very successfully. These are the instructions I give to my personal coaching clients and my group coaching members to successfully manifest more in all areas of their lives: love, health, money, and peace of mind. Some of the following materials came from one of my very best-selling audio programs called *Overcoming Unproductive Behaviors*, which outlines how to stop being discouraged, derailed, and sidetracked when you want to break any bad habit or behavior that is holding you back from the success you want. You can find this resource at my web site: *www.leemilteer.com*, along with other valuable resources.

Law of Vacuum

It is said that nature abhors a vacuum. To have the opportunity to attract what you do want, such as a better relationship, more attractive clothes, or furniture, you must make room for your desires to manifest.

I am big reader of prosperity books and there is one piece of advice in all of them: the way you create prosperity is to rid yourself of what you don't want in your life, because that makes room for what you do want. This includes negative thinking, sour attitudes, beliefs that hold you back, as well as material objects. This activates the Law of Vacuum.

If you're living in fear of lack and tightly holding on to everything—your material possessions, your time, your love, your energy, or your ideas—you're shutting yourself off from the flow of life. When you dam up a stream, the water becomes stagnant. When you close off the flow of your life, *you* become stagnant. The more unwanted things clutter your life, the less room there will be for the things you want to be able to appear.

A great universal secret of prosperity is passing along to others those things you no longer need. The more you give away the material possessions that you no longer need, the more love, appreciation, and praise the world will surprise you with, increasing your abundance in all areas of your life. Make it your goal to gift to others the material things that are no longer of use to you. Your junk can be someone else's treasures.

When you move things, people, or situations that no longer serve you out of your life, you're clearing the way for what you *do* want. It's difficult to know what you do want until you get rid of what you don't want or what is no longer working. Let the universe fill the vacuum.

"The STUFF Diet"

Now let's have some fun and play The STUFF DIET. Keep in mind that you are going to have to prioritize and be honest about your "stuff." It's essential to get clear about what's important in your life and what you really want out of life. To do this you have to be honest about what you really need, really use, and really want to keep in your space. We create our own clutter and we are the only ones who can clear it up for ourselves.

One of my pack rat coaching clients, Eric, reported back to me that he finally took my advice and did "The STUFF Diet" in the home in which he had lived for over ten years. After he completed the purge of all the junk he had accumulated, he felt the urge to get a professional decorator to help him get the Zen feeling he wanted. For the first time he felt so good about his newly cleaned house that he started to have small Friday night parties. This dramatically expanded his social life which, to his surprise, gave him back the joy of entertaining that he had denied himself. One evening one of his friends brought a guest over to one of his parties and he met the love of his life, whom he married in less than a year. He reported to me that he would never have met her if he had not cleaned up his life and started being more social again.

Eric was so sold on "The STUFF Diet" that he created a contest at his business office to motivate his staff to clean up the office and remove unnecessary stuff. He very happily reported that his staff's attitude went from tired, irritable, and short-tempered to more cooperative, relaxed, and creative about problem solving. He said he noticed a lighter energy at the office and his business improved dramatically. Eric's letter to me confirmed what I have personally and professionally experienced: Simplifying home and work space clutter reduces stress and frees up your energy.

Organization is key here and when you find and implement systems that work for you, you create a much more orderly environment. You will no longer feel overwhelmed by all the things you own and all the things you have to do to live your life.

You'll want to take these suggestions and modify them to best fit your style and personality. I want to remind you here that you will receive from this exercise exactly the energy you invest in it; if you only halfway do something please expect halfway results. All of life is the result of your focus so get excited about this new tool for success. Release what is not working so you can manifest what you do want. I promise you great results if you participate in how your environment is designed and maintained.

1. *"The STUFF Diet" (Or Home Diet/Office Diet):* Before you start, decide where you will take things to sell to consignment shops, or donate to charity, and also how you will have the old trash removed. This is a follow-up phase but setting it in place at

the beginning is very important. Don't just let this old stuff hang around and become another burden. Set a deadline for completion of this "diet."

2. Create a holding place for things to be released. Make it easy to get rid of stuff. Designate separate spaces for items you want to sell, donate to charity, give away, or trash. I personally set up a place in my garage, although it can be a spare room or any place you can allow things to gather for a week or so. I like to do it this way because if you change your mind and think of a reason why you are really not ready to part with something, you have a grace period. That way you won't regret letting something go.

3. Use big baskets, bins, or large strong boxes. Label them STORAGE, SELL, DONATE, THROW AWAY, and RECYCLE.

4. Set up a reward and accountability system. It's important to get everyone on board. Make a commitment to releasing things and decide how many things per week everyone will commit to releasing. Everyone should have a DAILY GOAL. *Something* has to go each day. It can be as little as a pen that no longer works, but everyone has to play the game.

The bottom line is to find ways to motivate your family or staff to release unwanted and unneeded things. For example: Kids love contests, so whoever can release the most gets a prize or special privilege. It could be anything from staying up later or a PJ party to horseback riding lessons. Try to reward with experiences, not more material things. Customize the reward so that it's something that makes them want to let go of the unneeded. Remember, we are all just big kids so find ways to reward and motivate every person who is part of the "The STUFF Diet."

I want you to live every day with the peace of mind that results from having your home or office *exactly* the way you want it. Remember: You are in control of your stuff, and not the other way around.

De-Cluttering Strategies

Un-manifesting really means that we are releasing things that no longer have value or importance to us. This is critical because these material items are draining us of time, money, and life energy. To motivate you, consider thinking of these strategies as a way to help your favorite charity and yourself.

Think of your time and efforts to clear out your spaces as actually doing something that could benefit others because of what you donate into the world. Many people who spend time working at charity functions feel a significant difference in their lives because of it. Clothing banks focus on giving clothes to foster children, children in orphanages, as well as children of low-income families. Many children and parents rely on these clothing banks to provide school and winter clothing, as well as blankets, school supplies, and shoes. Some of these groups do more than just clothing; they also offer basic furniture, like beds and recycled refrigerators, to families in need. When we give back to society by donating things, money, and time, we improve the lives of those less fortunate which, in turn, improves our own lives.

De-cluttering a whole house can seem overwhelming. BUT if it's broken down into bite size chunks, it can be handled with ease.

1. Start by de-cluttering for ten to fifteen minutes a day. It's enough time to achieve something. It's short enough that we can all fit it into our busy schedules. If you do this one thing, it becomes a good habit. It

will also ensure you keep your home or office clutter free in the future.

2. De-clutter storage space first. Once you get control of drawers, cabinets and closets it will be so much easier to find a home for everything that needs a space.

3. Pick one room for your fifteen-minute daily sessions and stick to it until everything is de-cluttered. It doesn't really matter which room you start with.

4. Be ruthless in deciding what to keep and what to let go. You can't succeed at de-cluttering and simplifying your life or office unless you are willing to let stuff go. To make it easy, take the attitude that you are prosperous enough that if you happen to get rid of something you find that you need in the future, you will give yourself permission to buy a new one, rent it, or even buy one from a secondhand store at a bargain. Go into this "STUFF Diet" with the mindset that most stuff can be replaced if absolutely necessary . . . *Because it can!*

5. Deal with paper. Little and often works best. Paper causes a lot of clutter. Bills, invoices, and receipts without a system get out of control fast. For example, you can stop paper clutter by creating a simple system for incoming mail. You'll need a bin and a two-tier tray. Designate one tray for items that require action, and the other for documents that need to be filed. Set up a filing system that suits your *own personality* and needs. Create reminders for scheduling actions like paying bills, appointments, and events. Use your computer or phone scheduling system for convenience.

6. As soon as you bring something new into the house or office, set aside storage space for it. Always keep it in its place when not in use.

It takes MUCH less time to de-clutter than it does to look at piles of clutter and feel bad day after day. The time we spend fretting about our clutter and berating ourselves is time we could be enjoying our surroundings and feeling like a winner.

To break up what could seem like an enormous task, choose different areas in your home or office and give yourself permission to go on "The STUFF Diet" one area at a time.

If there are clothes in your closet that you have not worn in the last twenty-four months—get rid of them! If there are clothes you don't like and don't give you a good feeling when you wear them—get rid of them. If there are clothes that need repair, have them repaired. Your one exception: you can keep your wedding dress or tuxedo!

Don't forget to clean out your attic and garage; inevitably there are things you're keeping that would cost more to repair than replace—throw it out or give it away.

Get rid of old furniture, toys, office files, magazines, and newspapers. Clear out the junk that robs you of your energy and time whenever you see or think about it.

De-clutter your life from the tangibles and intangibles that are no longer adding to your well-being. New substances, new relationships, and new opportunities do not flow easily into a cluttered environment.

Releasing Outdated Habits of Thought

We started "The STUFF Diet" to open ourselves up to more life energy and clarity. So far we've been focusing on material "stuff" but keep in mind that it would also behoove you to do some mental clean-up.

Mental de-cluttering and emotional de-cluttering are also extremely important because if not done, they can lead to self-imposed blockages, resistance, and massive frustration and stress. Holding on to grudges, anger, or bitterness blocks you from noticing and receiving good things in your life, as well as causes you to be frustrated, discouraged, unmotivated, and depressed.

How do you de-clutter in this way? Well, start by recognizing the predominant thoughts running through your mind and then the subsequent feelings you have as a result. What's your general opinion and belief about your life and abilities to co-create it? What is your view on manifestation, your friends, your family, money, etc.? Go through each area of your life and make a list of all the beliefs and feelings you have that pertain to each one. Let it all flow. Don't hold back. The more honest and candid you are with yourself, the better. No one has to see your list; it's between you and you.

Allow yourself to gently move away from acquaintances and friends who are no longer really friends. Just because you were close and had a lot in common at one time does not mean that you're destined to be friends forever. Give yourself permission to really see and let go of relationships that have grown in different directions. By continuing to spend your time with people you no longer really have a rewarding relationship with, you are preventing yourself from opportunities to meet and spend time with people that you would really enjoy or learn from.

Point to Consider

Most of us don't remember "stuff" but we do remember experiences. Why not start creating your life with good memories instead of things that have to be insured, cleaned, or repaired!

There is nothing in this world that feels quite the same as looking around your home or office and seeing it in order. And there's nothing more energy-draining than living with clutter, but it goes far beyond your own environment. De-cluttering will open new opportunities for you in your personal and career life because it frees up your life energy for new things.

De-cluttering releases the blocks that have been holding you back. It ignites the fires of energy within you—energy you didn't even know you had! The stress in your face and body will ease and your confidence will return when you feel more in control. Things start to fall into place in every area of your life when you de-clutter your surroundings.

The truth is many of us have some pack rat or hoarding tendencies and it is not healthy for us. I want to leave you with this thought: Having too much stuff in your life causes confusion. Confusion creates complications, which is the opposite of simplicity. Letting go and releasing what is no longer needed or wanted allows your life to be more organized and less stressed, and you will gain a sense of clarity. Apply this concept of "The STUFF Diet" to every area of your life and watch the clarity unfold for you, too.

One last suggestion: When all else fails and if you are really struggling with organizing your life or getting rid of stuff, please do reach out to a professional organizer to get the insight on how to organize and assistance with knowing what to lose and what to keep. You do not have to do this alone, nor do you have to suffer in old habits of creating clutter or disorganization. We all need coaches and helpers in our life, and if this is an area in which you are really challenged then, by all means, it would be a good investment for you to reach out and get professional assistance.

Magical Essences . . .

- If you really want to reclaim the magic and manifest the lifestyle you desire, it is time to have some discernment about what you keep—both in your physical and your mental space.

- All the unnecessary stuff you have is draining time, talent, and creative thoughts from you!
- There are tons of reasons why we all end up with way too many material things, which sooner or later may become a burden, physically, financially, emotionally and mentally.
- Really purge your life of anything that binds you to the unpleasant memories of the past.
- The purpose of Feng Shui practices is to change and harmonize your environment to improve your well-being in your inner and outer life.
- To have the opportunity to attract what you do want, such as a better relationship, more attractive clothes, or furniture, you must make room for your desires to manifest.
- If you're living in fear of lack and tightly holding on to everything—your material possessions, your time, your love, your energy, or ideas—you're shutting yourself off from the flow of life.
- When you move things, people, or situations that no longer serve you out of your life, you're clearing the way for what you *do* want.
- Simplifying home and work space clutter reduces stress and frees up your energy.
- Mental de-cluttering and emotional de-cluttering are also extremely important because if not done, they can lead to self-imposed blockages, resistance, and massive frustration and stress. Holding on to grudges, anger, or bitterness blocks you from noticing and

receiving good things in your life, as well as causes you to be frustrated, discouraged, unmotivated, and depressed.

- There is nothing in this world that feels quite the same as looking around your home or office and seeing it in order. And there's nothing more energy-draining than living with clutter, but it goes far beyond your own environment. De-cluttering will open new opportunities for you in your personal and career life because it frees up your life energy for new things.

- Your new motto: *If it doesn't serve a purpose, have meaning or monetary value—out it must go!*

SIX

The Magic of Envisioning

Our culture holds widespread skepticism and even disbelief about the power of the mind, and that we can use it to enhance our abilities and potential in life. Some people say this stuff is "woo-woo" but nothing could be further from the truth. There are universal wisdoms and natural magic that have been taught throughout history in Mystery Schools, in books by famous and well-respected authors, and in the Bible.

This lack of belief in what is possible or in the magic available to us has kept most people living in a very limited mindset about what is possible for them to achieve. We are programmed from birth by society, school, and contemporary science to trust the brain's logical functioning much more than its imaginative functioning. If we only trust our logical mind, we leave out the inner connection to our brain's intuitive abilities and knowledge. In today's world we need all our brain functions to be successful.

Our physical world—our entire universe—is made up of energy and matter. Physics tells us that neither matter nor energy can be created nor destroyed. Both matter and energy can be transformed, however. Think of the various states of common water: it changes from liquid to ice, or liquid to steam and back again. We don't think twice about this phenomenon, but it is matter changing form, isn't it?

All of the objects that we see appear to be solid and separate from each other. Though our physical senses perceive objects as solid, science has shown that they are really made up of particles moving in space, which eventually turn out to be pure energy vibrating at different speeds. Energy vibrates at different rates of speed. Light vibrates with different qualities, from very fine to very dense.

We, and all the matter we see, are parts of a large constantly moving energy field. Further, all forms of energy are interrelated and can affect one another.

Matter is considered to be compact energy and is relatively dense; therefore, it is slower to move and change. A perfect example would be a rock: though it appears to be unmovable and unchangeable, a rock is changed over time by the natural energies of water, light, and wind. On the other hand, our thoughts, which are made of very light, fine forms of energy, are very easy and quick to change. So, by controlling the thoughts we are predominantly thinking, we can change our feelings and our patterns of behavior, which will change our experiences in this world. It seems so simply logical, doesn't it?

In studying the metaphysical laws of our universe, we learn that the Law of Attraction is often stated simply as "like attracts like." Thoughts and feelings have their own energy, which always attracts energy of the same nature. For example, positive-thinking people tend to attract other positive-thinking people; negative people seem to be attracted to other negative thinkers. Some refute this, saying that like charges repel each other, but that's only true when it comes to electromagnetic forces. In 1935, Nobel Prize winner Dr. Hideki Yukawa discovered that there's a force that's a hundred times stronger than electromagnetic force, where like attracts like. Confirmed as more than theory in 1947, physicists today accept this as principle, and it is known as "strong force." Not only does this theory of strong force relate to atoms, but it also applies to our thoughts. Because of decades of research by physicists like Dr. David Bohm, today it is a widely accepted premise that thought creates particles, which are affected by strong force.

As Columbia University theoretical physicist and string theorist Brian Greene states, *"While quantum mechanical effects are most noticeable at micro/tiny scale, I'm made of atoms and so are you, so quantum mechanics is not just telling us about small things, its telling us about reality."* (Nova, *The Fabric of the Cosmos*).

You are constantly creating your personal reality with your thoughts, which have energetic properties to them. Your thoughts act like energetic blueprints of the image you want to create. The energetic blueprint guides the physical energy to flow into the form you have imagined, allowing you to manifest your desires into reality. Consciously holding thoughts and images of what you want to manifest in life is known as mental rehearsal.

Metaphysicians call mental rehearsal The Law of Radiation and Attraction. This is a simple principle you already know: as you sow, so shall you reap. As in your thoughts, so in your life. You always attract into your life whatever you strongly believe, think about, or imagine most vividly.

Researchers at Stanford, Yale, and Harvard conducted studies of high-powered executives to see if the technique of mental visualization was beneficial. They found that a shared trait among "super achievers" was the ability to sense what they wanted before they got it. These "super achievers" have the ability to translate their ideas or goals into actual physical visions; they create pictures of what they want, down to the smallest detail. Knowing exactly what they want, they can see it, taste it, smell it, and even imagine the emotions and sounds associated with their main desires or goals. Their sharp sensory vision allows them to pre-live their goals before they become realities. Among the "super achievers" studied, mental rehearsal was found to provide a tremendous boost to performance and the achievement of goals.

Your performance can be improved at any level and at any time in your life. Use your mental abilities . . .

- to imagine a "new you,"
- to help you reduce the effects of stressful situations,
- to rehearse an important call,
- to ask for a raise or a job interview,
- to cope with difficult people,
- to lose weight,
- to quit smoking,
- to improve relationships, and
- to perform better at sports.

All of these areas in your life can benefit from internal mental imagery. It doesn't matter what level your goals are on: physical, emotional, mental, or spiritual.

One of my favorite celebrities who has certainly made himself successful is Arnold Schwarzenegger, movie star and former governor. He said, *"The mind is the limit. As long as the mind can envision the fact that you can do something, you can do it—as long as you really believe 100 percent."* He also said, *"I used weights to tone my body, but I used my mind to shape it."*

Mental rehearsal or visualization techniques can improve motor skills and muscle memory according to athletes who use it to improve their scores in competitions. Most world-class athletes utilize mental rehearsal, according to golf legend Jack Nicklaus, who said, *"Good golf is 50 percent physical coordination and 50 percent mental rehearsal."* In his book *Golf My Way*, Nicklaus describes how he never took a shot without first playing it out in his head like a movie. He would play the scenes starting from the end result—his ball on the green—fade in to the ball's course and trajectory to reach the green, and the final scene of the swing he would take that would make his goal a reality.

Based on Jack Nicklaus' success and the empirical evidence of the power of visualization, this is a skill that everyone should use before doing anything important. We have this magical, inborn talent of creating mental images, and we hear from successful, talented people about how well it works, yet people still don't take the time to use it for their own lives.

There is so much research about using the power of your mind to help you succeed at your goals. At Stanford's Business School one of their professors who taught creativity, Dr. D. Thornburg, wrote: *"In mental rehearsal you're engaging your subconscious as an ally in pursuit of goals. With imaging reinforcing the goals' importance, the subconscious will put that goal very high on your priorities, making it far more likely that you'll unconsciously begin adjusting your actions in ways that will make that goal happen for you."* The mind is a marvelous tool. When freed, it will find so many ways for us to achieve what we want.

One of the secrets of success is to not work so hard with your physical sweat, but instead use your mind to work out the details of how to be the person you want to be. The difference between average people and outstanding people is the degree of motivation within them. By deliberately creating the picture of the upcoming experiences of success in your mind, you can turn aspirations into realities.

Frankly, it is the magic bullet that makes conscious manifesting work in your life. Are you motivated to spend just a few short minutes a day envisioning the future you want to create for yourself? You are a self-fulfilling prophecy and the images you create in your brain determine whether you will go for your dreams or not.

Dare to break away from the old, limiting programming you were given as a child and young adult, and give yourself permission to co-create with your Infinite Intelligence Source. You can create an exciting and rewarding future for yourself. Your destiny is more in your hands than you have been led to believe. Life really is about creating yourself. You can start today and move beyond the limitations you have felt in the past.

Napoleon Hill stated, *"Whatever the mind of man can conceive and believe it can achieve!"* I took his advice seriously! My attitude is this: if others can accomplish something, and I study them and model their actions, I have a much stronger chance of succeeding. I am a farmer's daughter with no advantages. I grew up in the middle of nowhere, without money, without connections, and with only a very determined spirit that I wanted to make something out of myself, regardless of the obstacles that stood in my way. I have used Universal Principles, Infinite Intelligence, and my Invisible Counselors (as Napoleon Hill says in the book, *Think and Grow Rich*), to break through all of the obstacles to emerge as an internationally known and celebrated author, professional speaker, and entrepreneur.

My success was not a fluke or accident. It was meticulously planned in the workshop of my mind. Once I made the clear decision that I was going to become the person I am today, I read everything I could on success, mental power, Universal

Principals, and I called in my Invisible Councilors (Helpers) to guide me into my purpose in life. If I can do it, I assure you that you can, too. You have the abilities, you just have to commit to developing a deep unrelenting focus on achieving your goals.

You have the power within you to re-imagine and to re-pattern who you will become. Re-imagining means to take charge of the images you allow into your Inner Energetic Blueprint (your mind!). Re-pattern means using your physical energy to make changes or create new patterns of energy that create a blueprint for your mind.

Keep in mind that there are no limits except the limits you put on yourself. You have the power, through your thoughts and imagination, to break through any barriers created by old limiting programs from society or your childhood. The more you use the unlimited power of your mind to visualize what you want (your dreams and aspirations), and then take *action* toward what you want, the more you can manifest new realities in your own life.

Fly into the Future: Re-Imagine and Re-Pattern Your Potential!

You have the power to fly into the future and imprint new operating instructions using your own workshop of the mind, your imagination. There are many terms used to describe using your imagination to influence your future: visualization, mental rehearsal, envisioning, and I like to use the term re-patterning. We have patterns in our brain waves (our thoughts) that have been installed by outside sources (see Chapter 3) and you can literally break free of these old patterns of thought, behaviors, and beliefs about what is possible. Using your imagination is the most powerful way known for influencing the outcome of circumstances, changing habits and acquiring better habits, and attracting success, love, and wealth. Your imagination is the workshop of your mind. Everything man-made had to be created in the mind before it could manifest into reality. When you take charge of your future and deliberately insert a new vision of the person you want to become, you are rewiring your self-image, your Inner Energetic Blueprint. This new vision acts like a magnet; once the image is fixed in the mind, your subconscious is alerted to bring about factors that will help you achieve the goal you've programmed. In time, with repetition, our deliberate visions become self-fulfilling. Mental training is simply a way of reprogramming the mind to achieve more positive feelings, behaviors, and results. It is said to be the truest magic on the earth to change your life's course and direction for the positive.

The more you practice using re-patterning, the better your brain can become at directing what happens in your daily life. This allows you to be in more control of your experiences. By using re-patterning, you can create a state of awareness in which you are not only using your logical, linear, or analytical thinking in your experiences, but are actually experiencing through your feeling nature.

You have the ability to create movies in your mind and you do it with total perfection. You do it every time you think of someone, remember something, or even daydream. Without being aware of it, you create pictures in your mind in countless different situations every day. As an example, try choosing an object near you, examine it in detail, and note its shape, color, and size. After you have examined it, close your eyes and picture in your mind what you just saw. If you can do that, you've just proven to yourself how you can direct your imagination and imprint a new pattern in your subconscious mind. That new image now re-patterns the vibrational frequencies of what we notice and pay attention to in daily life. We each use our inner movie screen slightly differently because every person is unique. The way you see or feel these new images is perfect for you. Some people see their pictures in color, while others see them in black and white. There is no right or wrong way. Today is the day to stop judging yourself against others. You are a unique energy field with different potentials and different purposes in life. You must follow your own heart and mind and not compare yourself with others.

It's important for you to understand that re-patterning or mental imagery is not a method of self-deception; it is one of the strongest tools known to date for self-direction and tapping into your potential. Do not confuse re-patterning with idle fantasies or grandiose daydreaming. Although both involve the use of your imagination, it's only when you commit yourself to a goal that you can truly take advantage of re-patterning your Inner Energetic Blueprint, your brain. Daydreams and fantasies are usually unrealistic thoughts that we really don't expect to happen or have little investment in, such as becoming an overnight success in a field in which we have no experience!

Re-Patterning Your Energy Field for Personal Success

The first step for effective re-patterning is to clearly define the goal you would like to have or to create in your life. You must have the faith and belief that you can realize your goal. This goal has to be one you actually can accomplish even if it requires a huge stretch. You can find more important information about setting goals in Chapter 7. Next, you will need to have a tangible picture of the goals you are consciously creating. Start to collect the symbols for what you want to create in your life from various sources, such as magazines or newspapers. These symbols can be in the form of pictures, sayings, or statements that represent the goals and dreams in your life. Put them in a place where you can see them several times every day to reinforce your true wants and desires. These are called "vision boards." To assist you to create a vision board, I invite you to go to *www.leemilteer.com* and look for one of my best-selling programs called: *Live Bigger, Dream Bigger, Your Guide to Manifesting with Vision Boards*. This program will help you create your own vision board with full instructions and templates.

In this step, your goal is to create a mental picture as if the goal were already yours; act as if the picture were real today, not sometime in the future. Be sure to fill in the small details of the sights, colors, smell, textures, and feelings; the more realistic the detailing, the better. If you can see, hear, touch, smell, and taste your goal, your picture will be that much clearer and will work that much better. Big hint: the more realistic the images, the better the results. Imagine yourself with the goal or in the situation as you desire it. Do not think about or reinforce negative pictures, thoughts, or feelings about the goal; just let those thoughts float away from your mind. It's very important to see what you want and to be willing to take action towards it so that you imprint the new pictures in your subconscious mind.

To get the best results, you must program your brain with the most empowering images and electrical energy possible. Doing this re-patterns your electrical energy to go in the direction that you have been actively shifting your vibrational frequencies toward so that you can attract what you want. Begin by getting your brain in the correct mode for re-patterning. The best method is for your body and mind to be deeply relaxed. This is called the Alpha state, where your brainwaves become slower and ready for programming and your mind opens to fresh ideas and new techniques. During this relaxed time your subconscious can re-pattern new programs that you have chosen more effectively. Two of the most effective times to use re-patterning are as you awaken in the morning-while your mind and body are very relaxed and receptive-and at night just before sleeping. Experts agree that having your body in a position so the spine is straight will help you come into the alpha state faster. You can do this in the middle of the day by sitting in a comfortable chair in a quiet place, to relax and renew yourself by playing your own mind's movies. The point is to go to a quiet, protected place where you can really relax, focus inward, and let the outside world take care of itself for a little while.

One of the biggest secrets of life is that you must *feel* successful before you can create it in your outer world. Our thoughts become our emotions; our emotions create our behaviors; our behaviors create our results and successes. Our lives are driven by our emotions and how we feel about ourselves and the world. When you *feel* a particular emotion, you vibrate at that frequency. You must feel confident and as if you are already the person you want to become, as if you've already reached your goal. As you do these exercises, you must *claim* the part of the play you are creating in your head to attract the circumstances into your life with the Law of Attraction. When you feel confident, you take more intelligent risks, and you use more of your available mental energy for solutions because you are not using your energy in wasted fear or doubt.

It is important to focus on your positive new mental picture as often as possible. Do this for one to two minutes at a time at least twice a day for at least twenty-one to thirty days. Research has proven that it takes a minimum of twenty-one to thirty days to effect any perceptible change in a mental image.

You can re-pattern yourself in small bite-sized chunks of time during your day. Whenever you have thirty seconds, if you're taking a break at your desk, are at a stop light or in the shower, envision the steps of what you need to do to get to your goal. It takes as little as three weeks for an old mental image to dissolve and a new mental image to form. By clearly focusing on what you want to create, you make this new image the blueprint for your future.

Napoleon Hill said in his book, *Think and Grow Rich*: *"Any idea, plan, or purpose may be placed in the mind through repetition of thought."* He also reminded us: *"Cherish your visions and your dreams as they are the children of your soul, the blueprints of your ultimate achievements."*

The point of this exercise is to create m*omentum*! Energy in motion tends to stay in motion and energy that is inactive tends to stay inactive. Accumulated energy has a cumulative effect. The more you re-pattern your brain with new positive images the more of that energy you are going to attract into your experience.

There are some schools of thought that have taught that all you have to do is visualize the achievement of a goal. From my personal experience and that of hundreds of successful entrepreneurs and coaching clients I have had the honor to work with, there has to be an *action* component to ensure your goals become a reality.

Recent research has shown that the reason people are not successful with using the process of mental rehearsal to achieve their goals is because they are substituting the fantasy of success for real progress. In other words they visualize the goal they want but do not take concrete actions towards the goals. Nor do they break their goals into a step-by-step process that helps them remove the fear and hesitation often associated with trying to achieve a life change or new goal. I call this naïve thinking because we live in a physical world. The old saying that God helps those who help themselves comes to mind here for me. Yes, we have to know what we want so we can aim our energy in that direction, but we need to do more than *think* it and expect it to show up in our reality. Thinking can create an attraction to the goal, but in the physical world, you have to assist the process by taking intelligent and consistent action to achieve the desired result.

Let's make a very large and important distinction here: Most of us have been taught to visualize the end result you want to achieve but there is more to the story here. You have to add the steps of how to get to the end result in order to make it effective. The chapter in this book titled "The Magic of Focus" will give you much more information on goal-setting and achievement, including a personal story from my experience.

Scripting to Pre-View Your Future

As we have discussed, most of us have internalized mental programming that clearly did not set us up for the success we aspire to in life. Here's another technique to upgrade your brain training. I call it "Scripting for Success." This process will rewire your Inner Energetic Blueprint to focus on and go in the direction you consciously give it.

If you take this information seriously, it will change the rest of your life. You see, I *know* this because using this method really changed my life—a truly magical tool. I was able to pull myself from being poor to being very successful and wealthy. If I can do it, you can, too, when you embrace this new mindset!

Most people spend their lives observing conditions and reacting to circumstances. Let go of this old pattern and step into your role as co-creator with your Divine Source. Get some traction on creating a new reality for your future. Be proactive and co-create instead of just trying to finance all your success with only your physical energy because, frankly, that old method is exhausting!

Boost your faith in yourself and your Divine Source. There are no limitations except the ones you put on yourself. My experience is a constant reminder that through Source, I can do many things that I simply cannot do all alone with only my human energy. Your true power is in your spiritual connection to the Divine Source. Today is the day to really connect with this unlimited power and increase your ability to make a difference in your world.

As a conscious person, your goal is to connect your spiritual nature with your daily life and work to create personal magic. Scripting is one of the most powerful ways to do it. Any message you regularly give your conscious and subconscious mind will imprint and start to become part of your life experience. These messages become part of your perceptions of yourself. They become your Inner Energetic Blueprint.

You must always remember that whatever you focus on expands and that you have much more magic power than our society has ever led you to believe.

Scripting for Success is a form of writing your personal and business goals in a story format. You can think of this technique as a form of written prayer. Any message that you give your conscious and subconscious mind *regularly* will imprint new references and will start to become part of your comfort zone. These visual messages become your own self-perception—your Inner Energetic Blueprint. Since you are a self-fulfilling prophecy, it behooves you to do as many positive things as possible to create a prosperous new personal image of yourself that suits the future you want to manifest.

We know that what we focus on expands. Scripting is powerful magic for creating your future because it assists you to determine the exact information on which your brain should focus. That focus enables you to have clear intuition on what actions to take to create the ideal future.

Your own thoughts are crucial to your success. Most people marginalize the impact of their mindset, which limits their ability to create the success and prosperity that is possible for those who know the magic mental codes to use. Scripting is a great way to create new references to what you want your future to look like . . . and to this end when I get up, every morning, I make it a point to "Script" my day, my month, my year, etc. It always works.

Scripting is one of the exercises I have shared with my personal and business coaching groups and I've had the most *amazing feedback* from my members about it. Some of the business folks in my group are very left-brained, and were a little hesitant at first because they thought the exercise might not be comfortable for them. They were all good sports though and took my advice. They started scripting every day and were amazed at *how the deliberate intentions they set for their lives changed their circumstances. It can do the same for you.*

I would like to share with you a story from my book, *Spiritual Power Tools for Successful Selling.* A salesman from New York who attended one of my seminars wrote to me four months after trying the scripting process to say:

> *"I have been a professional hardcore salesman from the old school for about twenty-seven years, and I am blown away with the power and impact of this technique you shared called Pre-Viewing your future or scripting. In truth, the only reason I tried it was because I was nearly desperate.*

Things were not going well for me. I could not understand what was going on. I was losing sales and customers daily. I was angry and frustrated. I was taking my hostility out on everyone: my family, customers, and my co-workers. My sales manager and I were at it tooth and nail. She gave me one month to pull myself together or I was out!

I started Scripting, as you suggested, and it felt weird at first. I felt like a liar to be saying all these good things about myself that were not true. But I kept writing. After about four pages of scripting my future, I felt a shift in my attitude. I realized that maybe my attitude was part of my problem. I started thinking about how lucky and blessed I was with my sales job. I felt much better that day. I now get up every morning and script. I can sum it up in one word. Miracles! I have seen my life turn around since I started focusing on what I wanted and asked God for help. My sales are up again. My relationships are the best with my customers and I feel younger and more alive. This is one process I will now do forever. As you say, the internal work is more important than the external! Well, I am a true believer now. Thank you!"

—T. L. Redmond, New York City, N.Y.

For me, the act of scripting is writing things out as if they had already happened, as if the acquisition or event is a completed part of my past. This is done to create a reference that something you want is not only possible but is now simply a fact of life. There is no doubt that you can achieve something *if* you have already done it in your own mind and you feel like it is part of your life experience. We don't have to hope we can do something if we have convinced our subconscious mind that we have already done it. This is very powerful to your mind and confidence level.

Most people have learned a manifestation process of acting as if you have the thing you want, the weight you want to be, the success now, etc., so you can *feel it now* and attract this new reality to you. I agree that this works and is a great exercise and way to train the brain. Since my focus in life is to manifest and do it fast, I have added a new element to the reprogramming of your Inner Energetic Blueprint. When you start to imagine and feel that this information is already in the past, you feel a sense of knowing and accepting this knowledge as fact in your life, so you stop doubting yourself. This "new you" becomes second nature and you are now really vibrating at that level so, yes, you do attract it into your life much faster, in my own personal experience.

I have been a speaker for well over twenty years and one of the things I sincerely wanted was to get to a place in my career that I only flew first class when traveling. I have spent decades in the back of the plane, to save money and I did not feel confident enough that I would get the speaking fee if I added first class airfare to the fee requirements. I sincerely was worn out beating myself up flying in coach so much. I started to script that I always now flew first class and described how I felt about it: how appreciative I was to be at a level of demand in my career that I could require it, my delight at the comfort first class afforded me, etc. I am happy to share that I do fly first class on 95 percent of my flights. Sometimes the flights are so short, there is no first class but I always seem to get in the front even on those flights!

Your true goal in scripting is to *feel* as you want to feel. As you visualize and write your desires, you create vibrational harmony by experiencing the thoughts and feelings associated with the achievement of your goals. The true magic power for manifesting your perfect life is to be able to feel as if you already have the qualities you want or the object you desire. Feelings are vibrational thoughts and are governed by universal law, which asserts that like energies attract. When you can create the internal imagery of feeling prosperous, you can attract the physical equivalent of being prosperous. You can create the internal imagery for feeling any way you would like to feel, and attract its physical equivalent.

When scripting your life desires, it's important to be as general in your word pictures as possible, but state enough to get a good feeling about your subject. You can become more specific as time goes on and you develop your skill with this process.

Scripting is a way to create *new references* of what you want your future to look like and to make your Inner Energetic Blueprint congruent with the future you want to manifest. Mental rehearsal of your desired outcomes increases your energy potential in that direction.

Scripting is easy, and can be done anywhere and anytime you have a few minutes to sit down and write out your vision and story of your desires for your future. You are the star, director, and producer of this story. If you give yourself permission to be true to yourself and honestly write down exactly how you would like to see your life unfold, this process can be exciting, productive, and magical. Also write down ways that you assist and empower others. Experiment and have fun with scripting for just thirty days, and keep an evidence book on the changes in your life. You will be amazed at the miracles that happen for you and for others in your life.

Guidelines for Scripting:

- *You are the star*—You are the director and producer of your life's story. It's up to you to decide what you want and what you will have. I encourage you to become the king or queen of your future reality—*really claim it.*

- *Clarity*—To have what you desire, you have to get clear and focus on exactly what you sincerely want. Think about this in great detail. The chapter "The Magic of Focus" will be helpful in getting really clear about your goals.

- *Feeling creates vibrational harmony*—The true magic power for manifesting your perfect life is to be able to feel as if you already have the qualities you want or the object you desire. Feelings are vibrational thoughts and are governed by universal law, which asserts that like energies attract. Your true goal in scripting is to *feel* as you want to feel. As you write and visualize your desires, you create vibrational harmony by experiencing the thoughts and feelings associated with the achievement of your goals.

- *Be general with your description*—When you begin scripting your life desires, it's initially important to be as general in your word pictures as possible, but state enough to get a good feeling. You can become more specific as time goes on and you have developed your skill using this process.

- *Experiment and have fun*—Enjoy playing with scripting for just thirty days. Keep an evidence book on the changes in your life. You will be amazed at the miracles that happen for you and for others in your life.

- *Write your story in the third person*—Start with a future date and write your story *as if it has already happened.* Always write using as many glowing adjectives as possible so that you *feel* the results you want. Use action verbs! The point is to create positive *feelings* in your body about the outcomes you want. This will create your point of attraction.

- *When to write*—For best results, script first thing in the morning to set the tone for the day or last thing in evening so your subconscious can integrate the information while you sleep. Create a time you can *focus* on what you want your future to look like. I often script on my computer sitting at the airport waiting for a plane. It is an attitude adjustment time for me. It is not how or where you script that is important, but the energy of focusing your attention on the positive future you are programming in your mind. I view scripting as stating my intentions and asking my Divine Source and spiritual helpers to help me manifest this new reality or something even better!

- *Record your writings*—Keep a notebook just for your magic script writings These are private writings and not for anyone else to read! I've kept my notebooks for years and it's rewarding to go back and see how I actually manifested things and events that I wanted through scripting them. It's also a wonderful way to build your confidence as you look back and view your notebooks as benchmarks of how far you have come in the world because *you* made the decision to do so.

I hope you will take my suggestion and begin scripting daily using the tips I have given you——mold them into your writing. It is my intention that this one simple daily act will have a *profound impact* on your life. It certainly did on mine. Remember to *have fun* with your scripting. *Realize you are co-creating your future with Infinite Cosmic Intelligence, so it always must be used towards divine good.*

I suggest that you be kind to yourself, and build your confidence by patiently taking small steps in the direction of your goals. Try something new every single day. It's very interesting to note that changing just a few small actions or habits in your life will compound itself. In a few months, these changes can produce dramatic results in your professional and personal life.

I suggest continuing to script about anything that has not come into reality that you want, no matter how long it takes. *Your scripting* is an ongoing story and it will evolve into the next story. Your real job is to keep developing the storyline.

If you don't like your present reality, script a new one. You have the power to create your future and scripting is a great tool to help get you there. This knowledge is information I teach in my Mystery School courses offered from Lee Milteer's School of Wisdom. It is very powerful. Be careful that you only use this knowledge for good and for light. For more information about Mystery School, sign up for my free weekly Spiritual Power Tools e-zine at *www.spiritualpowertools.com/freenewsletter*.

There is no right or wrong way to tell your improved story. It can be about your past, present, or future experiences. The only criterion that is important is that you be conscious of your intent to tell a better-feeling, improved version of your story. Telling many good-feeling short stories throughout your day will change your point of attraction. Just remember that the story *you* tell is the basis of *your* life. So tell it the way you want it to be.

Reminder: Dreams are renewable. No matter what our age or condition, there are still untapped possibilities within us and new beauty waiting to be born. You are the writer of your own future reality. Don't forget it is *your* story. Make it a good one because *no one* can decide your destiny but *you*!

To give you an idea of the type of writing I do daily to insure my future success, I am going to share a sample of excerpts from my personal scripting notebooks. Let these excerpts serve as an example of what a new story can look like. I personally do quite a bit of scripting, but I want you to remember that quality counts more than quantity. It's not how much you write but what you write that gives you a *feeling* you're already there that counts. Create the story you want!

> *And so it was:* the healthy, happily married, super successful, joyful, enthusiastic, elegant, timeless, connected to spirit, prosperous Lee Milteer was so thrilled and excited about the progress of her new beach home being built. Lee just loved daily walking on the building site and seeing the amazing progress. Lee loved all the workman and trades for the amazing efforts to make this house a show-stopper! Lee was in total harmony with everyone on the building site and was so grateful for all the effort and problem-solving the building crew did daily to make her new home strong and beautiful. Lee loved that everyone was so cheerful and cooperative and did their very best work daily. Lee was so grateful to have found the perfect contractor who sincerely took care of all of Lee's needs. The house was flying up and was going to be completed way ahead of schedule and under budget. Lee was amazed daily at the ways her contractor found the best discounts on exactly the materials she wanted and how magical the experience was to finally have the home of her dreams manifest right in front of her.
>
> Lee was always in harmony with her neighbors who understood about the noise and disruption of the new home being built. Everyone was looking forward to the big housewarming party being planned for the fall to see the end result of the construction. Lee found the perfect caterer

and was enjoying planning the big housewarming party. She had the perfect theme in mind and was so thrilled and excited to finally show off her Bucket List new home! A sixteen-year dream comes true for Lee and Clifton!

Lee's new Spiritual Power Tools for Profit and Purpose e-zine was a huge success with many people subscribing and recommending it to others. Lee loved coming out of the spiritual closet and showing the authentic spiritual part of herself. The new e-zine introduced many light workers to her Lee Milteer's School of Wisdom programs and her classes were always filled to the max with waiting lists of people around the world who wanted to utilize their spiritual knowledge with their business life.

Lee loved working with her personal coaching group. What an amazing group of really successful and conscious entrepreneurs! Lee always looked forward to the meetings and always came home feeling so thrilled with the results everyone was getting and the new mindsets and references that were being established so everyone in the group was not only making more profits, but were feeling much more confident of their abilities.

Lee adored her personal one-on-one coaching clients and all the progress they made because of working with her. She looked forward to her time with each client and hearing the results of her wisdom and experience integrated into their businesses and lives. One of the things she enjoyed was the stories of how her personal coaching assisted not only her clients but their staff, business, and family life. It gave Lee such a sense of fulfillment to be of service to people she admired.

Lee's Millionaire Smarts® coaching program was now serving more clients all over the world with inspiring and educational monthly programs that impacted people's abilities to use their natural talents and resources to become more financially and emotionally successful. Lee was thrilled at how people were attracted to her and her business. Month after month her business grew more and more successful and rewarding.

Lee was so enjoying her speaking and writing career more and more. She no longer had to hide her spiritual knowledge on stage and she was rewarded with more people doing business with her because her authentic self had showed up!

Lee was sincerely happy about completing her new book projects. She had such great time writing and they became best-sellers very easily. As always, many wonderful new clients for coaching, speaking, and events came from her books. Lee was sincerely thrilled when her new books were translated into many languages so people from around the world could benefit from Lee's knowledge.

Lee was most grateful for her publisher Rainbow Ridge, who contracted her to write a new book on manifesting called: *Reclaim the Magic: The Real Secrets to Manifesting Anything You Want* that was finished by the end of summer. Lee loved getting up early every morning and sitting down with her special Hawaiian Coffee and writing. The ideas for the book came easily and effortlessly because Lee understood that she was a channel for light and she had helpers who assisted her. This book was a much easier book to write than her last books and Lee was joyfully looking forward to the book's success when published in 2015.

Lee loved exercising and taking care of her physical body by walking on the beach, working out, and eating healthy food. Lee now released food and old habits that no longer served her and was craving now healthy live food that nurtured her to be creative and filled with vitality and health. Lee felt more energy and creativity daily! Lee's old non-beneficial habits dropped away easily and effortlessly.

Daily, everything Lee wanted and needed showed up in her life. The right clients who were suited to her talents and knowledge showed up, and money and wonderful opportunities that made her heart sing flowed effortlessly to her.

Lee recovered from the trauma and grief of her mother's passing and was at peace with the loss. She now only remembered the good times and released the painful times.

Lee Milteer, Inc. had one of the best years and more and more speaking engagements flowed in that were the perfect match to Lee's talents. Lee now only flew first class and always had a beautiful suite at all engagements. More and more of her products sold on her website.

Lee's Personal Speaking Events now always sold out easily. Lee loved her business and her staff and she felt so grateful for her creative staff that always took care of all her needs and treated her clients like kings and queens. Everyone always appreciated the magnificent first class treatment they received from working with Lee and her staff.

Life was truly blessed for Lee and she felt like a million bucks; things were better and better daily. Lee was always treated with respect and love, she always felt appreciated and valued, Lee was excited about the future and all the amazing things she wanted to do were becoming reality.

Lee now took more time to play and enjoy her life. She was now painting more in her art room and enjoying giving away her creations as gifts.

Lee was more mindful to take the time to nurture her mind and body by mediating thirty minutes per day. Lee was enjoying more new friends and exciting new fun adventures daily. Lee was living happily ever after. Life was good and getting better daily. There was harmony, prosperity and peace in Lee's life. Lee was more grateful every day in every way for all her blessings and potential.

Magical Essences . . .

- If we only trust our logical mind, we leave out the inner connection to our brain's intuitive abilities and knowledge.

- Thoughts and feelings have their own energy, which always attracts energy of the same nature.

- One of the secrets of success is to not work so hard with your physical sweat, but instead use your mind to work out the details of how to be the person you want to be.

- By deliberately creating the picture of the upcoming experiences of success in your mind, you can turn aspirations into realities.

- Re-imagining means to take charge of the images you allow into your Inner Energetic Blueprint (your mind!). Re-pattern means using your physical energy to make changes or create new patterns of energy that create a blue print for your operating system.

- The more you use the unlimited power of your mind to visualize what you want (your dreams and aspirations), and then take *action* toward what you want, the more you can manifest new realities in your own life.

- It is said to be the truest magic on the earth to change your life's course and direction for the positive.

- One of the biggest secrets of life is that you must *feel* successful before you can create it in your outer world. Our thoughts become our emotions; our emotions create our behaviors; our behaviors create our results and successes.

- Your true power is in your spiritual connection to the Divine Source.

- The true magic power for manifesting your perfect life is to be able to feel as if you already have the qualities you want or the object you desire.

SEVEN

The Magic of Focus

You must be the king or queen of your own reality! If you truly want to co-create your life with Infinite Intelligence, you cannot allow yourself to be controlled by the outside world and its needs and wants. You have to take care of yourself before you can take care of others, which takes some courage to do, but you cannot give what you do not have. If you are not willing to love, nurture, and protect yourself from the crisis demands of others, you will get sucked into the chaos with them.

If you allow yourself to get into the drama or crisis mindset, you cannot help yourself or anyone else. You won't be able to see or feel appropriate directions or solutions while you are upset, freaked out, or frustrated. In negative states of mind, you vibrate at a low frequency and will attract more low frequencies. The spiritual solution to this situation is to first realize you are in a low vibrational state. Become aware, and then make a conscious effort. When you are in a low vibrational state, breathe and calm yourself down, distract yourself if you need to, and find a way to feel grounded. Clear your mind of the problem and connect to your intuition to ask for solutions.

I challenge you to awaken the real power you have within yourself. You can live without drama, crisis, or depression. You must take back your spiritual power to practice the art of deliberate creation. That simply means you claim your conscious awareness of personal control of your life through focus of energy. Accepting this one thought, that you have the power of deliberate creation within you, will transform your life forever. Knowing you have this internal power will give you confidence and help you to optimize your choices on how to use your life energy effectively.

The secret to manifesting what you want is to have one foot planted firmly in heaven and one foot planted firmly on earth. In other words, use your inner thoughts, images, self-talk, and goal-setting activities to create a vision or blueprint of your desired outcome. Once your foundation of the new Inner Energetic Blueprint is created, then you take informed, well-timed action in the physical world. You must be the writer, set designer, head of casting, director, and *actor* in your own script of reality. This is your play so you get to create and publish a good story of success, love, health, prosperity, and a blessed life. Or you can create a life story of unfilled potential, missed opportunities, poverty mentality, and a mediocre life. This is *your story*, so why not write a good one? You hold thc pen every day with your thoughts, beliefs, focus, and life energy. Ask yourself what is really important and then have the wisdom and courage to build your life around your answer.

The True Magic of Crystal Clear Objectives

Goal setting will transform you from a thinker with good intentions to an active achiever. You'll be more motivated and optimistic, and you'll feel more in control of your life than ever before.

When you set clear goals you give Infinite Intelligence and your own Inner Energetic Blueprint a clear picture of what you want. Purposeful goals help us measure our lives and provide feedback to let us know how we are doing. They give us something specific to aim for with our life energy. For our goals to be fruitful, they must be anchored in something that arouses our courage, creativity, persistence, and sense of purpose.

As a performance coach I have found that some clients believe that God has ordained everything about their lives and that they cannot escape the mechanism of fate. The problem with that line of thinking is that if you believe life is pre-destined, you have placed a cap, an upper limit, on what is possible for your future. Any time you put limitations on what you can do you are sabotaging any possibility of transcending your old behaviors and creating a new life for yourself. Nothing in life is predestined because you create your reality with your thoughts, actions, and emotions every single day as you co-create with Infinite Intelligence.

One of the reasons for setting and reviewing goals is to reassess your progress on this journey of life. Whether you have achieved a high level of success in life or not, it is common to find that the attainment of material possessions does not lead to a mature and healthy lifestyle. Create a mission and vision for yourself that drives you forward into your future. Don't be afraid to reassess and readjust your goals. Sometimes we make career choices that ultimately lose meaning for us because they were based solely on financial gain. With maturity, our lives tend to focus more on the need to be of service to others, which can encompass ethics, nobility, compassion, concern for the planet, and shared responsibilities for human problems.

The question of whether to choose a career based on materialistic or idealistic income is a question every spiritually conscious person must decide. My view is that you can find a balance between altruistic purpose and material achievement. You can have the best of both worlds if you set your goals and intentions in that direction. I certainly have taken that path.

Goal-setting brings results because it is governed by specific mental laws. That to which you give your attention and believe in fully will become your reality. Because it is so important I want to share with you some truly down-to-earth tools, as well as spiritual tools, for setting and achieving your goals. Again, the secret to manifesting what you want is to have one foot planted firmly in heaven and one foot planted firmly on the earth to take inspired action.

Five Basic Steps to be a Deliberate Co-Creator

It has been taught by spiritual masters that there are five basic steps to creating your life from a deliberate, conscious point of power. To become a deliberate creator of your life you must start to *feel* your life instead of just thinking about your life. Here's what to do:

Step One: Identify what you do not want—period. Get clear about what does not work for you in life or in your work. Write it down.

Step Two: Knowing what you definitely don't want, identify what you know that you do want. Write it down.

Step Three: Close your eyes and find the good feelings that you associate with your desired goals. Enjoy this state of feeling; enjoy feeling as if you have exactly what you want. Write down how you feel so you can remember it easily.

Step Four: Write out your goal(s); create a clear intention to bring these goals to yourself. In your mind's eye, create a vision of the end result, of the way you just felt in Step Three. Once you have set the clear vision, relax and become unattached and let Infinite Intelligence assist you to make it happen. Create a daily mental rehearsal of your upcoming success.

Step Five: Focus and take action towards your goals daily.

The above steps put an end to the generations of programming about struggle and blame being the causative factors in our lives. If you will simply change the way you think, you will change the way you feel. Changing the way you feel changes the frequency of your body/mind vibrations and that changes the way you attract life events.

Envision and Feel the End Result

Success is not like a book where you start at the beginning, read the middle, and finish with the end. Success is achieved backwards; you must look at what you want in detail and then listen to your intuition about what paths to take and what tools to use. Leonardo da Vinci emphasized the importance of setting clear goals and following through to completion to be successful in anything. He wrote repeatedly, *"Think well to the end"* and *"Consider first the end."* Whatever is dominant in our thoughts is going to come to pass. In his famous book, *The Seven Habits of Highly Effective People*, the late Steven Covey said, *"Begin with the end in mind."* When you focus on positive results, you are putting your vibration in the same wave as the physical positive results you desire. When we focus on the crisis of the moment, we are simply creating more crises for the future. When setting goals you must focus on the solutions and outcomes you want, not the problems.

Re-Patterning your Potential

For some, trying to reach goals by visualizing only the end result can lead to overwhelm and discouragement. New research shows that goals are more attainable when we not only visualize the end result, but also the steps we need to take along the way to reach them. This is especially true if the goal will require or cause a huge life change or if you don't have any past references for it in your mind. The challenge here is that if you have a goal and have no personal experience for how to reach that goal, you are just vaguely imagining something, not actually imprinting a strong picture on your subconscious mind of something you believe. Vague energy is weak energy, and weak energy gets weak results. Plus, when you only use the end result, you may adopt an all-or-nothing mindset about accomplishing the goal rather than being able to break it down into manageable steps your comfort zone can absorb, which will motivate you to keep working until you reach success.

The late Zig Ziglar, who was a famous motivational author I had the honor of sharing the stage with on national lecture tours, used to say: *"People don't tend to wander around and then suddenly find themselves at the top of Mount Everest."* All successful people break down their goals into a series of smaller goals, and create a step-by-step process that assists them to remove the fear and doubt that is often associated with trying to achieve a major life goal. While working with many successful entrepreneurial clients and business owners, I have personally found that when setting goals, it is important to make sure these smaller goals are concrete, measurable, and have a timeline to them.

Let me share a story from my life: After I had been a professional speaker for a few years, I got a huge opportunity to speak in front of 5,000 people with some of the biggest names in my business at the time, like the legendary late Dr. Norman Vincent Peale and other well-known and respected speakers like Brian Tracy.

I was the only woman and the greenhorn on stage with these polished veteran professional speakers. The largest group I had spoken to was a thousand employees for AT&T in New Jersey. Until then, I had been speaking to smaller groups, and a group of 5,000 people was clearly beyond my comfort zone. The truth was that I felt intimidated by the idea of speaking to such a large group and being featured with such legends.

I went to see a very successful coach and hired her to become my mentor. I told her how every time I even thought of standing in front of 5,000 people my body felt weak and my confidence faded. My mentor's advice to me was the best I've ever gotten from anyone. She said to me, *"You must prepare mentally, physically, spiritually, and emotionally for this life-changing event. First imagine yourself in front of those 5,000 people and see the end result that you want to happen, then work backwards and create a strong plan of action so you are truly prepared."*

Her advice was:

> *You have already successfully spoken to an audience of 1,000, now just mentally adjust your comfort level to this new number. The mind needs to go in baby steps to adjust to the new image. Envision yourself in front of 1,500 people for 21 days. Then 2,500 people for 21 days, then 4,000 people for another 21 days. Next see the 5,000 people in the audience. Then let's work on the back story: Envision yourself traveling to the event, checking in to your hotel, and having a meal with the other speakers. See yourself in the*

> *Green Room waiting to speak. Feel your excitement in this amazing opportunity as you wait with these very famous speakers to go on stage. Feel yourself walk out on stage with those 5,000 people listening to your introduction. See your strong body language, as you confidently walk on stage and smile with great sincerity. Observe the audience giving you big smiles, positive body language, and actively taking notes while you are on stage sharing your speech. Then see the end of your talk where they applaud you and rush back to the back of the room and invest in your products. Imagine yourself signing your autograph on your books and products that people invest in. Feel that feeling of pride to be signing your materials for the audience members. Imagine the meeting planner coming over to you and patting you on the back for a job well done and handing you your envelope with your check inside of it. Feel the positive adrenaline and excitement from accomplishing your task."*

For the next few months I followed the instructions she offered for readjusting my self-image using mental rehearsal, which I call re-patterning my potential. When I first woke in the morning, I stayed in bed for an extra five to ten minutes and imagined myself standing in front of those 5,000 people. I saw myself as a confident speaker and "saw" the end result that I wanted—the group clapping enthusiastically after I finished. In the evening, just before I went to sleep, I played the same scene over and over in my mind, creating as many details as possible of the sights, sounds, and feelings of the entire process. Throughout the day whenever I had a few minutes, I would stop and imagine myself getting a standing ovation at the end of the presentation. Sometimes I'd do it for as few as twenty seconds at stop lights. This rehearsal assisted me in creating a new picture in my own mind of what was possible for me.

During this period, I also did the tangible work of physically timing out and practicing my presentation. I recorded my rehearsals and my coach critiqued them and provided feedback about how to improve my stories, power points, physical timing, and body language. In other words, I did my due diligence and homework to make this new vision of me a reality. My coach and I broke down all the components of my goal to speak as a platform salesperson in front of an audience this size. We made sure I covered all the bases of being a successful speaker and being totally prepared when it was time to speak.

I am a visual learner so one of my coach's suggestions was an unusual one: she had me call The Grand Ole Opry in Tennessee, which was the venue for the event, and ask for some photographs of wildly successful speaking rallies that had been there before. With a little bribe for the photographer, I received a package of photos of speakers on stage with the audience giving a standing ovation. I cut out photos of myself and put them on the stage in front of the audience and then pasted my modified pictures on my personal vision board. I hung it in my office so I could see it while I worked every day, which exposed my subconscious to the new images of a full house at The Grand Ole Opry being really excited to hear my presentation. I kept this poster up long after I spoke there.

My coach had not only gotten me to prepare by visualizing exactly what I wanted to happen, she also had me desensitize my reactions to these famous people by having me research how they all got started in the speaking business and what their journey had been up to this point. She helped me make them human and not super-human. She was also very confident that I would be successful in my undertaking because I was willing to do whatever necessary to succeed. She often said: *"If you want to successfully use visualization, it is better to actually visualize taking each step in the process. This helps you maintain your motivation. Yes, imagining the end result is critical to the process, but the step-by-step process of how you are going to get there to reach the goal is equally critical to your success."*

We started the entire process by creating a written plan with timelines, rewards, and clear instructions for what to do at each step of the goal. Every week, I worked on goal sheets and turned them in to my coach. I wrote out my huge goal in detail (working with these famous speakers and successfully speaking at the Grand Ole Opry in front of 5,000 people with comfort and ease). I then mapped out each step of the goal, which we'll call sub-goals. My criteria for each step of my goal, or sub-goal, was that it must be clear, concrete, measureable, and realistic with a timeline that can be met.

On my weekly goal sheets, I made it a point to answer the big questions:

- What's my major goal?
- What are the benefits for me of achieving this goal?
- Who will I share these goals with to hold me accountable?
- Who will I share my successes with?
- Why do I believe I can achieve this goal?

Sub-Goal #1:

- Actions I will take toward sub-goal one:
- I will complete sub-goal one by this date:

- My reward for achieving sub-goal one will be:
- The penalty for not achieving sub-goal one will be:

My goal required nine sub-goals, so we created a nine-week plan. Each week, I followed the above format for each step or sub-goal. I turned in the first week's sub-goal and moved on to sub-goal two, and so on until I finished my nine-week plan.

The plan was designed so I could break my major goal down into bite-sized pieces and think about how I would achieve each step, see the reward I'd receive for meeting the deadline, and keep me accountable for finishing on time by telling the supportive people in my life about my timeline and the end result I was going to achieve. I personally wasn't big on the idea of telling other people about my goal, but my coach insisted I share this goal to keep myself honest! If I'd kept the goal to myself it would have eased the fear of failure, but it also would have been easier to avoid making the big changes that meeting the goal would require of me. Not sharing the goal would have opened the door for me to drift back into old habits and routines. On the other hand, sharing the goal with supportive people I could trust ramped up the internal pressure to do the work, and kept me from failing. People tend to better stick to achieving a new goal when they share the goal with a support system that holds them accountable.

My coach was big on rewards and always wanted me to focus on enjoying the benefits associated with my imagined future, instead of fearing what might happen. Her attitude was the more you remind yourself of the benefits of achieving your goals, the more focus and energy you will use to get there. This was why my weekly report included what I was doing to reinforce the rewards of the work to change my self-image from a small room audience to a large group. The biggest benefit of accomplishing the goal was that it would launch my career to a new level of success and income from speaking. My coach was very clear that my focus had to be on a positive future, not fears or doubts.

The last piece of the plan my coach gave me was the written work I did daily. To make my plans, benefits, progress, and rewards as concrete as possible, I had to write them out in a script form either by hand in a journal or on my computer. I had to create pictures to post on my Vision board and bathroom mirrors to assist with the motivation to do the work. Her advice was that in order to achieve the goal you want to manifest, you have to reinforce these new images using your learning processes, both visually and kinesthetically.

The day of the biggest and most important speech of my life to that point, I was nervous and had butterflies. But within just a couple of minutes of walking on stage, I felt right at home with those 5,000 people. I confidently delivered my speech and received the standing ovation I'd envisioned. I made lasting connections with the famous speakers, and the event led to even bigger speaking engagements. I had successfully re-imagined and re-engineered my comfort zone to reach beyond 5,000 people and sharing the stage with those famous speakers! This event changed the course of my career destiny.

I was successful because I chose not to go into a big life change alone. I worked with a professional coach, who focused my attention away from fear and doubt and instead helped me re-imagine and re-engineer my mental programming about what was possible. She assisted me to create a cohesive, well-thought plan to achieve my goal.

If you are not part of a mastermind group or have a personal business coach to assist you to move past your current reality, I highly suggest you add this valuable component to your life to move you to the next level.

This experience helped shape my future because I realized the power of the mind and what I could create when I focused my energy on a single goal. I realize I could have never had the confidence to go for the goals in my life without the help of mental rehearsal. This tool allowed me to break through barriers that I had set up in my own mind of what I could and could not do.

Practical Magic Manifesting Methods:

Thank God In Advance

Thank Infinite Intelligence daily for manifesting your goals. When you thank Infinite Intelligence for what you want before you get it, you are programming your mind and the universe to accept that you already have it. Then you start to vibrate at the same frequency as your goal, which makes the law of attraction work for you, bringing you exactly what you want.

Think Big

Your success or lack of it reflects what is in your mind. Your current success or lack of it is the sum of all the thoughts you have had about it. If your life seems small, it's probably because your dominant visual picture of your life has been small. If you think big you will get big results. To reclaim the magic, you map out a new way of thinking bigger about your goals, which will attract new resources and options for a better future.

Give Yourself Permission Manifest What You Want

Desire is the starting point for all achievement. It's the greatest motivator of every human action. Again, dream big! Infinite Intelligence has a way of delivering to you exactly what you ask for, so ask for what you want. Put pictures of what you want around you where you will see them. Say out loud, with emotion and enthusiasm, daily, *"I am now easily and effortlessly attracting everything I want and need."*

Don't set a goal for yourself that your spouse (or anyone else for that matter) wants for you. You will never be successful achieving goals that are not motivated by your own desires. Don't compare your goals to other people's goals, either. You are a unique soul who has come to the earth for your own life purpose. Be unique, be original, and go for what you want!

Action is the Key!

The secret of getting ahead is getting started and moving towards the goal you want. If you become sincerely engaged, your intuition will inspire you to books, resources, and opportunities to learn more. Make it a point to take action on at least one of your goals every day. Reward yourself at the end of the day for moving ahead. Do not just sit and think about what you want to do. *Do it*!

Amp Up Your Passion and Enthusiasm!

If you have lost your passion and enthusiasm for your life, relationships, work, or goals, you need to rekindle the fire and remind yourself of what is good about areas of your life that you have let become tarnished. Take the time to write a list of the positive things about these areas of your life. Post this list in a place where you can see it daily to remind yourself that *you* are choosing how to spend your life energy. Truly passionate and enthusiastic people tend to achieve their goals faster. It's a wise person who is invested in both the journey and the goal. Don't lose sight of your partnership with Infinite Intelligence and the fact that your life is your ministry. Remember the king or queen within you! Where is your kingdom and how can you reignite the love for yourself and your life again?

Associate with People who Inspire, Love, and Support You
Realize that you cannot be all things to all people. You must surround yourself with a group of people who want you to succeed. Surround yourself with like-minded people who have the same type of goals, abilities, skills, and talents that you do or want to have in your life. Reward the people in your life who help you manifest your dreams. The truth is that no one becomes successful all alone. It is also important to be aware of who you associate with.

Magical Essences . . .

- You can live without drama, crisis, or depression.
- The secret to manifesting what you want is to have one foot planted firmly in heaven and one foot planted firmly on earth.
- Once your foundation of the new Inner Energetic Blueprint is created, then you take informed, well-timed action in the physical world.
- It has been taught by spiritual masters that there are five basic steps to creating your life from a deliberate, conscious point of power.
- When you focus on positive results you are putting your vibration in the same wave as the physical positive results you desire.

EIGHT

The Magic of Truth

"Circumstance does not make the man; it reveals him to himself."
—James Allen

There is an old saying that the truth will set you free, yet so many people today sincerely don't know the truth about themselves or reality. If you are watching mainstream media, you may think you are getting the real story, but that is not the case. The real truth is that the "news" is written with a fear based agenda to divert your attention. It is only loosely based on facts. You have been lied to by not only the media but others in your life such as the society you live in, religious intuitions, government, schools, families, friends, and business associates. I am not saying these people mean to tell you lies but they share the view of the reality they believe, which may or may not actually be reality. They may be telling the truth as they know it but that doesn't mean it will be truth for you.

One of the rewards of the spiritual path is that you question what truth is. You learn not to blindly accept what everyone else believes is true. You learn to pause and discern what information is the truth. Your intuition and your connection to Infinite

Cosmic Intelligence will be more of a guide than listening to what others say.

How important is truth in today's world? Dan Kennedy, my best friend and business mentor, has written many business books. I recommend all of his materials. Find him at *www.gkic.com*. In his *NO B.S. Business Success* book, published by Entrepreneur Press, Dan suggests that maintaining integrity and high ethics are some of the most important aspects to long-term success. He says, *"Personal faith is not usually a topic entrepreneurs discuss openly, but just about every highly successful person I've ever known has a very definite set of spiritual beliefs and, as a result, acts with faith. For me, faith is based on four simple ideas:*

1. *There is a plan and purpose behind our lives.*
2. *We're here to learn some things and to accomplish some things.*
3. *We were intended and are invited to live prosperously.*
4. *When operating within certain parameters, we have every reason to expect positive results."*

He went on to say, *"This solid expectation of positive results empowers you to cut through the clutter and confusion of self-doubt, fear, criticism, cynicism, negativism, and other obstacles."* The point here is that when you pursue your goals, they must be achieved by enriching others, not at the expense of others. You must accept responsibility for your own actions.

William F. James, founder of Boys Town, Missouri, said that there are only three things necessary to success: first, normal intelligence; second, determination; and third, absolute honesty. One cannot be a little dishonest; it's all the way or nothing.

Know Your Personal Truth

François de La Rochefoucauld, the French nobleman and writer, has been noted to have said that because we are so trained to mask ourselves and present a certain façade to others, we actually eventually get lost in the façade and no longer know who we are. As children, we are told what to do and who to be until we believe it about ourselves. We are rewarded for becoming what is expected of us and punished when we don't. He goes on to explain that:

> *"Eventually we no longer even know who we truly are—only what we believe ourselves to be. The disguise is complete, our integrity and authenticity gone, traded for a biscuit or a shred of love."*

The problem is that most people really don't know their own personal truth. As kids we were taught always to tell the truth and that honesty was the best policy. The bad news is that kids watch adults lie and get away with it all the time on television, in the movies, and in real life. Kids notice that sometimes, when you tell the truth, it can upset people and you might even get punished.

Since most people want to avoid conflict and confrontation we get in the habit of not telling the truth to avoid any upset it may cause. The truth gets told only when it is to our advantage to share it. Without realizing it, we sometimes don't tell the truth just so we can fit in with society's expectations. We sometimes stretch the truth to make someone feel more comfortable, including ourselves, or just to complete a business deal.

This serious problem of inconsistent truth-telling blurs moral and ethical lines. When we lose our morals and ethics, which are our own personal truth, we actually lose the essence of ourselves. As spiritual beings when we stop telling the truth, we lose integrity with ourselves. If you cannot trust yourself, you cannot trust anyone. This sad state of affairs will never bring you peace of mind or happiness, much less success!

To truly reclaim your magic, you have to stop worrying about what others will think of you if you speak your truth in an appropriate manner. If you really want to live an authentic life and be proud of yourself, you must not let anyone tell you who you are or what your truth should be. It's important for you to know your own truth and to speak your own truth. Become truly who you are and act only from what you truly believe. If you don't believe in what you are saying, you will not be able to live by your words.

Yes, I know it's easier to go with the flow than to stand your ground when problems occur. But after a while, if you don't stand your ground, you won't even know what you believe or think.

Our society and the media feed us an enormous amount of "shoulds" every day. We are told what we should like and should not like, how to think and how to fit in so that the "majority" accepts us. As of today, wake up and realize that, though it might be difficult to speak your truth at first, you will have more respect for yourself if you do. And once you get in touch with your own personal truth, you will not allow others to walk on it.

It's important to take back your power in life and understand that you do not have to conform to what everyone else is thinking or doing. You have the power and responsibility to decide what you believe, what your personal truth is, and how to stand within that truth. Be proud to be an individual.

When I urge you to speak your truth, please do not let that be an invitation to be offensive or difficult or to feel that you have to defend your truth. Always speak your truth with kindness and love. Who you are speaks loudly without words.

Understand that you may not always agree with others and that each individual has his or her own personal truth. No one has to agree with yours or join you in that truth. Realize that, once you let your own real truth come out, people around you might be upset that you are no longer "playing the game." You cannot control others and the good news is that they no longer can control you.

Do you know your own personal truth? Often in social situations I hear people give their opinion about certain subjects, yet I know it's really not their opinion. I know they are repeating what they have heard from others and have not taken the time to decide what they really think or feel about a subject. People tend to look at just one side of a subject and then parrot back in a conversation what they think other people want to hear and will find acceptable.

When I was very young and unconscious about who I really was, I found myself trying to be all things to all people. If I was around a set of people who thought one way, I found myself agreeing with them. In the same day I could be around another set of opinions and agreeing with them, too, just to be part of the group. I had no clue to who I was or what I believed. It was easier for me just to go along with the crowd of the moment. Thankfully, I moved toward a quest for truly knowing who I am and what I personally stand for and believe.

Do some soul-searching and ask yourself some life-defining questions. It takes a great deal of courage to examine your own beliefs. Do you really just want to follow the masses and believe what the media spoon-feeds you? Question your old beliefs about what feels right to you and how you want to live your life. I recommend *The Hard Questions for an Authentic Life* by Susan Piver (Gotham Books), as resource book for your personal investigation. Piver's *Questions* can help you sift through your beliefs and know what you want to keep and want to discard.

To begin to define your own truth, you might go into a quiet place, maybe out in nature. Get centered (quiet your mind) and ask yourself some soul-searching questions to help define what your truth is for you as an individual. This won't keep you from being open-minded to new views on life but it will help you to know your personal truth, how to operate in the world in the way that is authentic for you.

Are you aware of it when you are not operating from your own personal truth or ethic? Keep in mind that living from your personal truth involves not only how you feel you ought to be treated, but also how you treat or protect others. For example: a family member says something untrue or negative about another family member. You keep quiet and don't correct the error—breach of personal ethic. Another salesperson takes over one of your accounts and you don't speak up about it—breach of business ethic. You are in a social setting and someone keeps making sexist jokes or racist comments and you think, "I don't like that but it doesn't have anything to do with me and they are not talking about me so I will keep quiet"—breach of personal ethic.

I suggest that you write your observations about your personal truth investigation in a notebook or journal. Write about the topics in your life that you talk about but rarely have made a clear statement of how you actually feel. Write about topics such as work, money, success, love, spirituality, nature, politics, war, poverty, marriage, children, homelessness, and add subjects as they come along in your daily life.

When someone asks you how you feel on a subject, really think about it before you speak. Don't just repeat what you have heard others say about the subject. If you don't know how you feel about something, simply state, "I don't know. I'll have to think about that." Then take the time to actually think about it and discover your truth about it. Remember that in life it's more important to be respected than liked.

In your business life, needless to say, it is smart not to discuss subjects that are truly hot topics, those that hardly anyone agrees on, such as politics, sex, and religion.

To reclaim your magic, do your best to speak your truth with kindness and avoid defensiveness. You don't have to defend yourself when you live from your authentic truth. Everyone has their own personal truth and no one has to agree with yours. You cannot control others and you don't want them controlling you.

Be Impeccable with Your Word

A book that has made a huge impact on me and that I recommend for everyone to read is *The Four Agreements* by Don Miguel Ruiz. He has a chapter in the book called "Be Impeccable with Your Word," in which he says, *"Your word is the power that you have to create. Your word is the gift that comes directly from God. The Gospel of John in the Bible, speaking of the creation of the universe, says, 'In the beginning there was the word, and the word was with God, and the word is God.'"*

Your word is the most powerful tool you have as a human being. Like a sword with two edges, your word can create positive experiences or destroy your peace of mind.

This concept of being impeccable is very important for us in our business world because we live by our honor. We honor ourselves by living true to our word, so our word needs to be reliable.

Unwittingly, our culture has allowed the negative habit of lying to persist in much of our interpersonal and public communications. The word "impeccability" means "without sin." It is said that a sin is anything that you do which goes against your true self. Any type of lying is certainly going against your true self.

Ruiz says in his book that when you are impeccable, you take responsibility for your actions, but you do not judge or blame yourself. He also says that sin begins with rejection of yourself and that self-rejection is the greatest sin (error) we can commit.

When I read that last statement—that self-rejection is the biggest sin you can commit—I had to sit with it for a while. I finally came to understand that lying is self-rejection. As Ruiz says, speaking the truth is the most important part of being impeccable with your word. Only the truth sets you free.

Don't Take Anything Personally

As the old saying goes, "Sticks and Stones may break your bones but words can never hurt you." In today's world, rejection is a part of daily life. One of the best skills you can integrate into your life is how to detach from other people's rejection—to not take it personally. You see, the very personal fear of being rejected is actually the fear of not being good enough. You must detach your self-concept from others' opinions about you.

If you take other people's words and actions personally, you are doomed because internally you feel like a victim. If you get rejected, a part of you is saying, "I am not good enough, poor me; I am not intelligent enough; I am not attractive enough; I am not worthy." These are damaging and false beliefs. What do they do to your creative energy? They squash it!

We judge and punish ourselves for not living up to our own arbitrary image of perfection. No one is ever going to be perfect. By not being perfect we often reject ourselves. We wear social masks to keep others from seeing the real us. Deep down we feel inauthentic and don't accept ourselves. We are our own worst judges. Trying to be perfect is unnatural and destructive to our souls, going against the spiritual concept that you are already a perfect child of God.

It takes a great deal of courage to challenge your own beliefs about rejection and perfection. Accept that thoughts of insufficiency are fear-based and that they waste your creative energy and power. Use your energy to change those thoughts and you'll change the feelings behind them and reclaim your personal power.

A massive amount of freedom and energy comes to you when you take nothing personally. You become immune to negative people and negative situations and to rejection of any kind. Understanding the game of life, you simply go forth and do not let anything bother you.

You know that your connection to God Source is never broken and no one has the power to hurt you unless you let them. Do not give your power away to others—*ever*! Detach from other people's world. You live in your own world.

Author Don Miguel Ruiz explains that it's selfish for us to take things personally because when we do, we're assuming that it's all about "me." Ruiz says, "*Nothing other people do is because of you. It is because of themselves. All people live in their own dream, in their own mind; they are in a completely different world from the one we live in . . .*" He is telling us that taking things personally assumes the other person is privy to what's going on in our world and at the same time, forces our world on them.

When a situation seems very personal to you, in reality it may have nothing to do with you at all. When others offer their opinions, they are coming from their own programming, feelings, beliefs, and views of life.

We do not have to let others' opinions be part of our inner world. People's opinions are simply the way they see the world. Nothing they think about you has anything to do with you.

They see you from their own beliefs. They see situations or reality from a different lens than you do. If someone is upset with you, they are really upset with themselves. You are just a focus point for why they are upset with themselves.

For example, I recently found myself annoyed with my mate, Clifton, because his home office was an out-of-control mess. Later, I admitted to myself that by being annoyed with him, I took the focus off the very annoying fact that *my* office was a mess. I had to admit that I was really angry with myself for not being more organized in my own life. It was easier to lash out at him than to face my own disorganization. I had moved the focus off myself and projected my anger at him. It was my office mess and myself that I was truly mad at, not him, but it was so much easier to find fault with him and focus my attention on his mess.

Understand that you have to trust yourself and choose to believe or not to believe what someone says to you. You must trust yourself to make the right choices about what to believe. If you feel rejected, ask yourself, "Am I taking this personally? Why? This situation has nothing to do with me at all." Give up guilt or self-judgment and follow your heart.

You can lose the fear of being ridiculed or rejected by others and stay in a state of joy and happiness by simply understanding that you are never responsible for the actions of others. You are only responsible for yourself. When you refuse to take anything personally, you cannot be hurt by comments or actions from other people. No matter *what* someone says or does, you can still follow your heart and soul and recognize that you are a divine child of God.

Here is a short synopsis I came across, of the material covered in the book *The Four Agreements* by Don Miguel Ruiz.

I have this on a 5 x 7 card on my bathroom mirror to remind me daily to stay in integrity with myself and not to take anything personally. What most people say or do in the end has no impact on your everyday life and therefore is not worth worrying over. If you adopt these agreements with yourself, you will find you are less stressed and have fewer negative people in your life. You will be far more at peace with yourself.

1. BE IMPECCABLE WITH YOUR WORD

   a. Speak with integrity.

   b. Say only what you mean.

   c. Avoid using the Word to speak against yourself or to gossip about others.

   d. Use the Power of your Word in the direction of truth and love.

2. DON'T TAKE ANYTHING PERSONALLY

   a. Nothing others do is because of you.

   b. What others say and do is a projection of their own reality, their own dream.

   c. When you are immune to the opinions and actions of others, you won't be the victim of needless suffering.

3. DON'T MAKE ASSUMPTIONS

   a. Find the courage to ask questions and to express what you really want.

   b. Communicate with others as clearly as you can to avoid misunderstandings, sadness, and drama.

c. With just this one agreement, you can completely transform your life.

4. ALWAYS DO YOUR BEST

a. Your best is going to change from moment to moment: it will be different when you are healthy as opposed to sick.

b. Under any circumstance, simply do your best, and you will avoid self-judgment, self-abuse, and regret.

Stop Gossiping

If you want to be conscious about your actions and impeccable with your words, you must delete gossiping from your personal habits. It's true that misery loves company and perhaps that's what has made gossiping a major problem in our society today. Since our word is power, every time we gossip negative information we are contributing to the pain and suffering of others. Go on a gossip-free diet for thirty days and notice the difference in your relationships with other people.

Again, focus on what is good in life instead of what is not working, for yourself and others. Your attitude and productivity will improve and, since all energy gets results, you will change your life's results because you are focusing on others' good. Use your time to write out your goals and think about them, rather than to entertain yourself and others with gossip.

Have Integrity with Yourself

I work as a speaker, coach, and consultant for all sizes of organizations and personal coaching clients. I am proud to say that once I'm hired, I am often asked to come back to work with the groups many times. One of the signs of success is when people want more of you.

I started getting feedback from some of my corporate clients that they had an increase in the number of people quitting after my presentation. Since I have long-term repeat contracts with many of these Fortune 500 companies, they loved my work but understandably did not want their employees leaving! They asked me to leave out of my presentation the part about *"if you are not happy here, if you do not love this job, you should leave after giving reasonable notice."* I was torn about what to do with this situation. I work and get money from the client who employs these people and I have a moral obligation to supply them with the materials we have agreed upon for teaching. On the other hand, it feels out of integrity if I don't offer the "love it or leave it" information to the people whom I am teaching to think at a higher level and to be aware of their options.

I explained to my clients that the real truth is that employers are much better off without employees that are unhappy and don't want to be there. There it is, *truth*, simple and to the point. It is best for a company's long-term health to weed out the weakest links in the chain. In this instance, I stayed true to my highest integrity and was rewarded with the creative energy to find a win-win situation for all concerned.

The Power of Detachment

One of the most under-used spiritual principles is to be detached from the outcome of your efforts. One of the greatest causes of suffering is attachment. The more easily you can let go of the old and embrace the new, the more quickly you can prosper in life rather than struggle.

When you're completing a project, you know you must do your best. After you have done the very best possible, you have to let it go. Do not be mentally and emotionally attached to the outcome. Release thoughts and feelings about the outcome. Move the energy of your thoughts and feelings toward your future.

The truth is that if you are attached to the outcome of anything, the heightened emotion of fearing the loss of it can repel the very thing you want the most. Being attached to the outcome will actually foster fear, frustration, self-pity, self-recrimination, and even anger. Hanging on to a fixed outcome repels it and once you release it, you must truly trust that it will either come back to you or something better will take its place. As you learn to work with these spiritual power tools, you will learn to trust that nothing ever leaves your life unless something better is coming, so there's no need to feel attached to the outcome of anything!

Having attachments takes a great deal of life energy and drains you of creative proactive energy. Once you become anxious about needing the outcome you want, you can sabotage it by pushing too hard or acting a little needy. Physically, you may not recognize that you are acting needy, but the emotional "charge" of subconscious needy feelings will repel the very thing you are after.

People are attracted to confidence. They want to "go with winners" because they like to see the winner in themselves. Needy, greedy, and grasping people are not winners. Trust me: other people's emotional radar detector can sense if you are attached to what you want regardless of the situation. If the other party feels your need or attachment for a certain outcome, that energy will actually repel them.

Detachment is not disinterest. You must remain engaged in the process at hand without being attached to the outcome.

Detachment creates an atmosphere of freedom for right action to occur. What's right for one person is not always right for another.

One of the greatest challenges of spiritual growth is learning to release old ways of doing things. Detach yourself from beliefs, people, and things that no longer serve you. Bless them as they leave, and embrace the new as it comes. Letting go is an important aspect of growing spiritually. As a conscious person, accept that new growth involves learning new skills, making changes, and creating new attitudes.

Just before I went into the speaking business, I was in commercial real estate. Interest rates were sky-high for commercial loans at that time and I was not selling much. I was forced to face myself and admit that I really did not like selling commercial real estate. It was a great job for the guys in my office who loved it, but I did not. By not being successful, I was forced to ask myself what I really wanted to do with my life. I talk about this time in my life in great detail in my book: *Success is an Inside Job.*

The bottom line is, I gave up my ego and my attachment to becoming successful in commercial real estate. I let that career go and jumped into the speaking business and now all I can say is "thank you, God." I found my real calling in life. If I had not let go of my attachment to my old career I may have never found my true passion and life's work. We all need to reinvent ourselves with what is calling us from the deepest part of our soul.

Start practicing non-attachment by observing your own thoughts and actions. In what situations do you feel an attachment to the outcome? Who and what are you attached to? Practice giving up your attachment one situation at a time.

As you grow spiritually, you must give up your dependence on your attachments. You will notice one day that you are happy without them, and then you are free. Then you can have the objects of your attachments (a certain dollar value, etc.) in your life without being controlled by them.

You must realize that your well-being is never really contingent on what someone else does or does not do. Your well-being is always your conscious choice. You must trust the process and release any desperate feelings. The old saying that the universe is perfect and there are no failures is true. Give yourself the gift of detaching from your worries and trust that everything is in divine order.

My first real sales job was broadcast radio sales and I was so excited about it that the sales seemed to happen like magic. With no experience and no expectations, my enthusiasm was so strong that I sold almost everyone I called on in the beginning. I was really doing well.

My sales manager at thc time believed the theory that the more salespeople were in debt, the more motivated they would be to make sales. With my sales manager's urging, I got a new expensive car, lots of new business suits, and a much bigger apartment. Suddenly I was deeply in debt and the pressure was intense to make more money. I did not realize it at the time, but his mindset of motivation-by-debt backfired on me!

With every call, I now felt pressure to make the sale. Before getting in debt, when I made sales calls I had been having fun, talking to people, and sharing success stories about how my product would benefit them. I was not overly concerned about whether this prospect would buy because I knew that I had a good product and that I would always have interested customers. Suddenly all these big bills were coming in each month and my only focus was my desperate need to make more sales to cover my bills.

The more I needed to make a sale because the rent was due, the less interested people seemed to be about my product and me. I was working harder but getting less positive results from my sales calls. I was confused. What had happened? I was selling the same product, working harder and longer, and yet making fewer sales. It seemed the more I really needed to make a sale the less sales I made.

I was lucky enough to have a spiritual advisor. In desperation I went to her and told her my story. She explained to me the law of detachment. She said I had a few options to change my luck but the best one was to become partners with God in my business. She shared with me the exercise of praying for my clients and putting their well-being over mine. She also explained to me how important it was that I was not held hostage by material things. I was not happy at the time about downsizing my life to get it under control, but that gave me the freedom of not having to make a specific dollar level of sales. When I shifted my attitude—sales soared!

Even today, after all these years, I still live under my means, which has always given me a sense of freedom. I will never have to do anything I don't want to do just because of money. By detaching from a requirement to have certain material goods, I can choose to keep my business affairs in integrity with myself and others. By doing my best and always taking care of my clients, I have attracted more clients to me than I can work with.

Rid Your Life of Friends, People, and Clients Who Do Not Honor You

Another area where the truth can set you free is to rid your life of outrageous, difficult, or dishonest acquaintances, those who will never be happy with you no matter what you do. You may be thinking, "Lose friends, what is magical or successful about that? Aren't I supposed to turn the other cheek?" The answer is: when you have done your best, when nothing is working and they are still unhappy, it's time to let them go.

When you stay in a false stage of hope that the difficult people in your life will change, you are giving away time and energy that you could be using to enjoy people who want to be more positive with you. Negative people do damage to your well-being and integrity. Remember that the definition of insanity is doing the same thing over and over again and hoping for a new result. When you continue to try to work with or be friends with someone who disrespects you, is impossible to please, and who gives you emotional distress, it's time to move on.

To reclaim your magic, you must honor yourself, your time, and your peace of mind. Develop your sense of observation so that you are aware of when you are in a no-win situation. There are always red flags if you are conscious enough to look for them and acknowledge them when you see them.

I decided long ago that I am no longer going to squander my creative energies trying to please someone who is not a match for me and my product or service. I accept the truth when someone else is a better match for that person. By letting these "energy drains" go I have freed myself to be a better friend to others who are a match to me or to give other clients exceptional service.

Case in point: I have a coaching program called the Millionaire Smarts® Program, where I supply salespeople, entrepreneurs, and business owners a CD interview each month and articles with other famous authors on different topics to support their "right thinking." I also offer sponsorships to other business coaches for their members to be part of my coaching program to keep them motivated. After several successful years with very good word of mouth advertising, a particular business coach called, wanting to add my coaching program to his members. He wanted to be assured that his people would warm up to me, so I happily spent ninety minutes on a live conference call with him and his membership group. I presented a seminar tailored just for his members and their needs, and received great feedback from his members and staff. However, I never got even a verbal "thank you" from him. A small red flag went up in my head. That had not been my experience with other business coaches when I had taken my time and expense to assist them.

This prospect then asked if he could have one of my coaching calls for free for his group before he signed a longer contract. We finally agreed on terms for his group and set a date. The day before the conference call, one of his staff people called, wanting to make major changes to the way we did the conference call. With huge expense and effort to make these changes occur, we pulled it off. And again, there was no appreciation for our time and effort.

When it came time to close this client, he started making more demands and was more and more difficult and critical of my service. More red flags! He was asking me to break all my own business rules to make him happy. The more I did to try to close the sale, the more he would find something additional to ask for or complain about. Red flags! He was the kind of person who felt that, if he criticized you and your product, you would lower your price to get his business.

After a long, exhausting conversation with him, I realized that if he signed a contract, my life would be hell dealing with him because nothing made him happy! I'd had enough stress with him and he was not worth it. I looked back over the red flags and assured myself that I had lived before I met him and I would live and thrive after he was gone. I meditated for a few days about what to do and when I felt clear about what I needed to do, I sent him a letter retracting my offer to do coaching for his group. As you can well imagine, that didn't make him happy, but you just can't win them all.

A few months later I found out that listening to my intuition and retreating from his business was a blessing. I talked to a vendor who dealt with him and was told that this man made a point of bullying people that he did business with. The poor coach who finally ended up working for him was totally miserable and could not wait until the agreement came up for renewal to be rid of him!

The lesson here is to honor yourself. When you see really big red flags from a friend or client, be willing to save yourself energy, time, money, and tons of aggravation by letting them go.

I will share from a personal point of view that working with friends or family normally never works out in the end. Everyone has a different perspective of reality. You have better leverage with people when you are not emotionally attached or involved with them personally. Sadly, I have had to learn this lesson way too many times. When you are "friends," you find yourself letting things slip that you normally wouldn't because you are afraid of telling the truth and hurting your relationship. You are better off to keep your friendships and business arrangements separate so you can have integrity with self and speak your truth. If you follow this advice you will be much better off in the long run. It is tempting to hire people you love and know but only do it if you are willing to release the relationship.

Work Only with Businesses You are Proud to Represent

In my mid-twenties, after several successful sales positions and one year into my career as a commercial real estate agent (in a time of deep recession), I woke up one morning and simply did not want to get out of bed. The cold truth hit me in the face—I hated my sales job. I had lost my motivation. Life was no longer fun. In fact, after a little soul-searching, I had to admit to myself that I'd only gone into real estate chasing the lure of big bucks. And unfortunately, not only was I not making the big bucks, but my life was filled with frustration.

What was occurring—though I didn't realize it at the time—was that my belief systems were changing. Up to that point, I had been moving through life determined to establish a life style that I believed meant success—money, titles, and lots of fancy trappings. Clearly, I was at a critical point in my life. I could sell out and continue working in a job that did not bring me happiness, or I could begin to reevaluate and restructure my beliefs about what was really important, money or happiness.

Why couldn't I have both? I had been poor and I had been rich, and I can say that money, as energy, is a handy thing to have to live a comfortable life. And now I was not bringing in enough to pay my bills. The real estate company loaned me more money than I was making so that, when I did sell something, I already owed it back to the company. That meant that I could not quit without owing them money.

Though I felt much pain and confusion at that moment, I heard a small voice inside—the same voice that had led me through other dark moments—telling me to examine the belief systems I was holding on to in my life that were not working. Then I knew I would have to spend time to get clear about my new beliefs and allow them to motivate me toward my next level of success.

So, after many long sleepless nights, I finally began to ask myself some of the most important questions of my life. What did I love to do most? How did I want to live each day? What could

I do that would allow me to wake up each morning excited about the day ahead? How could I earn a living and love what I do?

Looking back, I realize I was trying to reclaim the magic of my life. It took a great deal of courage to face the reality that my life was not working and to attempt to do something about it. I knew in my heart that whatever I decided from that point forward I would have to only sell something I totally believed in with all my heart and soul. I was ready to do something that really excited and fulfilled me.

Long story short, that is what started me on the path to becoming a speaker, author, and business coach. Now I sell ideas and training on success-thinking concepts. I can honestly say that I believe in myself and my work 100 percent. Taking the risk to give up operating my life the way others felt I should and taking control of my own destiny allowed me to truly love what I do. Because I love what I do, I attract people who want to do business with me. I have never been more successful than I am now, doing what I truly love, in a field in which I have natural capabilities.

Life is way too short to work for an organization or be in any relationship that you feel out of integrity with. All too often, we put our needs on a shelf to serve others' needs and desires. We are the supporters of others, yet we do not give ourselves permission to pursue our own dreams and desires. Now is the time to look honestly in the mirror and ask, "What do I want? What can I do today to really live my life, not just go through the motions?"

If you feel you cannot continue your work or anything else in your life with pride, then you are out of integrity with your own truth. You need to do some serious soul-searching and ask yourself whether you want to stay where you are or move on to an environment in which you feel you are in integrity with your truth. Don't discount the pride aspect of being involved with something or someone; if you don't feel it, you need to keep looking for something that brings you a sense of honor.

Get clear about why you are happy or unhappy. The truth will set you free. Remember, destiny is not a matter of chance; it's a matter of choice. That means when you examine your beliefs about what is possible, you acknowledge that you have a valuable contribution and that your talents, skills, and abilities can serve you, your acquaintances and loved ones, and your clients.

One of the most magical acts you can do is to believe in yourself and listen to your own intuition. Belief in yourself is the one basic, absolutely essential ingredient for anyone who wants to reclaim their own magic. To have belief in yourself, you must know that you stand in integrity with your life choices.

In my coaching program and speaking engagements over the years, I have heard many stories of people staying in jobs they hate. Everyone gets stuck for their own reasons. Many people would rather be unhappy than risk looking or feeling foolish trying to get another job. For some people, the fear of the unknown is just too big for them to conquer.

If right now you are not feeling honest with yourself about your work or anything else in your life, what are you waiting for? You may have noticed that your Infinite Intelligence does not offer a neon light in the sky to guide you! Take some time to write out on paper how you feel and what you want. Knowing your own truth will give you the power to fund the necessary changes in your life.

If you have done your self-discovery process and truly don't see a future for yourself where you are, be true to yourself and sincerely start the search for your new life. Don't wait for life to come to you. God helps those who help themselves. If you do leave your current job for greener pastures, do so with integrity, professionalism, class, and proper notice. Be willing to help train the next person taking your position. Never burn your bridges because you never know when you may need one.

Don't just read these materials and say to yourself, *"She is right; I need to get out of here, I need to make changes in my life."* All success comes from studying, planning, and then taking action. It's just not bright to quit a job before getting another one, or having a solid action plan in place. Go to school at night or take online classes; prepare yourself for your future. Become a person who does not have to actively look for a job because your talents, integrity, professionalism, and good personality draw recruiters to try to hire you away from where you are now!

Today is the day to get yourself into a proactive state of mind and start an improvement program for yourself. Just as you would start an exercise program, choose the behaviors that will assist you to achieve your personal and business goals. For more tips on retraining your mind and motivating yourself, you can read my book, *Success is an Inside Job*, for a quick-start guide. I share my personal story of how I overcame the odds for my success by becoming self-employed. If you want to improve your life, be proactive towards planning your future.

All Relationships Have Imperfections

As Dr. Phil says, *"Get real."* Don't set yourself up to desire perfection because there are no perfect jobs or relationships. Furthermore, there are different personalities in every family and everywhere you work it's not humanly possible for people to agree all the time. In reality, there will always be difficult people. It's absolutely magical to look for the good in people first, and focus on the good in people to attract more good to yourself.

Claim Your Own Truth—Acknowledge Your True Nature

Another area for the truth to set you free is accepting yourself as a child of God. You are perfect in the concepts of heaven, though you are a human on earth. We are all on this journey to learn from life and enjoy the process. To reclaim your magic, accept the truth that your job in all situations is to simply offer the best of yourself. Yes, you will forget to pay attention to the messages of Infinite Intelligence, as all of us do from time to time, but you can easily turn your thoughts to the still, small voice within you and resume your path.

Some days, you may be the only person who knows you have stayed in integrity with yourself. You can look yourself in the mirror and know you did the best you could in every way. The only person we ever really need to impress is ourselves. And that is enough!

Magical Essences . . .

- Most people really don't know their own personal truth.
- You have to stop worrying about what others will think of you if you speak your truth in an appropriate manner.
- It's important for you to know your own truth and to speak your own truth.
- Do your best to speak your truth with kindness and avoid defensiveness.
- Your word is the most powerful tool you have as a human being. Like a sword with two edges, your word can create positive experiences or destroy your peace of mind.

- You must delete gossiping from your personal habits.
- You must honor yourself, your time, and your peace of mind
- When you see really big red flags from a friend or client, be willing to save yourself energy, time, money, and tons of aggravation by letting them go.
- Get clear about why you are happy or unhappy. The truth will set you free.
- To have belief in yourself, you must know that you stand in integrity with your life choices.
- Look for the good in people first, and focus on the good in people to attract more good to yourself.
- Your job in all situations is to simply offer the best of yourself.

NINE

The Magic of Your Intuition

I wish I could say that I have lived my entire life using my intuition and trusting that my still, small voice would consistently give me answers to my life problems when I needed them.

Looking at parts of my life in hindsight, I can see that if I had listened more to my intuitive insights, my life would have been easier and more profitable. It would have saved me time and difficulties on my path. Being human means you are always a work in progress. I have now learned to respect my intuition as priceless wisdom and to allow myself to connect with what I call the Intuition Network (which is connected to Infinite Intelligence). I have given myself permission to tune in to my innate voice over all the distraction and the noise of logical left-brain programming. I have learned that if I am in a state of mental uncertainty, emotional upheaval, or spiritual unrest, it is hard to plug in to my intuitive source and receive accurate information.

If you really want to reclaim the magic within you, then you must develop and use this powerful, natural skill of intuition. Most of us weren't educated about how to truly capitalize on our gifts. In this chapter, you will learn how you can take your life back from indecision, fear, doubt, and lack of confidence by allowing yourself to receive your own intuitive guidance.

The truth is you are connected to your intuition all the time. Your higher self and your spirit guides, or helpers, are always giving you information. Your job is to learn how you can personally access, receive, and then discern the useful information from mind chatter. You were born with a spiritual resource to assist your path and true purpose, and you have just forgotten this. It can be one of the your most powerful tools in life.

Intuition is called many things: heart, gut feeling, a hunch, sixth sense, instinct, and strong feeling. It speaks to you through insights, revelations, and urges. Intuition, or listening to that inner part of yourself, is clearly one of the most important areas to develop in your life if you are interested in success, prosperity, and well-being. Intuition goes beyond that which is known, and into the unknown. Intuition can help you make financial decisions, be a better entrepreneur or parent, capitalize on opportunities or save you from bad investments, and even save your life. It's a natural human function and is your closest advisor when you take the time to develop and use it.

If you want to reduce your stress and be more successful, you must make the effort to listen to your inner voice. You have built-in natural abilities to sense danger. You can use these abilities to make better choices and know when to trust or not to trust someone.

Amanda Owen, author of the book, *Born to Receive: 7 Powerful Steps Women Can Take Today to Reclaim their Half of the Universe*, said about intuition: *"When the body is relaxed and the mind and nervous system are calm, we become receptive and can feel and intuit subtle information contained in the energy received from external and internal environments."* She explains that when we are receptive and calm, it engages the parasympathetic nervous system, which allows us to hear our intuition. However, when we're lost in the hustle and bustle of daily life, it engages our fight or flight system. As we discussed earlier, an engaged fight or flight system shuts down many of the body's processes, including intuition. When we don't take time to slow down and calm the mind, we can't hear the subtle but important voice of intuition.

We have allowed our lives to accelerate to the point that we just don't have time for the way we used to communicate or conduct life or business. We have to step up to the plate now and adapt to the new economy we are living in, and we have to do it *fast*. That means seriously taking back control of our lives by being responsible for ourselves. It's imperative that you learn to trust *you* more than you trust others, who may have serious agendas that are not for your highest and best good.

Wake up to the fact that there is a great limitation to using logic, rationality, and scientific methods as the sole means of guiding your life. Our world is very unpredictable, with many hidden layers of what we call reality. People have lost the ability to discern whether people are telling the truth or a lie. Daily we see evidence of the bad advice by money advisors, banks, and corporate and government leaders! People are disappointed with the betrayal of those they trusted who have let them down, killed their dreams, and jeopardized their futures. Sadly, integrity and ethics have not been valued. Greed and desire for fame have taken over many people in our society.

Frankly, to truly thrive in our current reality you have to become aware—listen to your intuition about what is going on in your life and business. Stop being a victim to people who have no integrity and pay attention to the inner part of you that knows truth when you hear or see it. You have to start paying attention to how you feel when you get information and to discern if it is true and good for you. You must stop allowing others to take advantage of you with misinformation that serves their agenda and not your highest and best good.

Intuition is one of the best tools you can use right now to discern truth and take back your power to make decisions that serve your needs. It is clear that the old way of simply trusting people (who may be morally bankrupt and lack ethics) with our future and resources is not working. The person you should be trusting is *you* and *your* inner wisdom before anyone or anything else.

Right now, it is urgent to become skilled in new ways of thinking in order to navigate the shifting currents of reality. One of the ways we can do that is to get back to our real internal power and use our instincts to know right from wrong, good from bad, and truth from lies. We have survived hundreds of thousands of years by using our instincts, but in our modern society, we have stopped using them and instead, allow ourselves to be programmed to follow the advice of others. We have been easily misled by deceptive connivers in the guise of good people who will take care of us—for a price. We can no longer take other people's word for truth and make a decision without some due diligence listening to our inner wisdom about the situation.

It is interesting that in our western culture, we seem to understand almost all of our experiences through the logical, linear, analytical thinking process. We use words to communicate this kind of thinking. Because words are our way of understanding our world, we've almost forgotten that we have an intuitive and creative part of ourselves. We're not trained to say *I feel* but rather, *I think*. If we deny and cut off our intuition, we get trapped by concepts learned through our programmed minds. *Yesterday's learned beliefs cannot solve today's challenges or capitalize on tomorrow's opportunities.*

Some of the most intelligent people in history have relied on their inner knowledge to achieve great success, such as Albert

Einstein, who said: *"The mind can only proceed so far upon what it knows, and can prove. There comes a point where the mind takes a leap—call it intuition or what you will—and comes out on a higher plane of knowledge."*

We've all been conditioned by society since birth, that if you cannot relate to something with your five senses, that is see, touch, taste, hear, or smell it, then it must not exist. Even our educational system values only analytical processes of thinking. Very little attention or support is given to those students with creative or artistic talents in our public school systems. It's no surprise that with all the past programming, we're afraid to trust those thoughts or feelings that sometimes just "come to us." It's only by learning to trust your inner knowledge that you can really reach your true potential in life. Our lifestyle has accelerated and many times there will not be time to do all the fact-finding to make a logical decision. We must learn to seize the moment and listen to our inner wisdom.

You must wake up to the fact that decision-making is not just an exclusive function of the analytical left side of the brain. To really be successful in making decisions you must now use the intuitive and creative, right side of your brain as well. You must integrate analytical and creative intuitive whole-brain thinking to successfully navigate today's constantly changing realities.

Trusting your intuition may mean taking a risk. You may not be able to find rational reasons for doing what you *feel* you should. It has been taught by all the great teachers of mankind that we should listen to our inner voice. All answers are within your own self. We all know this is easier to say than to do, but we must make the time and effort to hone our intuitive abilities because there are times when we simply cannot TRUST what others are telling us.

Now that I use my intuition and do what I feel I should do (instead of what my brain or others have told me was right), I live my life with great success. As I mentioned before, I have painfully learned that if I do not listen to my inner voice, I nearly always regret my actions and there is hell to pay.

Learn to Trust Your Own Intuition—It Works!

One of my favorite books is Richard Bach's *Jonathan Livingston Seagull.* This book would have never been the success it is today if Eleanor Friede, an editor with Macmillan at the time, had not listened to her intuition and taken action. Ms. Friede's associates called it a *"nothing book."* One Sunday morning she was sitting on the deck of her beach house and suddenly sensed that *Jonathan Livingston Seagull* was a story for adults, not children! She then realized her strategy had been all wrong; it was an uphill battle, but she finally got it published with a very small printing. The publishers didn't want to do a second printing, even though it sold out its first release in just a few months. And even though the book received no national attention, she believed unfailingly in its message. She pushed hard for the second printing because she felt this book would become a best seller—and she was right. The book has sold over 11 million copies in dozens of languages.

We all have a bucket list and one of my biggest bucket list items was to buy a certain piece of beachfront property. After many years of working hard and saving my money, I finally had enough money to purchase it. It took several years to design a custom house plan, find a contractor, get permits, and start the home's construction. I was over the moon to have finally bought this land after over ten years of wanting it. I was busy working on the plans, talking to contractors, and saving money to build the new home, when suddenly I felt like I was not supposed to go forth and build on the property. I remember the arguments with myself: what the hell, I thought; I spent a decade of my life working on this goal and now feel like I am supposed to wait. I have been waiting and waiting, already, and I am tired of waiting, I thought. Something had shifted and I put the entire project on hold until I could figure out why I was spooked by building. As it turned out, my gut instinct to stop was 100 percent correct and my life may have had a huge disaster if I had logically pushed ahead and built my dream home.

Little did my conscious mind know, but at the time I was going to start to build the forever dream home, the local contractors started using a drywall manufacturer from China. However, it was exposed later that the drywall being imported at that time was contaminated. If I'd started building then, I would have been caught in one of the worst building disasters of our area.

The poor folks who built using the contaminated materials got seriously ill and had to abandon their homes, but still had to pay the mortgages on them. To this day, the lawsuits from these folks rage on without a clear solution to the problem, and the manufacturer in China won't accept responsibility for the defective and poisonous building materials. It seems the only way to deal with the homes is to tear them down, and sadly, people's health and life savings are being destroyed because of this.

Ours is a world in which science has succeeded in explaining most observable phenomena, which makes it hard for many to accept anything that is unobserved as being real. I'll bet you have personally experienced some instance of mental telepathy and still consider it just a coincidence. Physicists and psychologists say there is evidence of an energy link between everything in the universe. Everything that happens is simultaneously encoded in this energy pattern, which makes telepathy and clairvoyance more plausible, and certainly gives us a deeper understanding of how intuition works. This might explain why animals run away when sensing an earthquake.

British biologist Rupert Sheldrake has submitted a very provocative hypothesis that whenever a member of a species learns something new, the "causative field" or behavioral blueprint is altered. If the new behavior is repeated enough, a "morphic resonance" is established that will affect every member of the species.

> According to Roy Rowan, in his book, *The Intuitive Manager*, *"New ideas spring from a mind that organizes experiences, facts, and relationships to discern a path that has not been taken before. Somewhere along this uncharted path, intuition compresses years of learning and experience into an instantaneous flash."*

> Author Michael Hutchison, in *Mega Brain*, writes, *"In recent years many have recognized the dangers of left-hemisphere dominance and have undertaken various ways to emphasize the right-brain functions. Meditation, yoga, chanting, dancing, running, guided dreaming, visualization, self-hypnosis, and many other techniques have been used to open up the right hemisphere."*

Keep in mind folks, you cannot fool yourself. Sadly, if you don't trust your inner wisdom, you are going to need to take small steps, one at a time, in order to rebuild your confidence in it. Without these steps, you won't be able to bring valuable and dependable information to yourself. There are certain activities or surroundings that can be very conducive to intuition. You'll need to experiment and find out what works best for you. It is important for your mind to be receptive to different ideas and to have faith in your own abilities.

In the book *Psycho-Cybernetics*, Dr. Maxwell Maltz wrote, *"You must learn to trust your creative mechanism to do its work and not jam it by becoming too concerned or too anxious as to whether it will work or not, or by attempting to force it by too much conscious effort. You must let it work, rather than make it work."*

I am not suggesting that you don't do your homework when you make financial or business decisions. It's important to do the research to support life decisions. What I am suggesting is that you also listen to your hunches, and then make a decision. Listening to your intuition is just adding another resource to your existing tool box of strategies. It's the New Common Sense: Honor yourself before you honor the information from others.

One of the best tips I can share with you for making a decision about almost anything is that *if it feels right,* if things seem to fall into place easily, if people are cooperative and you have a very positive feeling, it usually means it's a go. However, monitor your feelings. If your decision feels unsure, if you feel anxious and nervous, if you experience a certain tightness in your body, then maybe you should postpone your decision until the uneasy feelings go away, or until you've gathered more information. It's very important to access your emotions. Keep yourself centered to feel in control of your inner feeling and do what you believe in.

Business Intuition

Intuition sounds almost mystical, but it's actually just the mind's ability to match patterns. You "get a feeling" about a new situation because it is subconsciously similar to an experience you have had before. That is how intuition tells us that an attractive business offer has hidden dangers or an associate doesn't have our best interests at heart.

Imagine this: You are sharing logical and intellectual reasons why your prospect, client, customer, or patient should invest in your product or service. But deep down, hidden away, you are feeling unsure of yourself. You have fears that your supplier cannot deliver on time or you don't feel worthy of a large commission, or maybe you dislike your prospect. Maybe you fear your supplier will let you down or your staff cannot handle the extra work. Something inside of you is insecure and not confident. Whether your feelings are positive or negative, they are energy that's being transmitted by you to your prospect. Your prospect picks up subtle energy patterns or thoughts, intellectually or subliminally, and can feel your doubts. Make sure you are aware of this important point. You must clean up your thoughts, doubts, and negative energy before you make presentations of any kind. Maybe your staff or sales people are having these feelings. If they are, I assure you these negative feelings are affecting your sales, profits, and results.

Your inner thoughts and feelings are just as important as your physical presentation because your inner thoughts affect your prospect's decisions. You must be aware of the feelings you are experiencing because others can pick up your energy transmissions. Keep in mind that when clients spend money, they want to feel safe to buy things. Just like you, they can sense danger or safety on a conscious and unconscious level. Human beings just seem to be "wired" to intuitively pick up fear, danger, or lack, just like animals sense fear.

Honor Your Inner Urges

Intuitive individuals are risk-takers, not motivated by a need for security. People who are good with using their intuition are normally confident and independent. If your self-esteem is low, or if you trust others more than you trust yourself, you are programming your intuition to fail you. You must start to trust yourself.

Pay attention to your self-talk because we are self-fulfilling prophecies. If you tell yourself regularly that your problems are too difficult for you or affirm that you will never find the answers, that's a sign that you do not trust yourself, and again, you're programming your intuition to fail you. Have you ever had a feeling that you should call a particular person or client? Then, after you ignored your inner nudging, later found out that, had you just called on that client, you would have helped with an important issue or made a sale? In today's world you must develop and use these natural abilities—your intuition—to be successful in whatever you do, from your personal life to business.

One of my clients, who is a top salesperson in the printing business, told me a story about how at the end of a very long day, she was driving from her last appointment and decided not to go to the office, but to just go home. Just before she reached the street she normally takes to go home, she had an intuitive hunch that she should go back to the office. Though she tried to talk herself out of the feeling, it was so strong that she finally gave in and went back to the office.

She said she had barely unlocked the door to her office when the phone rang. It was a prospect that she had been pursuing for about two years! She was surprised when she heard the caller say, *"Our company just landed a huge international account and we need a huge printing job done as soon as possible."* As she was writing down his needs, he said to her, *"This is your lucky day because if you had not been there tonight to get this started, I would have had to call on one of your competitors to get this project done. I am leaving tomorrow to meet this new client in London to sign the agreement."*

This sale turned out to be the largest volume sale of her career! If she had not listened to her inner urges, she would have missed it entirely. She told me later that this account alone allowed her to pay for her son's entire college education. After the call and large transaction, this client consistently did so much business with her each month that she was almost always the top producer of her office. She said she would never doubt her intuition again!

I hope you will remember this story because it could assist you to make better decisions when faced with listening to your own inner urges about business. Most people have lost the ability to "hear" their intuition simply because they don't use this natural faculty. As we all know, when you don't use something, you lose it.

Build Your Trust by Reviewing Your Past Successes

One way to motivate yourself to take the leap of faith and start to listen and act on your intuition is to look back at all the times you've acted on your instincts and were amazed at your success. You were listening to your intuition! Following your intuition requires you to love and have trust in yourself. The payoff for listening to those inner whispers and acting on them can make the difference in how fulfilling your life can be.

After being robbed one time, as you can imagine, I became very security conscious. Since I was away from home a great deal of the time, I started hiding the jewelry I had left when I would leave town for a few days.

Every week I would try to outdo myself on finding good hiding places. One week I created such a good place to hide my jewelry that I lost it! For several weeks I looked and looked for my jewelry but with no success. One night at dinner, I was telling a good friend about how I had lost my jewelry when she said to me, *"Lee, I cannot believe my ears. You teach people to use their intuition and you are not using yours!"*

That night, just before I went to sleep, I said to myself, *"Self, you know where that jewelry is and I want you to tell me when I wake up."* Well, "Self" was being a bit stubborn and I had to do this exercise for several days. One morning at exactly 2:45 a.m., I sat up in bed and my intuition told me to look in my garage, in an old chair that Goodwill was picking up that morning! Thank goodness I listened to myself and checked out that chair for the jewelry, or you can bet I would have been down at Goodwill buying it back!

I would like to remind you that you can also use the same strategy I used in the above story. Ask yourself: "Where did I leave my car keys, report, etc.?" If you keep asking, the answer will come to you.

Do not keep reinforcing the negative: I cannot find my (*fill in the blank*). That self-talk only tells your mind *not* to see or find what you're looking for!

I know in my heart that the most profound answers to my problems in life have always come from my intuition. My inner guidance has always led me to the right resources, or the right people who could give me the answers. Give yourself permission to let go of fears and connect to the inner part of yourself. Utilize the part that has more wisdom and knowledge than your conscious mind. You will see new results in your life. When you take the time to listen to your inner wisdom, you will feel more peace of mind, more confidence, and you will have a sense of knowing that you have what it takes. Know that you will make good decisions and move in the right directions to live a successful life.

When you ask your extrasensory perception to give you answers, you will find that the answers will come faster and become clearer with practice.

Shortcuts: Applying Intuition

Opening your mind and heart to using your sixth sense, one of your natural talents, can assist you in creating more prosperity and give you more information to make better decisions. I use a formula that you should write down and put where you can see it daily:

HEAD—HEART—GUT CHECK

Quick Tip: Pause to check out your head, heart, and gut before making any type of important decision. This makes common sense when you think of it. Simply make it a habit to ask and check your indicators before you go forth on a choice. Your reliable indicators are your head (your intellect), your heart (your feelings), and your gut. They warn you about danger.

Head: I ask questions about a situation, problem, or challenge. I use my conscious mind to discern questions I need answered. For example, is this person telling me the truth? Do I have enough facts in this situation?

Heart: I listen to my heart, my emotional self, and ask, "Is this the right direction for me? Do I naturally feel attracted to this? Am I hearing truth?" The internal part of yourself, the voice inside, tells you when things feel right or wrong. For example, I equate my heart with how I am feeling. Am I relaxed around the person I am asking the question about or do I feel uptight and uncomfortable? Keep in mind that your body does talk to you. For me personally, if I feel shut down, tight, and not good, I know something is not right. However If I feel open, light-hearted, and relaxed, I trust that my "heart" is telling me all is well. You have to pay attention to your own signals.

Gut: Trust your "gut feeling." You know, that icky feeling you get in the pit of your stomach if something is just not right in a situation. It could even appear somewhere else in your body, but usually it's the same place every time. If it doesn't feel right, chances are, it's not right for you. What may be right for one person can be very wrong for someone else. Your gut instinct, your inner voice, is always there for you when you take the time to pay attention and listen.

Go with Your First Choice

When you ask yourself a question, it is good to *listen to your first impression*. This is because your intuition is able to communicate more clearly *before* you begin to cloud your mind with all sorts of other details. When you're clouding your mind up like this, you are focusing more on the conscious part of your brain. Fear and indecision can then run rampant, and deliver incorrect information. This leads to a decision based upon partial, tainted information. Your intuition knew the answer *before* this clouding began. Trust your first choice.

Don't "Force" Decisions

That's right; there are times when perhaps you should not make an instant decision, and you must give yourself permission to wait. If you are confused about an issue, then your decision will be confused, and you don't want to make a decision when you are not clear. Learn to relax, let the situation go, turn it over to your subconscious mind and let it go to work for you. Your subconscious mind knows a lot more than you may give it credit for, so please learn to trust it. It keeps your body systems running twenty-four hours a day, seven days a week, and is always paying attention. Let the decision go for right now, the answer will come to you.

Be Open to Answers That May Surprise You

The purpose of developing awareness of your intuition is that it helps keep you safe in all ways. Think of your sixth sense as a power that encapsulates a dimension of awareness outside of space and time. It gives you extrasensory perception that, when developed and used, allows you to make much better choices both in business and in your personal life decisions.

Now more than ever, you must learn to use your instincts and tune in to feel the true nature of another person's intent. When you use your intuition correctly, you will be able to read the unsavory energies of morally bankrupt people's lies and deceptions. Avoid a great deal of heartache in the future by taking time to read between the lines. Don't just analyze what they say and do, pay attention and listen to these people with your intuition. Remember, pause to check out your head, heart, and gut before acting.

Famous people like Isaac Newton and Albert Einstein felt that using their sixth sense helped them find answers and solutions to problems that they could not find in their normal state of mind. Most millionaires and highly successful people from all over the world have shared over and over how they use their intuition or sixth sense to determine the choices they make.

If you sincerely want to develop these talents, you have to let go of your ego for a while and be open-minded to trying new ways of thinking and feeling. We must go back and rely on the old inner knowing of the tribal people of our history. The knowledge is not lost but it certainly has been put on a back burner and not valued as it should have been. It's time to take back our power and be able to tell truth from lies.

The truth is that having a sixth sense is not rare. Almost everyone has had some kind of sixth-sense experience. Have you ever thought of someone's name in your head and suddenly that person called you? We have a great gift and we should make use of it more often.

Psychologist Carl Jung said we are all linked through what he called the collective unconscious. Everything is energy. The marketplace of business, relationships, money, products, your actions, creativity, music, art, everything is energy. You can pick up information about that energy via your subtle senses and by paying attention to it.

In his book *Sixth Sense*, Stuart Wilde wrote about how logic alone is fallible. He explained that because logic is linear, "it can't see around corners" the way intuition can and because of that, using it alone leaves us worried and insecure about our decisions. Instead, the best way to be sure of our choices is to incorporate intuition—the use of our "subtle feelings," which comes in the form of impressions and extrasensory perceptions. Because our feelings are our guide to whether or not we're on the right path, we can always trust that all is well when we feel it is so.

Wilde continued, explaining how intuition is the result of the subliminal or unconscious information we've picked up along the way. As we established earlier, the subconscious mind picks up an enormous amount of information that the conscious mind can't comprehend. Accessing intuition is stilling the mind so that deeply buried information can surface from where it's filed in the subconscious. Wilde encouraged us to fine-tune our intuitive abilities by regularly asking our subconscious mind to tell us what it knows that the "intellect" or conscious mind doesn't.

The late Mary Kay Ash wrote and spoke about how she was almost disastrously mislead by an articulate, but largely incompetent marketing expert as she was beginning her Mary Kay cosmetics company in 1963. This man, whom she had agreed to hire, sounded like a marketing whiz, with enthusiastic plans for launching Mary Kay Cosmetics into the marketplace. One day as she stood talking to this man outside her office she said, *"I suddenly changed my mind; I had no reason, just intuition."* She added that within six months she was thrilled with her decision when she found out this man had been indicted on a felony charge.

Conrad Hilton, who was well known for using his intuition in his hotel business, wrote the book, *Be My Guest.* In it he stated, *"I know when I have a problem and have done all I can to figure it out, I keep listening in a sort of inside silence until something clicks and I feel a right answer."*

> *Quick Tip*: I am giving you a few simple and proven exercises to kick start your intuitive abilities. Remember, the goal here is to have fun and allow yourself to develop your inner talent. Learning anything new at first may feel awkward and uncomfortable, but with time and practice, you will become good at it. *If* you will work on developing your skills to listen to your

inner self, your heart, and incorporate them into your daily life, you will have more confidence and awareness and will manifest more profitable results in your business and life with less stress.

Kick-Start Your Intuition

First, outline exactly what solution you need. For example: You have interviewed several new possible candidates for an assistant position. It appears to you that they are all equally qualified according to their resumes. They all passed your internal office tests and you liked them all equally. So you are stumped as to which one to hire. Who fits in the office the best? Who will be your best choice?

Before you make your decision, allow your mind to play with each possible choice. When you envision your office in a month, does any one of the choices pop into your mind? Can you *see* that person in your office? If so, do you *feel happy*? Do you feel frustrated when you *see* that person? Ask your intuition to give you a *clear sign* or *impression* on who to hire. Always remember that your intuition is kick-started when you *ask* for help. Now relax and let it go. Then allow yourself to play, take a walk, or just enjoy nature. Hang out with your pets, kids, or do something that engages your creative right brain. Ask it out loud to help you find solutions and then wait for inspiration if you can. Play hooky for an hour and then come back to work on the problem.

Adopt a childlike view of the situation. Let go of your ego. Stop being an adult for a few minutes! Children often see the obvious where adults make things harder and more complicated than necessary. Look at the problem from as many different angles as possible. Ask other people. Oftentimes, people who know nothing can give you a gem of an idea that will turn into the real solution!

When trying to get information from your intuition, pay attention to your dreams and your daydreams; they are your personal, non-verbal imagery. Keep in mind that images are the language of the brain. You might get a dream that answers your needs if you are paying attention, or you could be at the movies or reading a book and get an answer! Intuition is stimulated when you ask a question, so do that often. You cannot get anything wrong when trying new ways to jumpstart your intuition. The real secret is to start communicating with yourself and your intuition. When you take the time to write out your questions, or even state out loud that you need help, you jumpstart your intuition to start working on the problem you want answers for right away. Now your job is to look, listen, and feel for the answer.

I would like to remind you that you have everything to gain and nothing to lose when you start to pay attention to, listen to, and take seriously the part of you that is connected with Source and gives you guidance. Life is too complicated to not listen to your inner knowing!

Intuition to Improve Your Decisions

From childhood, we've been taught to do what authority figures told us to do. We've been warned about the disastrous results that might happen if the rules aren't followed. The bottom line is that we've been taught to give our power away and not trust our own judgment or inner power, our intuition or sixth sense. There is loss in forfeiting our power of choice to the bevy of professionals to whom we've turned over our affairs, such as lawyers, accountants, and financial advisors. Many times we do not even question doctors who may perform unnecessary operations or prescribe drugs with side effects that do us more harm than good. Many people have lost the ability to trust their inner wisdom.

That is precisely what I want to remind you of: intuition is one of the best tools you can use right now to discern truth and take back your power to make better decisions for your business and personal life.

Face Facts: Intuition IS Your Sixth Sense

We don't deny our five primary physical senses, touch, sight, smell, hearing, and taste, that we use to gather information from the world around us. Everything you do gathers information for you to navigate in the world. For example, you might be reading this on paper and feeling the pages in your hands. You hear the pages as you turn them; your eyes receive the light reflected off the page. The light goes through the lens of your eyes and stimulates your retinas, which in turn, send messages along the optic nerves to your brain.

The big difference between using your physical senses and your sixth sense is that intuition perceives things without reliance on your other five senses. Intuition is nothing more than a process of gaining information that does not rely on your senses, your memory, your feelings, emotions, your experiences, or your logical thought processes. However, intuition does rely on all of them to interpret that information.

In her book, *Practical Intuition*, Laura Day says that:

> *"The popular image of a practicing intuitive ("psychic" or "medium" in pop vernacular) doing a reading is an eccentric individual in some altered states of consciousness. That may be Hollywood's idea, but intuition is a quite ordinary state of*

> *consciousness. Intuition is not something vague but a specific physical state in which you're open to intuitive information."*

She explains that accessing intuition only requires a small shift in where you place your attention, and when you do so, you then interpret the impressions you receive with your rational mind. She simplifies the concept, stating that intuition is a two-step process: 1. Receive, 2. Interpret.

As I've said before, we all are intuitive and you have to pay attention to how you personally receive intuitive information because it is different for everyone. One of the best tips I can share with you for making a decision about almost anything is *if it feels right*—if things seem to fall into place easily, if people are cooperative and you have a very positive feeling, it usually means it's a go. However, monitor your feelings. If your decision feels unsure, you feel anxious and nervous, if you experience a certain tightness in your body, then perhaps you should postpone your decision until the uneasy feelings go away, or you've gathered more information. It's very important to access your emotions. Keep yourself centered to feel in control, and do what you believe in.

Sanaya Roman, in her book, *Personal Power through Awareness*, wrote:

> *"Intuition talks to you in present time. Through urges, flashes of ideas, insights and feelings, intuition moves you in certain directions. To hear it, pay attention to your inner world of ideas and feelings. If you are forcing yourself to do one thing while your feelings are urging you to do something else, you are not paying attention to your intuition."*

Roman also said that the messages your intuition gives you are messages that will guide you to more "aliveness and a higher path.

Power in Noticing Things: BECOME AWARE!

Your sixth sense becomes sharper by simply taking the time to consciously notice things. The mind is known to be lazy and will ignore everything except those things that scare it or please it. When you force yourself to notice things, you are engaging your mind. You are telling your brain to be aware of life. When you take the time to notice, you are requiring your mind to come away from its own self-talk and self-absorption. Your observation skills improve and that will improve your sixth sense. Truth in details are important for your well-being.

I want to share with you some knowledge I learned very early in my life because of growing up on my family's ranch. We were out in nature and my father was not a trusting society kind of guy. He taught me the discipline to be aware and to take stock of my situation every time I found myself somewhere new. For example, he taught me to walk into a place and pause to look around. What is my first and overriding impression? What was the feeling there? Is it safe or will I find danger? Could I feel happiness, anger, boredom, indifference? He taught me that my feelings *were always right.* I was taught to trust my first feelings and act on them.

I was given a great gift as a child to have the right to ignore social programming. If I felt that I was in danger in any way, I was taught to remove myself or run to safety if need be. I was taught not to trust what people said but what they did, and trust the gut feelings I got from them. Of all the success skills I have, this is undoubtedly one of my most important skills. Anyone can adapt their life to incorporate listening to their sixth sense. All you have to do is give yourself permission to listen and feel. As my grandfather used to say, *"It's always better to quickly remove yourself from dangerous situations than to test your luck."*

Intuition is also a Warning Device

Just a few years ago I flew into New Jersey and got in line for a taxi to take me to my speaking destination. I was alone and as soon as I got into the cab, I felt that something was very wrong. The cab driver was loading the luggage so I could not see him with the trunk up. As soon as he got into the cab, every hair on my head screamed, my body felt total fear, and I jumped out of the back seat as fast as I could and went to the closest airport security officer. I knew I was in danger. I told the airport security officer that I was not going to ride with this driver and I felt danger from him so I wanted a different taxi. When the security officer told the cab driver I did not want to ride with him, he screamed and cussed at me that I had to ride with him because he had loaded my luggage. I refused to be intimidated and got another taxi. The first driver ended up throwing out my baggage, kicking it as hard as he could to express his extreme frustration and outrage and drove off without waiting for another customer. Later that week, the news reported that a cab driver, one fitting the description of the guy I'd refused to ride with only days before, murdered two flight attendants from that airport. I don't know if it was him or maybe the car where it happened—all I know is that I was not going to wait around and be nice or test my luck. I got out of there, and fast.

We often give in to prevent making a scene or to make someone else happy but it is very important that we honor our *feelings*. I suggest you start to pause and feel situations before you act. The simple act of asking yourself a question such as "is this safe" can benefit you and kick-start your instinct.

Pay Attention to RED FLAGS!

On a business front, I had a situation not that long ago where a financial advisor was chasing me for my business. We scheduled an appointment to discuss the products he was representing that he wanted me to invest in. He walked into my office and the first thing I noticed was his very cheap shoes and that his shirt sleeves were frayed. A red flag went off in my head: *"Successful people in the money world do not wear super cheap shoes."* These details made me ask many questions about whether or not he invests in the product he was trying to sell to me. He told me in great detail about his wealth and success. He was a good talker and told me of his great abilities to create money for his clients. However, when you looked at the details of his clothes, I knew he was stretching the truth. After the guy left my office, I called all his references and to put it mildly, he was desperate for a sale to the point where he would say anything for a client, including lies. Now this story sounds obvious, but it's shocking how many people only take others' words for facts and don't look for incongruent details or check references! You might say, "Well, that is not intuition." Well it is a way to *know* something is not right and start to notice reasons to back up those feelings. Intuition can tip you off that something is not right and your logic can take over.

Tips for Allowing Intuitive Signals

Your subconscious mind is picking up millions of signals in every moment . . . the feeling of the chair against your back, the temperature of the room, all the things in front of and around you.

Consciously, you only tune in to some of those things. Peripheral information or stimulus is filtered out of your immediate awareness. Your awareness is focused on the present, on the immediate. However, all of that peripheral information is acknowledged and to a certain extent, stored in the subconscious mind. Those license plate numbers that you weren't paying attention to, the billboards, the lady at the bus stop with a yellow raincoat—all of this information is processed and filtered unconsciously. While the conscious mind is busy with the practicalities of everyday existence, the intuitive mind is constantly absorbing every bit of information that it comes into contact with, be it ever so subtle. Our intuitive self is not only absorbing information but processing it, cataloging it for future reference, and making instantaneous decisions about whether or not to share this information with the conscious mind.

Distinguish Your Impulses from Your Intuition

Here are some suggestions to help you discern real intuitive information from wishful thinking.

1. True intuition is quiet and calm. It's never pushy, grandiose, obsessive, or manipulative. It does not advise us on what other people should do, but on what we should act on or do.

2. True intuition is supportive and directive, never judgmental, critical, shaming, or blaming. It sees the world as cause and effect. Beware of your ego: A message or voice that appeals to the ego, to the personality, or to stature in the world is not coming from intuition.

3. Real intuition is a complete thought, a statement. Intuition does not lecture, explain, and elaborate in

great long detail. You get simple, direct information. Beware of the ego that gives you logic on the arguments and reasons why we can't follow our hunches.

4. Real intuition always has your best interests at heart. Feelings or thoughts come to you and through you, without your feeling as though you are generating it. Intuitive thoughts may challenge and divert you from a path you have started by giving you warnings. Intuitions are never misleading and should be seen as messages and spiritual communication. If we believe the sacred is benevolent, intuition should also be regarded as benevolent. The challenge to the rational mind is to accept intuition and to use it as though you've been given a gift of direction and grace.

Developing Intuition

The most important thing you can do is to program yourself to listen to the messages you get and to then check them out. Intuition should add to good judgment, not replace it. As much as I believe in my sixth sense and have shared with you many stories of my own life, I would never allow intuition to be the sole guide in my life, any more than I would allow logic to be the sole guide. I think intuition gives you more data to make good decisions but it's a misconception that it should be used alone to make decisions.

The best use of intuition is not to decide whether you should do something but simply to add information to what you already know and feel. Intuition information should not be considered in isolation but then neither should logical, emotional, or sensory data! We need all those factors to make a good decision. Again, your intuitive abilities help you in effective decision-making when you add other factors in the mix. Sometimes a predominantly linear thinking process might be preferable when clear, empirical information is available to you. When you have little data to make a decision but need one right away, an intuitive process may be more efficient.

In her book, *Practical Intuition*, Laura Day says:

> *"For maximum effectiveness, use your intuition selectively. Modern psychology has moved in the direction of integration. But when using your intuition, you want to keep the various inputs—your senses, your knowledge and judgment, your feelings, and your intuition—separate."*

She explains that by keeping these inputs separate, you can use them as a checks and balances system. When the messages from your intuition, judgment, and feelings all line up, you can feel confident that you'll experience a good outcome.

I just want to remind you that intuition is a skill that can be strengthened. You can make your intuitive thoughts more accessible and more vocal. You can use a technique that is thousands of years old. Meditation is one of the simplest and most effective means of achieving these goals. Meditation is a method of slowing down and quieting the conscious mind, the mind that is full of the emotion and judgment we absorb from our daily existence. Quieting this insistent self-talk babble allows for a clearer communication with the wisdom of your intuitive mind.

Six Tips for Developing Intuition

1. Recognize it and encourage it. Get in the habit of paying attention to and studying your intuitive feelings.

2. Study it to make it more trustworthy. Start questioning your hunches. Where does your intuition work

best? If you're always right about your intuitive business decisions, give a little credence to them. On the other hand, if your hunches about stocks are usually wrong, don't follow them. Just pay attention more, and you'll develop experience using your intuition.

3. Give it good information to work with. Your skills, knowledge, and experiences determine the potential effectiveness of your intuition. Learn enough about a subject before expecting to receive good hunches about it, or before trusting the hunches. Work in the area you want more intuition in. When enough information is in your mind, it will go to work for you with or without your conscious participation, so feed it well with education, coaching, and mastermind groups.

4. Another strategy is to avoid the same routine every day. Just like muscle memory, you're mind creates its own set of repetitive systems called neural pathways. You want to keep changing things up so that they don't become too well established and stop serving you. Brainstorming, reading new types of books, painting, writing, and changing up your physical activity are all great ways to create these new neural pathways, and give space for your intuition to come through.

5. While all these tools and suggestions are excellent, they won't matter if you don't trust the messages you're getting. One way to build trust is to start small. Journal your ideas, hunches, and gut feelings and then keep looking back to confirm they were right. This will build your confidence and you'll be more willing to act in the future. Your intuition will tell you everything you need to know.

6. Relax. Step away from the computer and quiet the mind. Take a few relaxing breaths. If possible, you can

even close your eyes for a minute. Give your brain a chance to relax and let your intuition talk to you.

Magical Essences . . .

- You can take your life back from indecision, fear, doubt, and lack of confidence by allowing yourself to receive your own intuitive guidance.
- Intuition is clearly one of the most important areas to develop in your life if you are interested in success, prosperity, and well-being.
- To truly thrive in our current reality you have to become aware—listen to your intuition about what is going on in your life and business.
- You must integrate analytical and creative intuitive whole-brain thinking to successfully navigate today's constantly changing realities.
- Intuition sounds almost mystical, but it's actually just the mind's ability to match patterns.
- When you force yourself to notice things, you are engaging your mind.

TEN

The Magic of Prayer

Prayer is a wonderful way of taking your inner thoughts to the flow of the unseen spiritual realms in order to be in touch with the Infinite Intelligence that many people call God. Through prayer, you direct your thoughts and needs to the higher power. Prayer can re-center your life in truth. Through it, you can cultivate a life that will bring you peace, serenity, enlightenment, contentment, and fulfillment. Prayers can allow you to create a vibrational state that is congruent with the life you want.

Since at least as long as history has been recorded, prayers have been a way of communicating with the God Source, whether it has been called Spirit, the Universe, or Infinite Intelligence. Prayer brings us the insights and resources to progress through and to overcome every single challenge that we face in life. There are no limits, no boundaries, and endless possibilities to prayer when we clearly understand how to use and direct this inner power.

Prayer acknowledges your connection with Infinite Intelligence. When you pray, you are enacting spiritual law. Infinite Intelligence is an indwelling presence and your prayers connect your consciousness with that presence. When you pray, you commune with Infinite Intelligence; you sense it and feel it. The approach to Infinite Intelligence is direct—through our own consciousness.

There is not just one way to talk to Infinite Intelligence. There are many paths up the mountain, as they say, and everyone needs to find their own way on their own terms. We all must discover our higher purpose in life and our own mission. Any way you decide to pray is perfect for you. The most important thing is to take time daily to talk to Infinite Intelligence. Hand over your problems to a higher source so you can receive guidance and peace about them.

As the Bible promises, *"Ask and it shall be given you; seek and ye shall find; knock and the door shall be opened."* When you ask, define your desires very well. It's very hard for Infinite Intelligence to give you the innovative ideas, directions, or answers to create the life you want for yourself if you are not clear on your desires.

The Bible also tells us, *"Before they call will I answer."* When you pray, you become in vibrational harmony with the answer you are seeking; in that way you attract it to yourself. So the act of praying—that is, thanking Infinite Intelligence in advance for solutions and intuitive insight—attracts the results you want in your life by matching vibration levels with that good solution.

From India comes ancient spiritual literature such as the *Bhagavad Gita*, or *The Divine Song of the Divine Krishna.* Its verses state that the key is to live a spiritual life and to have an awareness of our spiritual being, and to let that guide us at all times. We are to know that Infinite Intelligence is all-knowing, all-powerful, and omnipresent, within every atom of the universe, including ourselves. When we pray, we set in motion the ever-mysterious forces that create the answers to our prayers.

Speaking about prayer in his famous book, *The Science of Mind*, Ernest Holmes said:

"We can be certain that there is Intelligence in the Universe to which we may come, which will guide and inspire us, a love which overshadows. God is real to the one who believes in the Supreme Spirit, real to the soul that senses its unity with the Whole. Every day and every hour we are meeting the eternal realities of life and in such degree as we co-operate with these eternal realities in love, in peace, in wisdom, and in joy—believing and receiving—we are automatically blessed. Our prayer is answered before it is uttered."

Prayer is often said to be a mental approach to the reality of spirit. We pray to demonstrate an invisible law that has power over the visible. It is often said that spiritual training begins with learning to pray.

Every day it would benefit you to take the time to pray for yourself and others. Great spiritual masters have suggested that we should always pray as we awake and pray as we go to sleep. These prayers connect us to Infinite Intelligence and help open the door to our own wisdom.

By thanking your God Source before you actually receive the blessings, you are accepting your good in the present moment. This works because, energetically-speaking, there is no future, there is only now. You are a co-creator with your God Source. Trust that It hears you loud and clear and will start to deliver your desires to you in ways you could never have dreamed.

When you declare your intentions to Infinite Intelligence through prayer, you impress upon your subconscious a heightened expectancy of the good you desire. You open the way for the manifestation of it to appear in your life.

Once you have prayed for someone or something that you need answers for, step back and allow the world to answer you. Your answers may come when you have quieted yourself down and you are observing the messages around you. They may come in a book, a song, a conversation with someone else, a movie, or a television show. As they say, God works in mysterious ways, so be open for messages.

You can pray for wisdom for yourself, or pray to send healing to the world or to yourself. I have always prayed for all the people in my life, both personally and in my business. It keeps me connected to my purpose in this life.

Tips for Effective Prayers

In my research and personal experience with prayer, I have found that when you put a group of like-minded people together who are attuned to the same goal, results from prayer seem to come faster. A Christian Bible verse speaks of this principle: Matthew 18:20—*"For where two or three are gathered together in my name, there am I in the midst of them."* Over many years I have been a member of prayer groups in which we meet on a regular basis and pray for others with specific intention. I have personally witnessed amazing positive results from these groups.

My office staff and I, who are all on board with the power of praying together on a regular basis, take a few minutes each week to pray for my business, our customers and clients, and each other. We do that so that our group can be of service in the highest and best way possible. I will share with you that it bonds us as a group to really put forward our best each day for everyone.

Remember that your mind is a powerful instrument and it has to be in the correct mode for programming. As mentioned earlier in this book, your brain emits electromagnetic waves in rhythmic form. It behooves you to take the time and effort to get your brain in the correct programming mode when you want to tap into the Infinite Intelligence or Universal Mind.

Another important aspect of prayer that most people do not seem to understand is that you are an instrument of the light. Your words are not as powerful as your *feelings* when you pray. It is very important to remember that you are in a vibrational universe and feelings generate a stronger vibration to your mental image. You must adequately *vibrate* your messages, not just mouth the words of unfelt prayers. Prayer uses your conscious mind and then transfers that vibration (information) to your subconscious mind to be connected to the Infinite Intelligence. That means that you have to be in the correct state of emotional connection in your mind as you send prayers to Infinite Intelligence.

The brain's electrical waves exist in four different frequencies: delta, theta, alpha, and beta. The beta state refers to the waking state when the conscious mind is awake. The alpha state is a "semi-trance state" where you might feel just a tad drowsy or altered. Emotions may be evoked in either state.

When possible, I recommend that your eyes are closed when saying prayers, as an aid to detaching your physical senses from the environment. Deliberately desire and take action to calm your conscious mind. Shift your brain from beta state (awake state) to the important alpha state (relaxed state). In this relaxed state, you will feel slightly altered. The purpose for this alpha state is that the subconscious mind can be reached by the conscious mind to offer prayers or clear directions for new programming or prayer. People often say that prayers do not work, but this is mainly because they have not deliberately taken the time to put their brain into the correct alpha state to connect with Infinite Intelligence.

One of my favorite things to do is go for a walk in nature or on the beach when no one is around, get into an alpha state of mind, and then start my prayers to the Infinite Intelligence. Once I know I am in that altered state, I know I am connected and I ask for my helpers to assist me with my prayers. I also ask for my request or the highest and best for *all* concerned. Then I let go and let God as they say. At that point I trust Infinite Intelligence that the highest and best will happen. I have only my own earthly view of life and know that my soul will always guide me to my highest path.

Once you have offered your prayers, be on the lookout for inspiration or validation from your intuitive nature. A great time to get this inspiration is when you meditate and your brain has once again entered the alpha state. Then you can enter the deep theta state, which is often when the subconscious mind may obtain information or impressions from Infinite Intelligence. Much of your intuition can be accessed at this time, along with your prayer requests, which are imprinted in the vibrational reality.

Remember that you are the co-creator of the reality that you are living right now. Whether you are successful or unsuccessful, wealthy or poor, happy or unhappy, healthy or sick, in some way you co-created these conditions. This is not a popular idea when things are on the down side. Most people like to think they are victims of life and not co-creating their reality.

The major magic tool to create what you want is to link the conscious mind with the immense powers of the subconscious mind. It is said that the subconscious mind is about 90 percent of your total mind power and that the conscious mind power you usually use in your normal waking state is the remaining 10 percent. The real truth is that you can pray for anything you want but unless you are a vibrational (emotional) match to that request, the prayer cannot manifest. We live in a perfect universe and it is governed by its own law of attraction. The universe cannot deliver to you something you're not ready to receive or something you're not in vibrational harmony with. Further, it cannot deliver a blessing to someone for whom you pray if that person is not a vibrational match to your prayer.

Think about prayer as a process which, when used in a proper manner, can be incredibly powerful and effective for you. Think of prayer as an art and as a science to help you manifest your goals.

As mentioned above, it's important to have clarity about your goals in order to convey them to Infinite Intelligence. In this equation—*Desired Goal = (Clarity x Energy) + Time*—energy refers to your own personal life force energy, often called Chi or Prana. To bring anything into the physical form requires energy. If you want to increase your wealth, you must increase your energy. Once you have become clear about your goals and have added your own energy to your desires, time will be needed for your goals to manifest, to show up in your reality. A huge secret to life is if you have high energy and high clarity, your goals will manifest faster.

To increase your energy and manifest faster, you first use your spiritual energy, which is why prayer is so important. When you pray you get inspiration and ideas that will be beneficial to making your prayers come into manifestation. Keep in mind that your spiritual self or higher self is connected to pure spirit. It is the part of you that desires to know Infinite Intelligence. Spiritual experiences are beyond words. It is because of your connection to spirit that you receive the inspiration for what you are praying for and how to manifest it. All you have to do is *ask* and Infinite Intelligence will answer in the form of ideas and inspiration. The more you are connected to Infinite Intelligence the more intuitive you will become and the answers to your prayers will reveal themselves.

Once you have completed your prayers, you sincerely need to know and believe they have been heard. Amen means, "So be it." As far as we are concerned, the matter is closed. We just thank God from that point forward. We know if we want results *we must not waver.* To waver is to doubt. To doubt is to not believe and all these prayers were a waste of energy if you do not believe.

In the Twelve Step Program, begun in the Alcoholics Anonymous program, the third step says, *"I made a decision to turn my will and my life over to the care of God, as I understand God."* The eleventh step says, *"I sought through prayer and meditation to improve my conscious contact with God as I understand God, praying only for knowledge of God's will and the power to carry it out."*

In his book, *Visionary Business*, Marc Allen wrote about the importance of letting go and letting God handle problems:

> *"Just say, 'Well God, I put the problem in your hands—I'm turning it over to you. Just show me what your will is. Let me do your will.'*

When you do this, and are receptive to listening, you will no longer need to worry because you will be shown the way.

In a sense, prayer is goal-setting using the Law of Desire and Intention. One of the most successful types of prayer that I use and teach in my spiritual courses (*www.LeeMilteerSchoolofWisdom.com*) is called God's To-Do List.

God's To-Do List

Make a list of things that you would like the universe to act upon. Include anything you are unable to act on immediately, either because you don't know how to get started, or don't have the time or resources to support it. Again this is a form of prayer. This is important to do so you can clearly identify your desires. This exercise allows you to set an intention, and then let God handle the details of bringing it to you. The universe has the ability to arrange details and circumstances much better than you. Your job is to clearly define what it is you want, to envision it clearly, and then be alert enough to see it when it presents itself to you! God will handle bringing you the knowledge, people, and opportunities necessary to accomplish your goals. You must acknowledge the inspiration and follow through on what your intuition tells you to do next. Then, take action. Yes, the universe is going to assist you through intuition, gut feelings, knowing, and inspiration but you have to physically take action. The old saying *"God helps those who help themselves"* comes to mind here.

By simply getting clear about what you want to happen during your day, you will be ready to see the opportunities when they are presented to you. In case you have never done a God's To-Do List, I'll share one of mine so you can see how easy it is.

- Attract to me the inspiration and motivation to improve my health through diet, exercise, and clean living.
- Attract to me the insights and wisdom to deal with all of life's challenges!
- Handle all the details to bring harmony and peace to my neighborhood.
- Attract to me only honest and easy to get along with clients and customers, who value me, are appreciative of my services, and pay on time.
- Attract the perfect staff to my office, people who are honest, hardworking, very creative, have initiative, and are motivated. Attract people for my team that I am thrilled to have working with me.

- Lead me to the perfect vendors that I will love and that can handle all the big projects my office has planned this year.
- Attract to me the information, skills, and knowledge to assist me in sharing the most beneficial materials to the world.
- Attract to me only the clients and customers that I am best suited to serve and I can give the highest and best value.

Trust that Infinite Intelligence will hear you loud and clear. Infinite Intelligence will start to deliver your desires to you in ways you could never have dreamed. Because you took the time to be clear about what you wanted, you'll recognize the opportunities as they come to you and be ready to take action towards those desires.

I want to share a prayer from Marianne Williamson's book, *A Return to Love: Reflections on the Principles of a Course in Miracles:*

UNDO MY ERROR Prayer
(*From A Course in Miracles*)

"I must have decided wrongly, because I am not at peace.
I made the decision myself, but I can also decide otherwise.
I want to decide otherwise, because I want to be at peace.
I do not feel guilty, because the Holy Spirit will undo all consequences of my wrong decision if I will let Him.
I choose to let Him, by allowing Him to decide for God for me."

Marianne Williamson wraps up by saying about the prayer: *"Miracles reverse physical laws. Time and space are under His command."*

This one prayer has given me a lot of comfort. It hangs over my desk at work. I have a very sparky personality and can get myself in trouble with e-mail by responding too quickly or "honestly." No one ever calls me shy, and I am known for my fearlessness. This is a good trait for business success but the flip side is that I can be seriously straightforward, which can cause discord. I can get myself into unnecessary drama, which is clearly out of harmony with my intentions. This *Course in Miracles* prayer for the universe to *undo* our errors has been very beneficial for me. Next time you realize you wished you could undo something, try that prayer for assistance.

One of my personal favorite prayer books is *Your Needs Met*, by Jack and Cornelia Addington, who have created over 150 prayers for all situations. The following is from the first page of their book: I hope you will add it to your spiritual reservoir.

"There is no power in conditions;
There is no power in situations.
There is only power in God;
Almighty God, within me right now.
There is no person, place, thing, condition, or circumstance that can interfere with the perfect right action of God Almighty within me right now. I am pure spirit, living in a spiritual world. All things are possible to God through me."

Sample Prayers

The following are a few prayers I personally use for different requests. Please notice I use different terms for God in different prayers. Your job is to rewrite these prayers and customize these words for your needs, wants, and desires, and use whatever terms feel right for you. If you want results, you must be fully present when using prayers, using honest communication with your creator and not just ritualistic phrases or repetitive requests. Remember to pray with emotion and feeling.

General Prayer

Dear Heavenly Mother and Father, please walk through my house and take away all worries, sadness, financial stress, and illness. Please watch over and heal my family, friends, and loved ones. Please bring quiet and peace where there is chaos; bring light and love where there is darkness, and put love in our hearts. Spirit, assist us to look beyond circumstances and look into each other's hearts to understand the unique challenges we all face. Please give me the ability to be non-judgmental and have more love, patience, and tolerance for everyone. And so it is. Thank you. Amen.

Prayer for Intuition

Dear God Source, I know I am always under your direct inspiration. There are no mysteries in God's kingdom and whatever I should know will now be revealed to me under grace. I am a perfect instrument to bring my perfect good into the world in perfect ways. Knowing this is true, I listen in the silence and know exactly what to do in all circumstances. I am connected with you and my intuition is the instrument that I hear you with. And so it is. Thank you. Amen.

Prayer for Direction and Guidance

Dear Infinite Intelligence, assist me to hear your divine guidance. Direct me to use my life energy in the most productive, profitable, and Spirit-directed ways possible. Give me confidence and faith that I am connected to you and to all life. I know that I am always under the direct inspiration of Infinite Intelligence. I make right decisions easily and effortlessly. So be it. Thank you. Amen.

Prayer for Clear Desire and Intentions

Infinite Intelligence: In this moment I know that I am a positive, powerful being, clear on my desires and purposeful in my intentions. The universe and my body-mind arrange for me to receive my every need and desire, and they come to me in wonderful ways. And so it is. Thank you. Amen.

Prayer to be of Service

Infinite Intelligence: Please give me the insight and perception to rise above the mundane and use my talents, experience, and abilities to share love into the world with my actions and thoughts. Give my life a sense of purpose and joy. Use me as an instrument of light for you in the world with every soul I encounter. I surrender my job to you. Assist me to remember that my real job is to be of service and to send positive energy into the world. And so it is. Thank you. Amen.

The Prayer of Partnership with God

Infinite Intelligence: I know that I am one with the Source of my being. I am one with all good things that are coming to me, and I am one with the good things I can provide for others. I bless all who come into my life this day, pledging myself to provide the highest service I can to them. All my relationships respond to me as a beloved partner, giving to me as I give to them. Thank you, my God Source, for the continuing revelation of this perfect law in my life. And so it is. Thank you. Amen.

Prayer of Detachment

Infinite Intelligence, *I am at peace.* I am God's perfect child. I don't take anything personally. I am at peace. I am undisturbed. I believe in the power of God in my life and there is no power in conditions or personalities unless I give them power. Nothing can upset or disturb me. I feel nothing done against me. I allow all souls to be on their own path and learn their own lessons. I give them permission to have their own opinions. Nothing in my past or future can hurt me. I trust the Divine Law of Life to take care of all my needs. I now trust the Infinite Wisdom of God working in and through me to bring me my good. I am undisturbed and always at peace. And so it is. Thank you. Amen.

Prayer for Prosperity

Infinite Intelligence's wealth is circulating in my life now. Infinite Intelligence's wealth flows to me in avalanches of abundance easily and effortlessly. All my needs, desires, and goals are met instantaneously. I am one with Infinite Intelligence and Infinite Love is everything. Everything I want and need comes to me now through Infinite Intelligence laws of action easily and effortlessly. Large sums of money and prosperity flows to me now from divine order. So be it. Thank you. Amen.

Prayer for Goal-Driven Behavior

Dear Infinite Intelligence, I am one with the Source of Infinite Intelligence now. Infinite Intelligence is filling me now with the power to define, clarify, and carry through with exactly the right and perfect goals for my life. I now pursue only those goals about which I have received clarity and direction from Infinite Intelligence. With Infinite Intelligence as my partner I have all the energy, focus, and right ideas I need to succeed in my goals. So be it. Thank you. Amen.

Prayer for Joy

Spirit; help me to take myself lightly so that I may play with the angels. I know that I bring the power of joy into my relationships and into each day and every environment. Thank you for reminding me to be "light" on my feet! So be it. Thank you. Amen.

Prayer for Health

Infinite Intelligence, I know it is your will that I have health. I now only think thoughts of health, vitality, and faith. I give no power to symptoms or conditions of dis-ease. Infinite Intelligence supplies me with all that I need and I see myself as whole and healthy. I am love and light. I am whole and my body and mind are restored. I am a divine, perfect, spiritual being, forever with Infinite Intelligence. So be it. Thank you. Amen.

Prayer for Forgiveness for Others

Infinite Intelligence, I forgive and release all those who have ever hurt or offended me. I now forgive them totally and completely. Forgiveness opens the door to divine right action in my reality. The Christ Consciousness within me works with the Christ Consciousness within them and all things are healed and forgiven. So be it. Thank you. Amen.

Prayer for Forgiveness for Self

I forgive myself for all my past mistakes. I release all condemnation. I release all destructive feelings about my past mistakes. I freely let go of the past. I am one with Infinite Intelligence and I am free. So be it. Thank you. Amen.

Prayer for Business Success

Dear Infinite Intelligence, I bless my business because it is God's business. I offer thoughts of prosperity, abundance, and the best service to everyone I deal with daily. Everything I need is drawn to me though God's sources. Customers, clients, ideas, solutions, and prosperity come to me easily and effortlessly. I bless all my transactions and the people I work with. Love permeates all of my business dealings. My business is God's business and God's divine energy leads me to success. I am in partnership with God, I cannot fail. God is my supply. And so it is. Thank you. Amen.

Prayer to Enhance Life Purpose

Dear Infinite Intelligence, assist me today to delicately guide my thoughts and images in my mind's eye to those of peace, harmony, perfect health, happiness, prosperity, and well-being in my life. Allow me to see myself as confident, filled with vitality and good health, and enthusiastic about my life and work. Allow me to work out any "problems" in my mind and to see the perfect solutions as they come to me. Thank you for your guidance and creative new solutions to fulfill my life's purpose. And so it is. Thank you. Amen.

I want to remind you that you must *ask for help* before help is delivered because your spiritual Helpers must honor your free will. You live in a free-will world and that means you can choose positive realities or negative realities. Infinite Intelligence is not going to assist or give information without it being requested. Your real job is to establish your awareness of your partnership with your God Source, then create the habits and rituals that will build a great life for you. You can reclaim the magic of being connected to Infinite Intelligence but you have to make the first move! All of these blessings from prayers will happen when you take the time to join forces with your God Source to pave the way before you. Don't take Lee Milteer's word for anything. Experiment with the use of prayers in your own life and enjoy your results.

Magical Essences . . .

- Through prayer, you direct your thoughts and needs to the higher power.

- Prayers can allow you to create a vibrational state that is congruent with the life you want.
- Infinite Intelligence is an indwelling presence and your prayers connect your consciousness with that presence.
- The act of praying—that is, thanking Infinite Intelligence in advance for solutions and intuitive insight—attracts the results you want in your life by matching vibration levels with that good solution.
- It is very important to remember that you are in a vibrational universe and feelings generate a stronger vibration to your mental image. You must adequately *vibrate* your messages, not just mouth the words of unfelt prayers.
- To bring anything into the physical form requires energy.

ELEVEN

The Magic of Meditation

There is an old saying: Praying is talking to God; meditating is listening to God. Meditation teachers say that one hour of meditation can be equivalent to a night's sleep. You will feel refreshed when finished. By taking some quiet time or meditation time, you will achieve a peaceful, relaxed state of mind. It is only when you are relaxed that you listen to your intuition (listen to Infinite Intelligence). Uptight, anxious, or fearful thoughts may hold you back from listening to those inner urges of what you really want for yourself. Taking time to meditate aligns you with your highest and best good. Creating a time each day for inner reflection and listening to Infinite Intelligence helps to reduce your stress, allowing you to feel more centered and in control of your life.

One of the greatest benefits of meditation is that it can remove you from your customary state of awareness and allow a new perception to flow into your consciousness. When practiced on a regular basis, meditation can relax and heal your body, too, making you more efficient mentally, creatively, and intuitively. Meditation also results in a more balanced, integrated, and harmonious personality. By maintaining a quiet time, we are stilling the ordinary habitual chatter of our minds and relaxing the tensions in our stress-reactive bodies.

Meditation is a very simple process, yet at first your thoughts will take off in many directions, telling you that this is a waste of time and you should be doing something productive. At first you will experience tons of unrelated thoughts as you try to quiet your mind. Just stay centered and imagine yourself as an observer of all of this inner chatter and unrelated thoughts. Within a short time, you will be able to sit quietly and allow the silence, to allow the peace within yourself to come forward.

When you are at peace, your body's energy vibrates at a different speed than when you are stressed out or depressed. Since similar vibrational energies are attracted to each other, it certainly makes sense to align our bodies and minds with the peaceful clarity that will attract that desired energy to us.

Dr. Wayne Dyer says it well in his book, *10 Secrets for Success and Inner Peace*:

> *"I include the embracing of silence as one of my top ten secrets for inner peace and success, primarily because it's the only vehicle I know of for making conscious contact with God. There's only one omnipresent presence called God. This presence is everywhere and is a force that creates and sustains life."*

He goes on to say that God can't be divided or separated, and is the only power in the universe. However, as humans, we constantly experience the duality of the physical realm—right and wrong, up and down, light and dark, front and back—contrasting components that can be divided. Despite the duality and division of the physical realm, there is one experience that can't be divided, and that is silence. Dr. Dyer explains that even when you slice it down the middle, you still have silence, and like God, there is only one. He surmises that silence is your avenue for connecting to the "*oneness and indivisibility of God,*" which is why you want to meditate. Through the practice of meditation, you are able to know God first-hand, and when you sit in silence, you will find the answers you seek.

I personally think being silent and peaceful is like having an invisible shield around you that negative energy cannot penetrate. I once heard meditation described as ". . . breaking out of a personal prison and finding paradise." A regular meditation practice can help to protect you from other people's crises and drama-laden behavior. You will find that as your meditation practice calms you, it has a soothing effect on those around you, too. You may feel less annoyed or negatively impacted by common situations. The reason for the good feelings is that when you feel connected to Infinite Intelligence, you feel at peace.

The point is to realize that your true power is internal and not external. If you make meditation an integral part of your daily life, it will become one of the more significant tools for controlling your life. When you meditate, you are quietly going within to discover the invisible intelligence and loving guidance that is always open and available to you. You are allowing yourself to be in direct contact with Infinite Intelligence.

When you go into a meditative state you can imagine or play out a problem or difficult situation in your mind. You can ask for divine guidance about a situation. For example, suppose you have a difficult client, boss, neighbor, or relative that you have to deal with and every time you are in their presence, you get tongue-tied and frustrated. You could go into a meditative state and seek divine guidance by asking, "How can I feel loving, kind, and open-minded, and act in this situation to ensure a win-win and harmonious outcome for everyone?" You will get answers, I promise.

When I meditate, I often ask about a problem for which I am trying to find solutions. I'll ask, "What is the lesson here? How can I benefit from this experience? How can I be of service? Whom do I need to forgive?" I view meditation as a valuable way to find solutions to real life problems. Meditating is also a great way to create a stress-free space for you to rejuvenate yourself and assist your body and mind to heal from the relentless movement of the world.

Quiet Time

There is a silence in the space between your thoughts, where your true spiritual answers lie. That is why using meditation as a practice in your life can literally change your reality! This is the space where you can find—or plant—true personal peace. It is said that the average person has up to 60,000 thoughts per day. Well, that doesn't leave much time for the silent spaces that brings us peace of mind, does it?

Spiritual teachers have taught us to go into the silence for all wisdom. When you can visit the silent spaces of your mind, you can open up an entire world of possibilities for your future. When you take the time to experience the silence, you are plugging into the Infinite Intelligence, acknowledging your connection with It. *"Be still and know that I am God,"* it says in Psalms of the Old Testament. All creation comes from the silence, and silence is what will recharge your life by removing stress, anxiety, and tension.

I sincerely urge you to demand more silence in your life. One of the most productive ways to create silence is to schedule time for it and make it a personal habit. If you do not take the time to connect with Infinite Intelligence you will be a "reactor" to situations, and you will be filled with the daily frustrations that come with life. One of the best ways to create and schedule quiet time is to cultivate the habit of meditating daily.

Simple Tips to Meditate

First let me share with you that there is no right or wrong way, no specific strategies that you must follow to start meditating. Learning to meditate is like learning anything else you do in life. You must want to do it and tell yourself that, by having quiet time in your life, you will access a valuable spiritual part of yourself that may have been hidden away.

The simple act of allowing your body and mind to relax is a form of meditating. For some people, walking in nature, playing with pets, enjoying a hobby, or gardening can lead to a state of mind that rejuvenates and allows the mind to stop the busy talk. I am going to offer some simple tips that will assist you to experiment with what works best for you.

Nature is one of the greatest places to find healing therapy. When you are feeling troubled, go out into nature and find peace and serenity. Nature has a marvelous ability to heal a troubled heart and mind. Make time spent in natural surroundings a regular part of your routine. You might work outside in your yard or take a walk. Whatever you choose, allow your mind to relax and become silent. Gently allow your spirit to commune with Infinite Intelligence.

Consider creating a spiritually nourishing environment in your home and office, if possible. It will assist the sensory side of your meditation process to add music, flowers, and beautiful scents. Try to make your meditation location as peaceful as possible, with symbols and colors that bring you heart-opening feelings when you view them.

Suggested Steps

1. Create a quiet environment where you will not be disturbed for twenty minutes or more. You may want to play very soft instrumental music or light a scented candle.

2. Wear loose, comfortable clothes or loosen your clothes so you are not distracted by them as you sit or lie in meditation.

3. You can sit cross-legged, or sit in a chair with both feet flat on the floor, or you can lie on a mat/bed or the floor. Your spine should be erect/straight, but comfortable. Your body should be relaxed and at ease so you don't focus on it. You may want to start to quiet the body by doing some relaxation exercises. Try some deep-breathing exercises; begin with a deep inhalation, hold your breath for a few seconds, then complete the cycle with a long, slow exhalation. Your objective is to relax your mind and body.

- Quiet the body. It is very important to utilize your body as part of your spiritual practices to facilitate access to the subconscious mind. Give yourself permission to relax all of your body. Starting from your head, focus your attention on your forehead and mentally say, "My forehead is relaxed." Next say, "My eyes are relaxed." Believe and feel they are relaxed and they will be. Do the same for ears, nose, and mouth. Apply it to the entire head, "Now my head is totally relaxed," and feel it be relaxed.

- Apply the procedure next to your neck, arms, torso, legs, and feet. Complete the exercise by thinking,

"My whole body is relaxed." Take your time and enjoy the process and your entire body will relax.

- Once your body is relaxed, then relax your mind. First, close your eyes and roll your eyes upward gently.

- Now mentally invite Infinite Intelligence. Imagine it as an intense and brilliant white ball of light above the crown of your head. Feel the rays of Infinite Intelligence enter your being by penetrating the crown of your head. This light fills every cell in your body with life energy. Concentrate on this for about a minute or two.

- Now feel this divine light covering you from head to toes. Then feel it going from your feet to the core of the earth and back up through your body, out of your head, to a few feet above your head. Know that this bright light is the energy of your Creator, who is just as alive as your spirit is within your body. This divine light pervades every cell in your body, and every space in the universe outside your body.

This imagery activity allows your brain to enter into the alpha brainwave state. You should feel a sense of peace throughout your entire being, resulting from this active attempt to establish a union with Infinite Intelligence.

On average, this practice should take just a couple of minutes. You are welcome to extend the time as you please.

4. Focus on a constant mental stimulus, such as a phrase, sound, or word repeated silently. You may close your eyes or fix your gaze on an outer focal point, such as a tree, a stream, a candle, or anything that is pleasing to you. This simply helps you to shift away from your logical, externally-oriented world.

5. Invoke a passive attitude. Don't work hard at meditating; you don't have to achieve anything, you're not in a competition. If distracting thoughts intrude, acknowledge them but let them pass through your mind; your goal is to be receptive. If you are uncomfortable, move; if you have an itch, scratch it, and return to the process. Again, you cannot do this incorrectly.

6. Allow yourself to just be in the quiet of your mind. Feel yourself going into your inner reality. Feel the centering, aligning, and balancing of the real you.

7. After your meditation period, bring yourself slowly and gently back into physical reality. Give yourself a few minutes to write down any thoughts or insights that came to you. You will always leave this state of mind feeling renewed in spirit, energetic, peaceful, and blessed.

One of my coaching clients, a stressed-out entrepreneur, reported to me that after a month of meditation practice, he realized that he was now enjoying the wonderful spiritual connection he had been seeking for balance and peace of mind in his life. He said, *"Meditation grounds you and sets you free. When you do it first thing in the morning you are able to think clearly for the rest of the day."* This daily quiet time tool had benefited him more than all the professional therapy he had received over five years. He went on to say that now he did not feel the need to stay in the crisis state of mind as in the past. He now mediates for thirty minutes every morning before his workdays, in order to be in a peaceful state. His relationships with his staff, clients, and family have drastically improved.

So, have you decided that you are willing to invest a few minutes a day to have quiet time to reinvent your life and connect with your source of inspiration, comfort, and peace? Once you learn to meditate, it is important to train yourself to be able to do it at almost any time in order to center yourself, such as the five minutes right before an important meeting. Any time you feel under siege from the world, take a few minutes to go back to your core, to your God Source, and become centered. This will assist you to make better choices.

When I expressed some doubt that I could meditate correctly, my first real spiritual mentor told me, "A bird sitting on a branch in the tree is never afraid of the branch breaking. Her trust is not in the branch but in her wings." I took that to mean I was capable of learning to master anything because within me is all the ability I need. So remember, every day is a new beginning. Take a deep breath every morning and begin again!

Reclaim Spiritual Time and Space for Yourself

I want to share something very personal. I had been a serious workaholic most of my life until I woke up and realized how unhealthy it was, and that it did not serve me. A few years ago I knew I was in deep trouble when I could never seem to relax. I felt that there was always one more thing that needed doing, one more deadline to make, and clients always in the front of my mind. I often had a hard time sleeping at night because I worried that something important was about to slip through the cracks. Clifton, the love of my life, finally had a "Come to Jesus Meeting" with me about working seven days a week as an entrepreneur. He was right; I needed to do something different. He asked me to just take off Sundays, except when I had to travel for a speaking engagement. So we went to my Google Calendar and marked off every Sunday as booked with Clifton. Within a short time of going back to the old-fashioned tradition of taking Sundays off,

I saw an immediate improvement in my clarity, enthusiasm for life, and my relationship with Clifton. By taking just one day off that was designed for family and spiritual work, I was able to relax and let go of some of the tension and frustration that often comes with being self-employed. The benefits have been really good for me. I realized that working too much was just a habit and I was the only one who could break it. I had to be the one who gave myself permission to actually take time off!

I now do my best to schedule at least one day a week just for myself, my family, and my spiritual work. I don't look at emails, Internet, answer the phone, or do mundane chores. I spend time with my loved ones, walk in nature, paint, meditate, pray, write in my journal, and maintain a state of great appreciation of my blessings. I take this quiet time to envision my future and write goals that I want to manifest in my life. Taking this one spiritual day brings me back to a centered feeling that assists me with the demands of the modern world. I go back to work feeling rested and with a sense of calmness that supports me all week long.

In our fast-paced reality, many of us have forgotten the tradition of keeping the Sabbath, where you set aside one day per week as holy. On these days you don't do any work and keep the day as a day of rest, rehabilitation, and prayer. Re-establish your connection to the deeper spiritual part of yourself and nurture that. It is said that even God needed a day to rest when the world was created. Yes, in one sense we can consider every day holy, but if you take just one day a week and make it *your* holy day, you will see miracles in your output for the other six days of the week.

There is great value for your mind, body, and creativity to regularly set aside one day a week as your day for rejuvenation, healing, quiet time, and to listen to your own wisdom. Answer this question honestly: When is the last time you truly took an entire spiritual day that you didn't get some work in or chores done? Don't you think you truly deserve one day of rest from the pressures of modern life? The secret to reclaiming the magic within is about you waking up to the fact that there is a magic in life that enables you to feel connected to the universe, and to all the blessings available to you.

Our culture, with its need to consume, now has everything available to us seven days a week, twenty-four hours per day. People who used to rest on Saturday or Sunday now spend those days shopping, working around the house, or paying bills. Our lives have become a course of endless work. This kind of nonstop "doing" eventually wears you down. As a society, we need to become conscious of the scope of damage that this stressful materialistic cycle has on our peace of mind, happiness, health, our communities, and our spiritual connection. Is this never resting style of living in integrity with your values? Is it a lifestyle that is healthy for you? Are you a human being or a human doing?

I'd like to suggest that you try an experiment for a month that, hopefully, will turn into a habit. Make your internal need to connect with Infinite Intelligence a priority. Choose just one day on which you do not answer your phone; you have devices for that. You cannot get it wrong. Infinite Intelligence is always connected to you, no matter what. It's your intention that counts, not the fact you may have no candles in the house on the day you reserve to commune with your Source. Do not make plans to leave the house; do not do any work. Simply take this time to create a quiet, reflective retreat wherein Infinite Intelligence is your focus. You, your family, and your loved ones are the only other things that are important. Do something that fills your soul up with the spiritual energy it needs to stay in touch with Infinite Intelligence all week. There are no other rules. You get to make up the day to suit you. Just make the experiences of this one day a week *feel good.*

How about creating a retreat for a day or week from time to time, to just do whatever gives your soul some good old "R&R"—relaxation and recreation. If you want to avoid non-resourceful states of mind, you must take time to be still and listen to your inner self. Creating retreats allows you time to heal from the insanely busy world we live in and get back to who you really are without all the material aspects of the world. When you take time to listen to yourself, you will find that most of your problems will resolve more easily and you will move away from operating from a crisis state of mind.

Magical Essences . . .

- Praying is talking to God; meditating is listening to God.
- Taking time to meditate aligns you with your highest and best good.
- A regular meditation practice can help to protect you from other people's crises and drama-laden behavior.
- If you make meditation an integral part of your daily life, it will become one of the more significant tools for controlling your life.
- Meditation is a valuable way to find solutions to real life problems. Meditating is also a great way to create a stress free space for you to rejuvenate yourself and assist your body and mind to heal from the relentless movement of the world.
- Once you learn to meditate, it is important to train yourself to be able to do it at almost any time in

order to center yourself, such as the five minutes right before an important meeting. Any time you feel under siege from the world, take a few minutes to go back to your core, to your God Source, and become centered.

- The secret to reclaiming the magic within is about you waking up to the fact that there is a magic in life that enables you to feel connected to the universe, and to all the blessings available to you.
- If you want to avoid non-resourceful states of mind, you must take time to be still and listen to your inner self.

TWELVE

The Magic of Rituals

Throughout history, all of humankind has used rituals. Rituals are simply tools, a link to the divine, and a huge part of our daily life. Rituals teach you how to access and harness the incredible natural energies that will empower you to experience a completely new, enlightening, and liberating dimension to your life. There is a sometimes dormant but incredible magic spirit that resides in all of us that can be utilized and enjoyed! Rituals are a huge part of reclaiming your magic and manifesting exactly what you want in life.

Rituals have an extraordinary potential to transform your thoughts and wishes into reality. They have the power to create healing transitions and restore peace and harmony within our lives. We are energetically connected to all other energies in the universe. When we take the time to use rituals, we open the deepest part of our soul to communicate with the spiritual realm. Intentional rituals can be compared to powerful prayers because, as in prayer, we are focusing the mind on a new outcome. Rituals are an extraordinary way to honor your magnificence and all you can be.

Rituals provide the bridge between our inner and outer worlds and provide us with comfort, balance, strength, and energy. Rituals can help us take on the next challenge in life and give us the courage to face whatever comes our way. Through the use of rituals we honor and release the past, reclaim ourselves, and focus our energy to be able to manifest our desires for the future.

Life is full of rituals. We do something almost daily that is based upon rituals, whether we're aware of it or not. We perform a myriad of rituals, although we may have forgotten their deeper meanings. We offer toasts to each other, say prayers, and offer gifts to celebrate holidays, marriages, birthdays, graduations, retirements, or the passing of someone, all of which all signify life transitions.

Even eating a meal can be highly ritualized. A holiday meal, for instance, is ritualized from menu planning through food preparation and dining, usually with an important set of procedures. In its simplest meaning, a ritual is a series of actions performed in a prescribed manner.

People often ask me what the difference is between a ritual and a regular chore or task. A chore or task is something you "have to do" and a ritual is something that has meaning to you—it becomes sacred to you. Rituals can cover a wide expanse of physical, mental, emotional, social, spiritual, and business success.

Ritual is often mistaken for routine, but it is actually the opposite. Routine helps us do things without thought, such as brushing our teeth. When we act consciously with rituals, we are seeking change, a desire to experience the unknown, or perhaps a new way of seeing life.

Most people never think of the rituals we do and how many are infused with the sacred dimension. Most people live their lives unaware of what their rituals mean or how powerful they can be in creating a magical life.

Each society has its own rituals. We pray over food, break bread to celebrate good fortune, and celebrate certain religious rituals surrounding Christmas, and Hanukkah, all designed to bring like-minded people together. These holiday rituals connect us with our broader support groups.

Personal rituals help you heal yourself. They can be very powerful and helpful in dealing with life transitions. I personally started to understand the power of rituals when my husband was killed many years ago. I reached out to many healing groups and found that rituals strengthen human bonds, provide a support system, honor the sacred, and encourage expression of our deepest self.

For example after my husband passed, my daily morning ritual to remember him was an unconscious response to my deep grief at the time. I honored him by creating a shrine in my home with photos of him, with his favorite pocketknife and cuff links, and adding fresh flowers as often as possible, since he was big on bringing me fresh flowers.

When my animal companions pass, I plant a flowering plant in my yard in their memory. Plants symbolize never-ending life to me. As I have taken care of these plants and watched them grow, I remember my sweet fur babies. In a place of honor in my home, I have all my animal companions' photos with their collars hanging on them, to remember them for the unconditional love they offered me. These are rituals that allow me to still feel connected to my four-legged fur children that I have lost, who I still deeply miss and love. Honoring them with small rituals gives me comfort and keeps me feeling connected to the love they brought to me.

Rituals help us recover from grief, give us strength, and allow us to honor loved ones' memories. Now when someone I love passes to the next dimension I always create a small shrine with a single fresh white candle, fresh flowers, and photos or items to remember the soul who has passed. This is my way to sincerely honor the love and appreciation I had for that person or animal.

When we create rituals we act with deep awareness and dedication to a higher purpose. In our modern world we have forgotten how to take time to honor our rituals. Rituals often incorporate prayer, song, drumming, music, dance, meditation, purification, invocation, and sacred love offerings like fresh flowers or new candles. All these actions open a way to touch our soul with Spirit and give life greater meaning. It is said when we use ritual, we channel the power of our intention, which unites with the power of our Spirit, opening ourselves to allow miracles to occur.

In her book, *The Art of Everyday Ecstasy*, Margo Anand says:

> *"Ritual activates, magnifies, and integrates the energy of our four centers: our body (through movement, gesture, and dance), our heart (through feeling, music, invocations), our mind (through holding a vision, invoking sacred speech), and our Spirit, which manifests through all of the above."*

I have been lucky enough to travel to many historical sites as a photographer and professional speaker. This has allowed me to witness many types of ceremonies and rituals all over the world. I have found rituals to be one of the most powerful ways to access a deeper connection to my own inner guides, spirit, and the Infinite Intelligence. Plus, rituals touch the subconscious and give our Inner Energetic Blueprint new directions for the future. Rituals enhance your magical connection to life and allow you to embark on your journey with renewed hope, which can be life-altering. Positive rituals give life more meaning by opening your mind to new sacred dimensions.

We create or enact rituals for many reasons:

- To celebrate or honor something or someone; to mark an important or significant event or passage, transition, or beginning or ending; to express gratitude; and pay tribute or mourn our deep appreciation or love for others.
- To open ourselves to our spirit connection, thus leaving the everyday world and entering the realm of spirit and cosmic energy for physical, emotional, mental, and spiritual healing.
- To ask for guidance and direction from our spiritual helpers and guides.
- To honor our family traditions and to feel connected with our past.
- To create new bonds with others using an agreed upon ritual when we are together.
- To manifest or change something we want to experience.

The Purpose of Rituals

When you create a ritual, you are creating a bridge from the invisible world to the visible world, so it's important for it to feel congruent with who you are and what you believe to be true.

You can think of the time you spend performing rituals as time in which you can switch off from everyday life and become connected to the bigger cosmic picture. Creating this time and space allows you to connect to new energies that will give you the motivation and desire to understand yourself and your deeper root challenges so you can overcome them. With ritual, you create a serious connection to your inner/spiritual self, which can give you intuitive guidance in a way that you cannot get while you are giving your attention to the everyday world. Once you get this intuitive guidance you can then make changes in your physical dimension to create more money, better relationships and health, and rewarding work. It is a time to live in the moment and allow your heart to remember that each moment of life is sacred if we just take the time to slow down and "smell the roses." Embrace the magic that is truly around you daily. Be in the Now.

Rituals help us pay attention to what is happening all around us right now. By allowing ourselves to create meaningful rituals, we can honor and release the past, reclaiming all of our awareness for the present, and then create possible futures for us to live. By taking the time to create a ritual that you do in a mindful way, you can take the next step in your life with the courage to face life's challenges.

One of the questions I get often is, "Is it really necessary to use some form of ritual when applying the universal laws of creation to achieving my goals?" The answer is yes. Intention, paired with deliberate action towards your intention with the expectation of seeing your goal manifested, can literally focus your energy in a new direction. To be successful, consistency of your uninterrupted focus and consistency of your beliefs and actions is required. Rituals have been around as long as history has been documented. They will be around long after our lifetimes and all the future lifetimes we can imagine, and there is a reason for that—they work very well to consistently focus our attention and energy.

All ancient spiritual traditions contain some form of repetitive symbolic action in order to access higher planes of consciousness. These actions are intended to trigger a corresponding effect within the individual to raise the consciousness. When you perform rituals, your goal is to be a co-creator of reality and to imprint your desires on the divine energy field. Most people cannot achieve the degree of success or speed in manifesting something they want without the use of a ritual or prayer to focus energy.

In most of my studies, I've found that using the same rituals as others before you makes it easier to access and imprint the divine energy field. Religions have done this for centuries, encouraging worshippers to tap into a pre-existing archetypal energy pattern. In other words you don't have to reinvent the wheel. There are many books written on ritual energy patterns that contain rituals which others before you have reinforced through repeated use. Using those proven actions and prayers will allow you to tap into the divine energy field faster because the older and more stable a ritual is, the more powerful it is. It's more powerful because the repeated application of it has imprinted a distinct energy pattern in the divine energy field that is consciousness. An established flow of energy that has already been assigned to a specific purpose is one of the fastest way to manifest your desired physical reality—but not the only way.

With that said, I always advise the use of rituals that feel right for you. It is very important that you only use rituals that resonate with your specific desires and your personal beliefs. I suggest that you listen to your intuition and find ways to create rituals that are suitable to your current lifestyle. Trust that you can create new vibrational imprints (rituals) that incorporate modern methods, knowing that you will be guided in the right direction by your own inner knowing and good intentions. Always listen to your personal intuition about creating or using rituals. For example, I have researched many old books on ceremonial magic and have read many ancient rituals that seem outdated today. Since the act of a ritual is done by focusing the mind, we have to consider that we live in a busy, time-deprived society in smaller spaces, with less privacy.

For me personally some old, traditional rituals are too time-consuming and it's difficult to find the accoutrements. I don't try to use old rituals if they are not practical for me to do. If a ritual is overly complex, or if it is difficult to do, it defeats the ritual purpose. It is not beneficial to get so caught up in the complexity of ritual-making that you are more concerned with doing it right than the end result. KISS (*Keep It Simple, Sweetheart*) is always the best policy when you are just getting started. You can always work your way up to more complex rituals if that is what calls to you, or work with an established group or teacher to learn more methodology. Since I teach courses for Mystery School at the Lee Milteer School of Wisdom, there are more advanced courses available at *www.LeeMilteerSchoolofWisdom.com.* If you are interested in more details, come visit me at Mystery School. There, I share much deeper knowledge than I can share in a book for the general public.

I try to connect with the divine energy patterns in the most effective and fastest way possible considering my lifestyle and my personality. *Your* truth is within you and you should always listen to your own intuition when enacting any rituals. Rituals are designed to make you think about what it is in your life that is holding you back. It could be anything from lack of confidence, lack of direction, your current job, another person, or confusion. By ritually releasing any heavy issues that you feel are holding you back, you are creating a space for more rewarding and positive aspects to flow into your life.

How to Create Successful Rituals

Think of rituals as an art form. Art is usually created from the inspirations and whims of an artist. When you create art you are transferring emotion and feeling from your mind into reality, and the same goes for creating rituals. Rituals are intense and powerful acts and should never be done casually. Only perform a ritual when you feel the time is right and you feel the need to change or get guidance.

Map out your intentions and actions before you start. Once you start, you need to be clear about what you are going to do. Always stay focused and centered. Remember your intention for the ritual, which is to manifest something new, change something into something better, or to heal a situation by bringing peace and harmony to it.

Your state of mind is critical. Remember that your mind can be your worst enemy or your best friend. It all depends on whether you are the master of your mind or your mind is the master of you. If your mind controls you, you will never achieve anything of significance. Success is based upon whether you are the controller of your thoughts, feelings, and actions. Most people use 99 percent of their energy as physical and only 1 percent of their energy for spiritual purposes. The truth is that your *real power* is 99 percent spiritual and 1 percent physical. Your mind power co-creates your reality.

Design your ritual so that it balances your needs for focus and for raising energy with your ability to imagine. Deliver your requests with heartfelt joy and gratitude. Before you embark upon any ritual you do, be sure you are in the proper mindset. Be fully aware and conscious that you are a light worker and your intention is only for good and light purposes.

Remember: What you focus on daily becomes your reality. If you focus on the good, you will find more of that in your life. Focus on what is lacking in your life and you will find more of that in your life. Rituals must be focused on what you *want* to create, not what you want to get rid of; this is a very important distinction.

Always be a light worker and never try to operate rituals trying to hurt someone or create harm. These are dark intentions and I will seriously warn you that what you send out will always come back to you. Never send out poison arrows to anyone, trying to hurt them, for that energy will boomerang right back to you. Remember you are always 100 percent responsible for your actions and choices. Use common sense, honesty, and fairness when dealing with other people, as whatever energy you send them has to come to and through you.

Develop your rituals to make yourself a clear channel for your own God Source. We as humans have internal battles. We get hurt by others and society promotes revenge but you must not go down that path. There is always an inner battle to stay in the light.

There is an old story that comes to mind here to make this point.

> *An old Cherokee told his grandson, "My son, there is a battle between two wolves inside us all. One is Evil. It is anger, jealousy, greed, resentment, inferiority, lies, and ego. The other is Good. It is joy, peace, love, hope, humility, kindness, empathy, and truth." The boy thought about it, and asked, "Grandfather, which wolf wins?" The old man quietly replied, "The one you feed."*

All rituals are the manipulation of symbolism as manifested through the use of cosmic or universal energy. The main purpose is to focus your intent and energy on your objective. You must clearly and precisely state the objective before enacting the ritual, whether working alone or within a group. If you are in a group it is imperative that everyone must be equally clear and agree to the value and purpose of the ritual.

Be completely prepared before you start. Choose a place that you declare to be sacred and devote it to your spiritual connection with your God Source. Create an altar in your home, your yard, or out in nature, anywhere you can create a quiet, uninterrupted place to do your spiritual work.

It is important to ground yourself before starting any ritual so you are clearly connected to Mother Earth. You can imagine a light at the top of your head going through your body and out your feet to the center of the earth and that energy connecting to Mother Earth. Then in your mind's eye, see that light coming back up from the earth going through your feet, and throughout your body to the top of your head and beyond, connecting you to earth. After you feel grounded and mentally focused, continue with your ritual by asking your guides and helpers who are of service to your soul to assist you in your requests.

I have studied Native American spirituality and rituals. Their rituals tend to be an attempt to maintain balance, peace, and harmony between the mundane world and the universal forces (energies) of spirit. I think including this dimension to your process is a good guideline to have when creating a ritual. In Native American rituals, you may call in divine Mother Earth, Father Sky, the spirits of grandmothers and grandfathers, or the spirits of the East, West, North, and South energies.

Call in the energies of light that speak to you personally. I just call in my personal spiritual helpers for whatever I need. For example: If I need help with money I call in my banker helpers, help with finding a lost object I call in lost object helpers. When I am writing a new speech, I call in my speech helpers. While writing this book I called in my spiritual writing helpers! I know this doesn't sound very spiritual but frankly, we all have helpers that are all assigned to different things. I just call in the helper for my specific need and ask for exactly what I need to know or want to do. Don't just take my word for this; check it out for yourself. The staff at my office, whenever they are being challenged with a task, now stop and just meditate for two minutes, asking the specific helpers to please come and assist them with a solution. I will share that my staff loves to let me know how "the helpers" have cut down on time, frustration, and have made the office challenges melt away faster.

I ask that divine love energy be with me during all work with spirit. You should ask for protection before each ritual and always thank all the light sources for their assistance at the end of each ritual. You can call in your higher self, guardian angel, or Cosmic Intelligence. There are other positive forces you might work with, such as the angel kingdom, and the divine Archangels: Michael, Gabriel, Raphael, and Uriel. I personally also call in for Mother-Father-Divine Cosmic Intelligence of love and light to be with me and to protect me from any non-beneficial sources.

All ancient spiritual traditions use some form of preliminary ceremony or repetitive symbolic actions in order to access higher planes of consciousness before proceeding to the spiritual or metaphysical goals. The reason for this is that a ritual is a prearranged set of symbolic or archetypal actions which are designed to trigger a parallel dimension or reality. Truly effective rituals are intended to trigger a new feeling about a situation, which in turn, creates a new energetic pattern in reality.

When you have asked for protection, or invoked a connection with spirit, you should specify your goal. Be as clear as you can with what good thing you want to occur in your life. As you are asking for help with your goal, see the completion of it in your mind's eye. Feel how good it feels to have it completed.

As you begin to feel that your ritual is complete, thank and dismiss your protectors, helpers, and spirit, as you called them in to help you. When you are ready, relax the focus of your mind and come back into your day, refreshed and thankful that your goal is underway. You may leave your sacred space and your altar or remain there to journal your feelings and thoughts about the ritual. You may either leave the altar as it was for your ritual or take it down, whichever is appropriate.

The Truth Serum Ritual

There is so much confusing information in the world, and many people have questionable motives and agendas. One of the rituals I use on a regular basis is the ritual I call: Truth Serum. With this ritual I ask for only the truth to be shown to me now, whatever the situation. Sometimes in the past I have ignored red flags or bad feelings about certain situations. I found myself being loyal to a fault or simply not wanting to see the truth about someone. In those situations I gave away my power, time, energy, and lots of money to people who did not have my best interest at heart.

Once you set the Truth Serum into action you must be truly ready to see and acknowledge the real truth of a situation. There is no need to keep sticking your head in the sand once you give yourself permission to be in integrity with your highest good. The truth will set you free of illusionary thinking and give you clarity. I have learned how powerful it is to know the truth about other people's intentions, motives, honesty, or integrity.

This one ritual can save you from disasters and negative consequences if you take the time to learn it and use it. I am often very shocked and disappointed that people are not what they pretend to be. We want to look for the good in people, yet we must be open to the truth about the underlying agendas. You must never discount your intuition if you have a bad feeling about a person or situation. Never take action until you have clear knowing. Always investigate why or postpone a decision until you are absolutely clear in your gut. False images or illusions are shattered with the cold hard truth. For your best interest and preservation you must be willing to see the truth from an observer's perspective and be as neutral as possible about it. Release your attachment to the person, thing, or outcome you previously desired so that whatever the real truth is can be revealed to you. By letting go of your preconceived thoughts, you become open for seeing the situation in a new way. Only then can you receive the information you really need to make informed decisions and take wise actions.

Be open to receiving your answers from other sources, other people, books, movies, etc., because your spirit operates within everything. If you pay attention, you can discern the truth that is hidden. It is very important to be patient and wait for the will of heaven to give you a clear answer before you assume anything, take action, or make a decision or commitment of any kind. Taking action on a decision when you have serious doubts will only create heartache. Some of my messages of truth have come through communication with the very person whom I feel is not sharing the truth with me.

I once was interested in buying a new beachfront home and all the numbers were really good. On face value, it looked like a good investment but I had big doubts. I felt there was something hidden that I could not see and I intuitively felt the owners were keeping something from me. I invoked this divine Truth Serum ritual about the purchase of the property. Then I waited for the will of heaven to give me an answer before I made a commitment. The next day, I went to one of my favorite breakfast restaurants that are so popular here in Virginia Beach. While waiting in line, I was behind a booth of folks who were real estate agents. I heard one of them talking about how one of her sellers did not want people to come to their beachfront property during full moons and high tides. It seemed the seller was painfully aware that when the water rose at these times, it was hitting the house or flooding the property. Suddenly I knew what I had to do. I had to visit this house on the beach during the highest tides and see how far the house was from the water. Sure enough, five days later it was a full moon and high tide and I went at midnight to see the house. To my shock and dismay, the water was actually hitting the house. This meant that in a bad hurricane, the house was toast. I did not buy the house, which was good because a few years later, the house was almost destroyed by a hurricane and had to be completely ripped down. The land is now so close to the water it is not safe to build on it. I had the serious hots for this house but because I took the time to notice my uneasy feelings about it and then call for a Truth Serum, I received information that gave me the motivation to take an action that saved me from this negative fate. Had I ignored my inner "something is wrong here" feeling and listened only to my emotional desire to live in a beachfront house, I would have taken a sincerely devastating financial blow. I have learned the hard way that trusting things at face value is not always the most intelligent way to live for prosperity, peace of mind, and success!

More Useful Rituals That I Use

Whenever possible, I always try to light a white candle with any ritual to acknowledge that through God everything is possible. To me, the candle represents spirit and the flame is light and love energy. It is not mandatory to have candles but the simple ritual of lighting them certainly puts you into a different state of mind and helps you focus.

Morning Rituals

Positive morning rituals are the secret to knowing and growing your inner self. Success is not a destination—-It's a *journey*! You are a work in progress with each new day so start your day right.

Each morning, at the very start of my day, I create a space to fill myself with the right thinking or mindset to create the best version of me each day. These morning Attitude Adjustment Rituals determine how I will respond to the "stuff" that happens in my day. I clearly have no control over the outside world or what challenges will be thrown at me, but I can control my responses to it.

I love to get up earlier than anyone else at my home and spend at least fifteen to thirty minutes alone to set the tone for my day. I feel that this creates more balance, happiness, health, prosperity, love, and success for my day.

My morning rituals vary and can include a combination of many things such as affirmations, prayers, visualization, scripting my day and future, reviewing or adding to my vision board, journaling, drawing, deep breathing exercises, meditation, and review of my daily goals. Yes, I know this looks like a long list but it allows me to manifest much faster than the average human being! What you focus on expands and multiplies so I look forward to completing these rituals each morning. You need to create your own choreography of rituals to assist you to manifest what you want in life versus just being a reactor and taking what life hands out.

It is critical to have at least one consistent ritual to improve your day. My one consistent ritual is to script out my future. If you will commit to do it every morning for at least twenty-one to thirty days, you can create a terrific habit of feeding your mind with new references for what is possible. I use my daily rituals to fortify my Inner Energetic Blueprint to manifest my desire. (See Chapter 6 about scripting).

Evening Rituals

It's important to review your day near the end of it, clearing away any leftover mental "spider webs" that you do not want to be caught by the next day. In my evening rituals, I include any of my regular practices that I did not have time to do in the morning. It's important to create whatever rituals will assist you.

My Journal

One consistent ritual I do daily is to write in a journal. Some of my usual questions to myself are: What did I learn today? What or whom do I need to forgive?

I light a white candle and I offer forgiveness first to myself and then to all others with whom I am not in harmony. I pray for their prosperity, success, health, and happiness. I ask for harmony, peace, and love. I have learned that the best way to sincerely heal with anyone is to first heal within my inner world. Then I can see results in the outer world.

You only need to do this prayer for a minute to three minutes.

Truth Serum Ritual

As I mentioned earlier in this chapter, I use this ritual when I am confused or unsure of the information I have about someone, a situation, or an event. I light a white candle. I meditate and ask for my divine highest and best connection with the Infinite Cosmic Force. I declare assistance for divine truth in a situation. Then I pay attention. What do I feel intuitively?

Ritual for Prosperity

I light two candles, green for abundance and white for spirit guidance. I then declare divine assistance for the ideas, human assistance and support, and creative thoughts that allow me to utilize my skills, talents, knowledge, and connections to the highest and best. I ask for spirit to assist me to give value and service to others for a fair exchange of money. I declare that opportunities will flow to me now to be of service and that my service will bring me the prosperity I envision. I place anchors or subconscious markers around my living space (symbols of money, for example, a novelty million dollar bill, objects that represent wealth and prosperity to me personally) so that my subconscious mind is seeing and getting the message to bring prosperity to me. I declare that I am one with the energy of abundance. I am always inspired by spirit in all my business endeavors and know I can create money and success whenever I call it forth and act on my inspirations towards my goals.

I can put objects on my altar that represent prosperity to me, such as jewelry, real money, or anything that gives me the feeling of prosperity. I keep an evidence journal of prosperity flowing to me. I envision myself at my mailbox and see checks coming in the mail. I notice how happy I feel to open the checks and deposit them in my accounts. I always thank the universe in advance for my blessings, therefore I have an expectation that good is always coming to me.

Ritual for Clearing Negative Energy

For clearing negative energy or thoughts, grudges, anger, frustration, or blame out of your energy field, I have two rituals to suggest to you, both of which I use.

Write out clearly and exactly what negative energy you wish to release and be removed from your energy field. In a quiet, undisturbed place of honor, light a white candle.

The first clearing ritual is for cutting away all negative energy cords with people and situations in your life. Have a ceremonial sword of some kind ready to use. A child's play sword can work here or a nice knife that has meaning to you. Even a fancy letter opener will do here! Use the knife or sword to mentally cut away any mental and emotional energy ties between you and the situation, person, or negative energy. Mentally seal the energy around you, so the old negative energy cords cannot be reestablished in your direction. Then seal the other person's energy around the other person or around the situation. Send love and light for healing to you and then to the other person or situation. Now envision the outcome that you desire which is for harmony and the highest and best for all concerned.

The other negative energy release ritual I use is to *bury* the paper or *burn* it using the same rituals as above. Be safe in whichever method you choose to release negative energy.

Ritual for Help with Organization

Light a candle. Call on your organizational helpers. Ask your brain for all the organizing information you have ever read to be recalled in an orderly fashion so that you can actually use it. Take three minutes and envision yourself easily finding homes for all the clutter and disorganization. Then see the end result you are striving for. Hold on to that image and give yourself permission to let go of all your resistance to get started. Forgive yourself for letting "so much life happen" and just move on to your real power, which is in this moment. Intend that the entire process is easy, fast, and painless.

Now for at least one full minute or more *feel* the project being done. Really feel it to imprint the energy field of feeling accomplished and proud of yourself for getting this done, versus the energy field of disorganization around you. You are traveling to the future and seeing the results you want right now. Envision what you want by seeing yourself do it as if you're recording on fast forward. Feel and see in your mind your desired end result: A place that has organization and a good feeling of light around the project.

Rituals for Advice

I have two rituals to share with you that are very helpful to me.

The Older Version of Me: Ask that the older, wiser version of yourself become available now to answer challenging life decision questions. In your mind's eye, imagine yourself at a much wiser, calmer, happier, and older version of yourself. Be sure to *see* yourself as healthy and filled with vitality and peace of heart. Present your challenge to the older and wiser *you* and ask for assistance to see the big picture. Ask to be guided in the highest and best direction for you. Now wait for the gentle hand of the universe to offer guideposts and intuitive insight. These guideposts can come while seeing a movie, reading a book, listening to someone else talk, or having a good friend share some intuition for you. The universe finds a way to answer your questions so be open and aware, and look for messages that will give you the inner knowing of what is right for you at what time.

Council of Wisdom: Call forth in your mind's eye your "workshop of the mind" or a Council Meeting. Call forth the spirit and higher self of people who could give you wisdom and knowledge about going forth on projects. For example, to write this book I called forth famous writers and spiritual leaders whom I admire, people whose good qualities inspire me to action in my own life. I also called forth writers and teachers with whom I feel a kinship and connection because of holding some of the same views of life.

I imagine them all in a meeting room around a large round table. I stand and thank them for coming

> at my request. I then ask for the inspiration, creativity, motivation, and connection to "hear their voices" about how to write, what to write to assist people to reclaim their magic, and how to gather the wisdom to do so. I envision these people nodding their heads and smiling, with a thumbs-up kind of attitude. Then I close the circle and release their energy from mine. I thank everyone again and then just meditate. I write down any information I get while doing the ritual and then just know I have "helpers" to assist me.

Your free will prevents your helpers from simply saving or helping you. You literally must ask for assistance and the more specific, the better. There's a really interesting book, *The Cosmic Internet*, published by Rainbow Ridge, which goes into great detail on this process. Author Frank DeMarco describes his conversations with his council of those who are now in the non-physical. I first read about this concept in *Think and Grow Rich* by Napoleon Hill. The concept that you can access other realities for information and guidance, what we call the "other side," was also reinforced in Jane Roberts' "Seth" materials.

I encourage you to consider different ways to expand your rituals using drumming, chanting, song, dance, and artwork. There are aspects of you that can be given a new platform to emerge if you give yourself permission to let the inner you talk and communicate more. The more you listen, the better information you will get from your own guides. Your life can flow in a much more enjoyable and easy way. Your world is a reflection of what's inside of you. If *you* don't value yourself, no one else will!

I recommend you get out of any old, stuffy programmed views you have of yourself as a limited human being and open up to the fact that you are truly a light worker who is on the earth to assist with raising the consciousness of our world. If you weren't a light worker, you wouldn't be attracted to reading this book. Consistency in practicing your own rituals will allow you to develop the confidence that the information you receive is real. You will find that you do have the power to manipulate and affect reality with your thoughts and actions. I encourage you to get started with some rituals that will allow you to manifest the life you really want to live. Always remember you cannot focus upon the unwanted in your life and receive the wanted. Take back your real power to direct your life in positive ways. I would like to leave you with this thought:

I am a wealthy woman not by accident, birth, marriage, or divorce, but by thinking and doing things others will not do. How about you? What is your legacy going to be? You have to understand that is totally up to you!

If you want something you've never had, you've got to do something you've never done!

If you are interested in more information on rituals, go to Lee Milteer's School of Wisdom for more advanced courses.

Magical Essences . . .

- Rituals are simply tools, a link to the divine, and a huge part of our daily life.
- Rituals are a huge part of reclaiming your magic and manifesting exactly what you want in life.
- Rituals can transform your thoughts and wishes into reality.
- Rituals have the power to create healing transitions and restore peace and harmony.

- In its simplest meaning, a ritual is a series of actions performed in a prescribed manner.
- When we create rituals, we act with deep awareness and dedication to a higher purpose.
- Rituals often incorporate prayer, song, drumming, music, dance, meditation, purification, invocation, and sacred love offerings like fresh flowers or new candles. All these actions open a way to touch our soul with spirit and give life greater meaning.
- Positive rituals give life more meaning by opening your mind to new sacred dimensions.
- By allowing ourselves to create meaningful rituals, we can honor and release the past, reclaiming all of our awareness for the present, and then create possible futures for us to claim.
- When you perform rituals, your goal is to be a co-creator of reality and to imprint your desires on the divine energy field.
- Rituals are intense and powerful acts and never should be done casually.
- Your *real power* is 99 percent spiritual and 1 percent physical.
- Be fully aware and conscious that you are a light worker and your intention is only for good and light purposes.
- Rituals must be focused on what you *want* to create, not what you want to get rid of; this is a very important distinction.
- The main purpose is to focus your intent and energy on your objective.

- Positive morning rituals are the secret to knowing and growing your inner self.
- It is critical to have at least one consistent ritual to improve your day.
- The more you listen, the better information you will get from your own guides.

THIRTEEN

The Magic of Forgiveness

"Inner peace can be reached only when we practice forgiveness. Forgiveness is letting go of the past, and is therefore the means for correcting our misperceptions."
— Gerald Jampolsky

Forgiveness has been taught by every spiritual leader since the beginning of written time. All major religions teach the importance of love, compassion, and forgiveness as part of our daily lives. While love and compassion tend to be relatively easy for most people, we often find true forgiveness to be a little more challenging. However, I think it's important to point out the fact that forgiveness is more about you than it is the other person. You don't forgive someone for their sake; you do it for yours. When you forgive your trespassers, you give yourself the gift of positive vibrational energy.

One of the most important tools for creating a more successful life is the awareness of how you are using your life energy. If you're exhausting your energy holding on to past grudges, anger, guilt, or any other negative feelings, you're wasting precious life energy and blocking yourself from manifesting a good life.

Using your life energy to hold on to negative thoughts prevents you from creating new ideas and from having the energy to take action on them. Holding on to anger, frustration, or revenge puts you in vibrational harmony with negative energy. Positive people feel turned off by your negative energy. The antidote is to forgive yourself and to forgive other people. That's great in theory, but most of us have a hard time with forgiveness, don't we?

You probably have a story about how something great would have happened in your life *if* someone had not done something to interfere with your success. We often blame others for our lack of achievement, but when you take a spiritual approach to the situation, you realize that you are either part of the solution or part of the problem. When we don't achieve something we want, we have to take responsibility for the outcome because our life energy is intimately attached to the energy pattern of our dominate thoughts. If you are vibrating a low frequency and are feeling upset and angry, you are going to repulse positive opportunities and people from you because you are not a vibrational match.

We have all been taught that it is important to forgive in order to heal from pain of the past and can move on in your life. We understand that the reason to forgive is because it is a give to ourselves to clear away the pain inside from the person or situation or person who harmed us. All of this sounds wonderful, but in reality, it's easier said than done.

That said, we must learn to release the cycle of being a victim. As stated by Lewis Smedes, "*To forgive is to set a prisoner free and discover that the prisoner was you.*" We all want to create a better life for ourselves, but we can't do that until we forgive the past.

What Forgiveness Doesn't Mean

Forgetting

You don't have to forget about a trespass in order to forgive it. Sometimes, it's a good thing to remember so you don't find yourself in the same situation again. If forgetting the situation won't put you in harm in the future, and you want to forgive and forget, then you certainly can, but it is not a condition of forgiveness.

Condoning actions or Negative Behaviors

You can forgive someone but it does not mean that you excuse or condone their actions or behavior. When someone behaves badly, betrays you, lies, cheats, or steals from you, forgiving them doesn't change what happened. Forgiving them allows you to be free from the pain and move on in your life.

Denial

Forgiving is not denying the fact that something has happened to wound you and cause you pain. Forgiving means dealing with reality and your feelings about what happened and then letting them go to free you up from old energy.

Reconciling

You can forgive someone without reconciling with them if you're not emotionally ready to do so. Forgiveness is about you being free from the emotional pain and it doesn't always require the participation of the other party. Reconciliation is not in your best interest if the person or situation can potentially cause you harm again.

Recipe for Forgiveness

"Forgiveness is not always easy. At times, it feels more painful than the wound we suffered, to forgive the one that inflicted it. And yet, there is no peace without forgiveness."

—Marianne Williamson

It's important to understand that when you have been hurt by a person or situation, forgiveness is a more complicated process than just saying "Okay, I forgive you." Words are meaningless; it is the vibration that the Inner Energetic Blueprint needs to feel to be able to truly forgive.

Here are some steps to help you move into forgiveness.

Acknowledge the reality of what happened.

Don't sugar-coat reality about what happened. Write out in detail exactly what happened and how you feel about it. Get out the pain as much as possible on paper. Create a ritual of writing everything out and burning the paper, ripping it up, or burying it. Acknowledge that you have been hurt and don't try to deny the emotional pain, or suppress or medicate it. If you do not sincerely acknowledge and feel the pain, it will only fester and cause more pain. It is what it is so acknowledge this pain so you can let it go.

Express your rage or hurt feelings in a safe manner.

Give yourself permission to really cry about this pain in a safe quiet place so you can let it out of your system. Many of us are taught to suck it up and not cry, but we are wired to cry when we're deeply hurt. It is healing to release painful emotions. Another technique that can be useful is to yell and scream your feelings out. Try punching a pillow or hitting a punching bag, anything where you can express your rage or wounded feelings without harming yourself or others. Always remember that feelings are a form of energy. If you don't find beneficial ways of expressing them, negative destructive energy will get stuck inside of you and will cause havoc in your life until you find a way to release it. If you don't express your anger, you may experience either depression (which is repressed anger) or suffer from explosive rage. If you keep this destructive energy trapped within, you could start to do things that are self-destructive such as overeat, drink, overspend, or lose your temper.

Release the pain and negative feelings.

Give yourself total permission to let go of being a victim. The past is a locked door and cannot be opened. Your future will depend on you now letting these feelings go. You cannot move forward if your head is turned looking backwards and reinforcing your old reality. Your point of power in life is this minute. Sometimes it will take time to truly forgive and let go, but it is a process that you have control over.

Compassion and understanding.

First, have compassion for yourself. Acknowledge that holding on to grudges and angry feelings only poisons you and your peace of mind. Once you acknowledge reality, express the stuffed feelings and give yourself permission to free yourself from victimhood. Then you can start to get into a neutral place inside of yourself and shift your perspective to start forgiving. Most people are not trying to hurt your with their actions, but are simply doing the best they can. If they knew better, most of them would do better. Let go of your perceptions of wrongdoing and you will free your energy to move forward with your life.

Who and What to Forgive

To really claim the magic that is within you, you need to forgive yourself for anything you have done that you still feel guilty or upset about. Understand that even when you've done something regrettable, you did the best you could at the time and no, you were not perfect. But who is? You were only equipped to react to a situation in ways you knew at that moment in time. Now you know you would act or react differently because you are at a different consciousness point in your life. You have evolved and grown since then and have new viewpoints and experiences you did not have before. If you cannot forgive yourself you will find it difficult to forgive others because how we treat ourselves is often how we treat others. Forgiving yourself and giving yourself another chance will improve your own life tremendously and will improve your own self-esteem and value of self.

There will be many people and situations or circumstances that you need to forgive to free up your Inner Energetic Blueprint to manifest new things in your life. You do not want to squander your life energy using it on negative feelings such as guilt, blame, anger, or grudges.

Ask yourself who you need to forgive:

- Yourself
- Your parents and childhood
- Siblings and other family members
- Current family, spouse, children, or ex-spouses
- Neighbors or friends
- Your job, coworkers, or bosses
- Others?

"When you forgive, you in no way change the past—
but you sure do change the future."
—Bernard Meltzer

Struggling to Forgive?

I've personally had some people and situations that no matter how hard I have tried to forgive, I've had lingering negative feelings. I realized that I was not getting to the root of the situation alone and I needed help. Whenever I find it hard to forgive, I ask my "helpers" to really assist me.

One of the best things I do to let go and forgive is to write a Release Letter, which is a letter you write to your Higher Self that gives you total permission to release all aspects of a situation that needs forgiveness or a person it's time to cut ties with. This letter can also help you in your self-forgiveness. After you write this letter, create a ritual and burn it to complete the feeling of it being done.

Here is my letter for you to use. Simply fill in the blanks:

Date: _______________
Name: ______________

Dear Higher Self,

I ____________, hereby grant you, my Higher Self, my soul, my connection to Infinite Intelligence and all my spiritual helpers, my cellular memory, and all parts of myself that are holding on to negative feelings for any reason permission to release all the pain, misunderstandings, and misguided emotions, in my conscious mind and subconscious mind, to now release me from these thoughts, emotions, and beliefs to be free now and forever from the bitterness, anger, and grudges.

I ___________, thank you for assisting me to release all thoughts and memories that have kept me from forgiveness. I am now willing to see the situation as a soul growth. I release judgment and now release all non-beneficial thoughts. I am free.

I ___________, do now totally forgive _______.

I release ___________ to their own highest and best good and set them free. I totally see them as my teacher and I am willing to release them.

I ___________, now forgive myself and I love myself as I am right now, I am a perfect child of God.

I ___________, claim my own right to be free and live a life of happiness, health, prosperity, and love. All is in divine order and so be it.

Forgiveness is a Priceless Gift

Think of forgiveness as an act of survival because when you forgive someone or a situation, you are the one who will receive its benefits. Your forgiveness may not influence a change in the behavior of others at all. Forgiveness is for you and for generating your own healing. You are the only player in your life that has any power. Forgiveness is an exercise in true personal power because the past cannot be undone. What you can change is how you feel about it. You have the power to choose to feel better about who you are and move on with your life and future.

"The weak can never forgive.
Forgiveness is the attribute of the strong."
—Mahatma Gandhi

"People are often unreasonable and self-centered.
Forgive them anyway.
If you are kind, people may accuse you of ulterior motives.
Be kind anyway.
If you are honest, people may cheat you.
Be honest anyway.
If you find happiness, people may be jealous.
Be happy anyway.
The good you do today may be forgotten tomorrow.
Do good anyway.
Give the world the best you have and it may never be enough.
Give your best anyway.
For you see, in the end, it is between you and God.
It was never between you and them anyway."
—Mother Teresa

Think of forgiveness as a huge gift to you for your present life and your future. When you give yourself the gift of forgiveness, you are actually allowing yourself to heal and let go. Holding on to old grudges only causes stress in your life because your body and mind are a continuum. When you relieve your mental stress, your body will also relax. Guilt and hatred resolve nothing, they just sustain the negativity that continues to obstruct from your goals and dreams. Forgiveness undoes the stickiness that binds you to an unhappy past. You no longer have to carry the heavy bags of the past injustices and keep telling that story of you being a victim.

We are self-fulfilling prophecies and every time you tell the story of you being a victim, you actually create a vibration to attract more of the same into your life. Today is the day to truly release the resentment, bitterness, and anger and start a brand new life.

Magical Essences . . .

- When you forgive, you release the thoughts, grudges, and anger that take up your time and eat up your energy.
- To really claim the magic that is within you, you need to forgive yourself for anything you have done that you still feel guilty or upset about.
- There will be many people and situations or circumstances that you need to forgive to free up your Inner Energetic Blueprint to manifest new things in your life.
- Think of forgiveness as an act of survival because when you forgive someone or a situation, you are the one who will receive its benefits.

FOURTEEN

The Magic of Your Attitude

When I was a small child living on that farm in Chuckatuck, Virginia, my great-grandmother used to take me on her lap when I was unhappy and say to me, *"Choose to be joyful, because when you are joyful God can send His Angels to guide you and help you with anything you need. When you are unhappy God is still there but you just cannot hear Him so you cannot get the answers you want."*

I have never forgotten her words of wisdom to an upset child and I have found them to be so true. The more joy and lightheartedness I feel, the more in touch with my God Source I feel, and the more I can listen to the guidance that I am offered. The more guidance I get, the better my response in any situation and the greater service I can be in any situation.

In a way, my grandmother was teaching me that my emotions arise from my thoughts. Somehow she knew that if I focused on being joyful, I could not feel overwhelmed by negative feelings that seemed to have no solutions. She was teaching me that what we focus on expands. When you are consciously looking for joy you will find it, and it will grow.

You know in your heart that when you are feeling joyful, difficult people or situations do not have a lasting effect on you. You are more resourceful and open to new solutions. You handle stress and rejection much better. Joy turns routine tasks into enjoyable experiences, no matter what you are doing. Having fun is an important tool for a conscious magician. Henry Ward Beecher said, *"A person without a sense of humor is like a wagon without springs—jolted by every pebble in the road."*

Your goal must be to become conscious of the fact that this very moment in time is a precious gift. You can get the most power from any moment if you make up your mind to enjoy it. Appreciate it. Honor it. You are not on this earth to be unhappy or to waste your time and talents. You must make choices that allow your enthusiasm for life to stay with you.

The great Norman Vincent Peale once said, *"There is real magic in enthusiasm. It spells the difference between mediocrity and accomplishment."* Enthusiasm for your work will assist you in finding solutions where there appear to be none. Enthusiasm for your life will help you achieve success where it was thought to be impossible. Keep this in mind: information does not move people to action, but emotion does. So, if you want to improve your life and create better relationships, you have to improve your enthusiasm for what you do and how you do it.

I live on the beach at the mouth of the Chesapeake Bay. The view is breathtaking and very healing for me. I bought an oversized rocking chair for my deck and started a ritual of taking the time to enjoy sunset on the water when possible. One night as I was enjoying the view I overheard a bunch of kids at the waterfront. Sound travels around the water and I could hear one child say clearly, *"Do you know what I love? I love it when the seagulls fly over the water low then fly straight up in the sky."* All the kids giggled. The next voice was a little girl saying, *"Do you know what I love? I love it when my mom makes real mashed potatoes."* For the next twenty minutes each of these kids took turns talking about what they loved. They tried to outdo each other. I was enjoying overhearing all these young souls expressing joy!

After it got dark, the kids went home and I started hearing adults coming out on their porches and talking. The first conversation I overheard was a man saying, *"Do you know what I hate?"* Then the entire conversation with these adults was about what they did not like about life. These adults were having a contest on how much they dislike life. To be honest, it was depressing. I was so struck by the difference between the kids and adults. The kids were focused very much in the present moment and looking for the good in their lives, and they were so full of joy. The adults in this situation were only focusing on what they did not like and they were miserable!

Today is the day to give yourself permission to take a step back and see the big picture of your life. The past is a locked door; the future will depend on what you do today.

Sometimes we take ourselves very seriously, which may lead us to get stuck in old attitudes, perceptions, and habits. But when we stubbornly hold on to old ideas of the way things should be, we shut ourselves off from new ideas, interesting people, and exciting business ventures. Conscious magicians are more spontaneous and can laugh at their own mistakes. They see the brighter side of life. They know how to have fun and turn routine tasks into enjoyable experiences. That's using the magical tool of Joy.

Take to heart the very old but true saying: Life is a journey, not a destination. How much we enjoy this journey depends on where we focus our life energy. We have no real power over the external world, but we do have power to choose how it affects us.

Cultivating a sense of humor and a sense of joy can protect you from the negative attitudes and actions of others. Sir Francis Bacon said, *"Imagination was given to man to compensate for what he is not, and a sense of humor to console him for what he is."* A good sense of humor can keep you sane in difficult times, it keeps you balanced, gives you a sense of perspective, and can get you gracefully through many situations in which you would otherwise want to tear your hair out.

Remember your point of power is always this very moment in time. To reclaim your magic you must honor yourself and become aware of how you spend your life energy. You have 1,440 minutes each day to be conscious that every minute of your day is a precious gift. The more you fill your life with joy, the more lighthearted you are, and the more enthusiastically you do everything you have to do, the more you are contributing to life.

You can choose to look at your life as one of adventure and fun. You can wake up in the morning looking forward to the day. Make a conscious choice that you are going to enjoy what you do and how you do it. It's important to reconnect with your funny button and allow the child within you to come out and play.

Learn to be flexible in your attitude, to see the humor whenever possible and allow yourself to be human. Flexibility makes it possible to respond to change by adapting to varying conditions. Flexibility allows for growth and excitement. Being flexible will allow you to see new opportunities and capitalize on them.

One of the questions I always ask in my seminars is, "How many of you have let an old person move into your body?" People always laugh, but it's a good question to ask yourself occasionally. Have you gotten stuck in your attitudes, perceptions, and life habits? Have you allowed yourself to be older than your years?

Think of life as an adventure and enjoy the moment. Look for the lighter side of every situation and don't hesitate to laugh at yourself. Every time you laugh you increase your body's production of endorphins. Endorphins are the "feel good" hormones which imitate the effects of morphine in the body. Research suggests that laughter can, in fact, help improve resistance to pain and disease. Laughter can clearly help people feel better.

A good sense of humor keeps you sane in difficult times, keeps you balanced, gives you a sense of perspective, and it can get you gracefully through many situations in which it's clear you have no control over the circumstances. Choosing to see the humor in your life nurtures your creative side. This creative, positive side of yourself enables you to see new opportunities and to keep your spirits high in times of trial.

It is said that a well-developed sense of humor is one of the most charismatic qualities a person can have. The happiest people are self-accepting, spontaneous, and laugh at their own mistakes. They see the lighter side of life. They know how to have fun and turn routine tasks into enjoyable experiences. Nurture and value these qualities in yourself because they are very attractive!

"Laughter is the shortest distance between two people," stated Victor Borge. When you can help people laugh, they relax and feel more in harmony with you. A trust level is set up. Humor is one of the most important of your magical attitudes because it can diffuse anger and hostility, conquer pretense, and subdue inflated egos.

As I mentioned earlier, your emotions arise from your thoughts. To stop taking yourself so seriously, it's important to create an internal environment that supports you. Let's face it, there will be a lot of things you cannot change and the better your sense of humor, the better you're going to feel about yourself. Humor keeps us sane and gives us a sense of balance. Remember when you were a child; children love the absurdity of life. They do things for the sheer joy of it—they don't care about what others think. They do things simply to have fun. When you choose to have an attitude of joy, you will find fun everywhere.

Don't worry if you feel your sense of humor has been dampened in the past. You can learn to see and to use humor with a little practice, patience, and a willingness to let the lighter side of life shine through. Begin the process of lightening up with these joy-creating assignments.

Creating Joy

1. Take time to learn to tell funny stories and jokes. It's just like playing sports; the more practice you have at it, the better you will become. If you have not thought of yourself as funny in the past, begin by reminding yourself daily to notice and appreciate more humor in your life and work. People love to laugh and it's important for your success that you look for the humor in life. People really do say and do crazy things, and real life stories are the funniest to share!

2. Make a commitment to yourself to go out and play more often, maybe a comedy club, or an entertaining play or movie. Everyone needs to let go of their troubles for a short time to just relax and laugh. One of the greatest benefits of laughter is that it enables you to gain a new perspective on your problems.

3. Give yourself permission to watch some funny television and movies to lighten your mood. Life is serious enough without compounding it by watching drama, soap operas, and the news.

4. We become like the people with whom we associate daily. Pay attention to who is upbeat, supportive, and positive in your life and choose to be with them as

often as possible. The people who are funny, optimistic, and enjoy life will help you stay in a joyful state.

5. Look for the good news. What you focus on expands. Don't let the daily grind of the news deflate your optimistic attitude. Do not dwell on the negative news on television, radio or newspapers. Balance your life with what you need to know, but do not focus on what you cannot control.

6. Look for funny cartoons and keep a funny file. Send funny cartoons to friends or clients. Keep them around the office for humor.

7. Start or join an e-mail joke list. One of my suppliers called me a few months ago and asked if I wanted to be put on his humor e-mail list. At least once a week, he sends me a collection of very funny jokes. It's an effective and unique way to advertise to me. Next time I need what he supplies, am I going to think of him? You bet! IMPORTANT: Make sure all jokes and cartoons do not create harm. Using humor to slander anyone is not a magical approach.

8. Create a new label for yourself. Learn to think of yourself as a flexible person. Give yourself permission—and lots of reminders—to rule your own mind no matter what the outside world throws at you. Commit to being a more flexible person for the next thirty days and notice how much more productive and creative you can become. When you choose to do things differently, you give yourself the opportunity to see your life and your work from a totally different perspective. You become more conscious of how your thoughts form your actions, which form your habits, and how these habits shape your future.

Framing Your Focus

Most of us go through life making things tougher for ourselves. Without realizing it, we have programmed ourselves not to enjoy our present moments. We ambush our minds with negative, self-defeating messages like, *"This job is too hard, and I wish I didn't have to do deal with these people. I'm not good at this."*

Behavior experts say that about 80 percent of our thoughts are negative. These negative, self-defeating thoughts literally program our Inner Energetic Blueprint to overlook the joy in our lives. Why are we doing this to ourselves? It's hard to feel motivated to keep going or to start new projects when you've pre-framed yourself to believe that things are going to be difficult. Stop programming yourself to believe that life is hard.

The good news is that you can program your brain to have fun doing something before you do it. Start paying attention to where you make your life and your job harder than they need to be. Since what we focus on increases, choose to focus on creating a life where you're lighthearted, have fun, and feel creative and relaxed. When you allow yourself to have fun, and to not take yourself so seriously, your performance usually improves because you are not so tense and stressed out.

The Magic of Gratitude

If you want true inner transformation then you must practice gratitude. It will raise your vibration and attract what you desire. Having gratitude is the single most powerful step towards inner peace you can invoke. We have established that everything is energy and everything and everyone are connected. The energy of gratitude has its own frequency and when you think thoughts of appreciation and gratitude, you can shift your abilities to manifest exactly what you want in life into high gear.

Gratitude tells the universe what you want and creates the feeling of having exactly what you want right now, which activates the Law of Attraction. Feeling abundance through gratitude gives you a magnetic vibrational draw to attract to you exactly what you want.

The old saying what you focus on expands is true. When you are in a state of appreciation and thankfulness, you will attract more magical experiences in your life. When you are in a state of negativity, entitlement, or resentment, you are going to vibrate at a rate that is a lower vibration and will clearly not bring light or prosperity energy back to you. If you want to enjoy more loving relationships, better collaboration and cooperation, better health, and live in a state of abundance, then gratitude has to be your attitude of choice.

When you take the time to identify what is good in your life, you are using your mind and your energy to feel good about yourself and others. That good-feeling state has a huge impact on your overall state of mind. If you feel happier and more content, you have more confidence. When you have more confidence, you'll naturally be more willing to step forward in your life. You'll be more optimistic and creative; you'll see new ideas and ways to capitalize on those ideas. This is the mindset that gives you the opportunity to truly see life with a renewed sense of love and enthusiasm that will then attract the people, things, and opportunities you want into your life. It all starts with your feelings of gratitude for your current blessings!

Webster's Dictionary defines gratitude as: "A feeling of thankfulness and appreciation." It is also described as a state of feeling or being grateful. Gratitude is a positive emotion that focuses on expressing appreciation.

An attitude of gratitude helps you put life into perspective and see how blessed you really are in the big picture of life.

Feeling a sense of appreciation of what is good in life will also help you get through life's big challenges. Gratitude helps you maintain that child-like sense of wonder and love of life. Being grateful lowers stress levels and helps release feelings of depression. Your mind can only focus on one thought at a time so deliberately focusing on what is good in your life pushes out of your mind what you are unhappy about.

Why are Gratitude and Appreciation Important?

"Cultivate the habit of being grateful for every good thing that comes to you, and to give thanks continuously. And because all things have contributed to your advancement, you should include all things in your gratitude."
—Ralph Waldo Emerson

1. Appreciation and gratitude cultivate and encourage positive immune responses, moods, relationships, and aptitudes of success according to university research. Gratitude helps you stay mentally and physically healthy, promotes connectedness with your relationships, and gives you an edge with your business.

2. Gratitude is at the center of all the world's spiritual traditions.

3. Gratitude awakens the heart intelligence. The power of the world comes from love energy and when you feel gratitude you literally stimulate the electrical output of heart intelligence.

4. Gratitude produces endorphins in your system. When you focus on what is good in your life you feel

expansive, energized, hopeful, comforted, and pleasurable freedom.

5. Gratitude is attractive. There is a true magic about appreciation that makes people want to be in your presence. When you carry thoughts of gratitude and appreciation within you, they radiate outward into your world and will attract joyous results into your life. You have to *feel* successful, worthy, and blessed to be able to attract those things into your life.

Suggestions to Practice Gratitude and Appreciation

Realize just how blessed you already are in this very moment. Start a list of the blessings you enjoy, even the simple ones you may be taking for granted. Many people don't focus on what is good in their lives and careers until they've lost them. Become conscious of all of your blessings right now and see how thankful you can feel.

1. Be thankful in advance: One of the most powerful forms of gratitude is expressing your appreciation for something before your actual experience of it. When you do, you shift your Inner Energetic Blueprint into one that attracts what you are grateful for.

"When you are grateful, fear disappears and abundance appears."
—Anthony Robbins

2. Find things to be grateful about in negative situations. No one says this is easy but since you are reclaiming the magic within you, start to look for things you can appreciate about the situation. If you are having a conflict with someone, be grateful that

the situation has forced you to grow or that you only have to be around that person every few months.

3. Write daily a gratitude list of what you are truly grateful for each day to guarantee you will attract more of that in your life. Commit to a consistent gratitude practice because it will shift any negative momentum you have going from being upset or stressed out. By simply taking the time to list everything you are grateful for, your inner experience will shift, which will cause a shift in your external experiences as well.

4. Start a Gratitude Journal. Dedicate a journal to appreciation and gratitude. By acknowledging the blessings in your life that you are deeply grateful for, you imprint your life energy to stay in high frequencies for your Inner Energetic Blueprint attraction. In his book, *A New Earth: Awakening to Your Life's Purpose,* author Eckhart Tolle said: *"Acknowledging the good that you already have in your life is the foundation for all abundance."*

5. Have some fun when you do social media posts or write letters. Start with celebratory beginnings: Start each line with "Hooray!" Note blessings, achievements, or anything going your way! This is a fun way to ramp up your energy, acknowledge the blessings around you, and be a grand example to others.

6. *Love Notes*: Take the time to write little notes of appreciation to all the people in your life you truly love and treasure. This can include your mate, friends, children, parents, co-workers, neighbors, employees, or people who help you in any way. I personally always slip love notes into my husband's suitcases when he travels, and put sticky notes on the pillow and his bathroom mirror. The gesture he seems to like the best is the ready-to-drink cup

of coffee first thing in the morning. I also write thank you on the paycheck stubs I give to my staff and vendors. One vendor recently told me I was the only person in his career who always thanked him for his invoices and services!

7. As I have shared in a previous chapter, when you script your life story out write how incredibly grateful you felt about the blessings in your life. *"[Gratitude] turns what we have into enough, and more. It turns denial into acceptance,"* writes Melody Beattie.

8. *Speak Gratitude*: When you honestly can say thank you, it is more than good manners because it is truly an affirmation of appreciation. Say thank you as often as possible, letting people know you acknowledge their gift of service or kindness.

9. Hand-write a sincere thank-you note for gifts, favors, and opportunities such as a job interview or someone sharing information that empowered you. The late President John F. Kennedy said: *"We must find time to stop and thank the people who make a difference in our lives."*

It's important to write a thank-you note anytime someone has gone out of their way to gift you their energy, knowledge, or time. I grew up in an era that if someone gave you a gift or did something nice for you, you sat down and took the time and effort to hand write a thank-you note to that person with real appreciation and feeling.

This concept may seem quaint and old-fashioned today, but I know that if I take the time to go out and choose a gift for someone, wrap it, buy a card, and either deliver it personally or mail it and I don't receive a handwritten thank-you note, I do not feel appreciated for the time and effort I put into the gift. There was no fair exchange of energy. This leaves the person who put forth the effort feeling a sense of lack of appreciation. That creates a lack of motivation to invest your life energy in people who are not grateful for your efforts.

In today's world if you get a get a text, e-mail, or just a verbal thank-you, most people think that is enough. It's tough to stay motivated to give another gift in the future when you don't feel appreciated. What you sow is what you get in the world. If people cannot take the time to sincerely show appreciation and gratitude for efforts for them, it shows a deep lack of caring.

Food for thought: A simple and sincere hand-written thank-you note can open doors, get you jobs, seal a deal, and express sincere love and appreciation in a way that no text, Facebook message, email, or any other electronic gadget can do. If you have fallen into the bad habit of substituting electronic thank-yous for gifts and opportunities, I will assure you that that message will be so energetically and emotionally diluted that it will not make an impact of gratitude. I love this quote from Brené Brown: *"What separates privilege from entitlement is gratitude."*

10. Express Gratitude and blessings for your food. When I was growing up we always gave thanks for the food on the table in front of us. We blessed it and gave it life force energy before eating it. We gave thanks to all those who grew it, prepared it, and served it. By taking the time to feel gratitude for your food, you will appreciate the taste, textures, and colors of it more and your body will receive the nutrients from the food since you have blessed it. Taking the time to pray over food has given me a foundation of knowledge of how lucky I am to have the abundance of good food in my life. If you are not currently taking a minute before you eat anything to offer thanks this would be a good time to start this life-enhancing habit.

Another positive habit you and your loved ones can adopt is when you sit down for a family dinner, go around the table and have each person share something they are grateful for that happened that day before you start to eat. It will become a very positive habit and shift any stressful events into the focus of how blessed you are daily. In her book, *Living with Joy: Keys to Personal Power and Spiritual Transformation*, author Sanaya Roman said: "*Whatever you appreciate and give thanks for will increase in your life.*"

Affirmations for Gratitude

- I am blessed daily with the wisdom, tools, skills, and assistance to be successful in all my undertakings.
- I am deeply grateful for all the people in my life who assist me.
- I am in profound gratitude for being connected to Infinitive Intelligence and my spiritual helpers.
- In gratitude, I am in harmony with the creative energies of the universe.
- I am grateful for all I have and all that is coming to me from divine sources.
- I am grateful to have my health, my intelligence, and vitality.

Please create affirmations to use daily to increase your ability to feel and acknowledge the blessings in your world.

"To be grateful is to recognize the Love of God in everything He has given us—and He has given us everything. Every breath we draw is a gift of His love, every moment of

existence is a grace, for it brings with it immense graces from Him. Gratitude therefore takes nothing for granted, is never unresponsive, is constantly awakening to new wonder and to praise of the goodness of God. For the grateful person knows that God is good, not by hearsay but by experience."
—Thomas Merton

Release Your Need to Be Perfect All the Time

One of the sources of stress in our lives is our own requirement to appear to be perfect to our families, clients, and bosses. Here are a few phrases for you to practice saying until you are completely comfortable with them. Knowing when to use them and how to use them with integrity will free you to be flexible and creative.

I Don't Know

Many times we won't say, "I don't know" because we're afraid others will think we're incompetent. It's okay to not know everything—no one does. What you might say is, "That is a very good question and since I am not 100 percent sure of the answer, I will find out and get back to you." Then, just be sure you do get back to them with the correct information when you promised. No worries!

I Need Help

Everyone needs help from time to time. No one can be all things to all people. People with no support system burn out early in the game. Create a support system that can be there for you when you need help. Think about the situations you face in your job and know in advance how you might need assistance and who might be helpful to you. And don't forget to be helpful to others in the process. What goes around, comes around!

It Was My Mistake or I Was Wrong

No one is right all the time. Even a genius will have the wrong information sometimes. When you're wrong, admit it, because if you don't, someone else will say it for you. I recommend that you apologize at once, then utilize your valuable emotional energy to go right into problem solving. Right away, ask, "What can we do to fix this situation?"

If appropriate, you might try a light-hearted response, acknowledging your mistake and joking about the predicament. When you resort to a gently self-deprecating demeanor and make fun of the situation, you are conveying grace under pressure, confidence, and credibility. Remember that the ability to laugh at your own errors gives you the flexibility to respond appropriately to difficulties and adversities. You will be better able to keep life in perspective.

No

It's hard to say "no" to people because we want them to like us. We end up giving too much of ourselves—or our profit—because we don't want to disappoint anyone. Setting appropriate boundaries is crucial in every aspect of your life. Everyone—and every job—has to have boundaries.

The position I now take is to be clear about my boundaries and to tell the truth with kindness (because the truth will set you free). In life, it's more important to be respected than liked.

It's Not My Job to Make Everyone Happy

There is no way on earth you can make everyone happy. You cannot be all things to all people. Your job is to be the best and do the best that you can.

I was presenting a seminar a few years ago called "Visionary Sales Training." We had a no-questions-asked refund policy and anyone could get a full refund of the seminar fee before noon of each day, for any reason. My program manager came up to me at lunch one day and said, *"I have now seen everything to be seen in the public seminar business."* She had been outside trying to catch up on paperwork and all she could hear from inside the ballroom was the audience just having a ball, laughing and enjoying themselves. On the first break, some of the seminar attendees told her it was the best seminar they had every attended and they were totally enjoying the day. Out of the blue at 11:00 a.m., a woman attendee came to the back table and asked for a refund. The program manager said she was totally shocked when the woman blurted out. *"I cannot learn anything in there; people are just having way too much fun!"* We happily gave her a refund.

Some people live with a belief system that requires that anything new they want to learn or to do has to be difficult and taught in a serious manner. I have just the opposite opinion. The more fun you are having as you learn or do something, the better your brain will function, and the better your work, your relationships, and your life will be.

Start Now!

Life can be a fun adventure. Stop putting off enjoying your life. There are no guarantees that we will be here tomorrow! Your attitude and your behavior affect the results you get in your daily work and in your life. What positive messages can you give yourself to keep yourself feeling good? How can you be a better role model? How can you have more fun and truly enjoy your life instead of just going through the motions?

While you can, tell the people you love that you love them and tell them often. Send flowers, write notes, give candy, do special things for the people you care about. Be nice to yourself. Realize that life is too short to sweat the small stuff. And, let's face it, folks, most stuff we worry about truly is small stuff in the big picture of life. It's never money or material possessions that really make you happy; it's your relationships with yourself and others. It's the quality of time you have in your life. It's your health and vitality to enjoy life that makes you happy. True peace of mind and joy come from the moments and feelings that count in life, not from material things.

Whatever you have wanted to do in your life but were waiting for the perfect time to do, stop putting it off—*start now!* Whether it's going back to school, starting a family, or enjoying a hobby, stop wasting your precious life away and start doing what brings you joy.

Magical Essences . . .

- Our emotions arise from our thought.
- When you are consciously looking for joy, you will find it and it will grow.
- Enthusiasm for your work will assist you in finding solutions where there appear to be none. Enthusiasm for your life will help you achieve success where it was thought impossible. Information does not move people to action, but emotion does.
- When we stubbornly hold on to old ideas of the way things should be, we shut ourselves off from

new ideas, interesting people, and exciting business ventures.

- Cultivating a sense of humor and a sense of joy can protect you from the negative attitudes and actions of others.

- Honor yourself and become aware of how you spend your life energy.

- A good sense of humor keeps you sane in difficult times, keeps you balanced, gives you a sense of perspective, and it can get you gracefully through many situations.

- You can program your brain to have fun doing something before you do it.

- The more fun you are having as you learn or do something, the better your brain will function, and the better your work, your relationships, and your life will be.

- The energy of gratitude has its own frequency and when you think thoughts of appreciation and gratitude, you can shift your abilities to manifest exactly what you want in life into high gear.

Afterword

The theme of this book is that *life is not happening to you*. Life is responding to you. Daily we have the opportunity to start fresh and reinvent our life, improve it, and manage our life energy so we get the results we want. Life always responds to who you are, and what you are thinking and feeling.

There is an old saying: If your path is more difficult, it is because of your high calling. Because you are reading this book, I know you have a high calling in life. You are from the family of light and our job is to assist the earth consciousness to evolve into a higher state. That means you must love yourself as you are right now. In order to love who you are, you cannot dislike the experiences that have shaped you. We do not attract what we want—we attract what we feel. Today you are who you are because of your past life experiences, so be grateful for them all. If you want to improve your life, you have the power to do so by taking charge of the information you allow into your world.

We're living in a whole new model of reality, a new paradigm, and by adding a spiritual dimension to your life and partnering with Infinite Intelligence, you can improve your ability to not only be of service to others, but to increase your own enjoyment and passion in all aspects of your life.

Now is the time for you to stop hiding who you really are and come out and be your authentic self. You have within you the ability to manifest what you decide you want.

If you would like some additional assistance, please come join me for my free weekly e-zine, Spiritual Power Tools for Profit and Purpose. Go to *www.spiriutalpowertools.com/freenewsletter*. I will be sharing more about the adventure of my life and weekly tips on how you can be a better manifestor. If this book has assisted you, I would love to hear from you. I would also like to encourage you to share this book with others so we, as light workers, can help bring light and love to the world. Remember your point of power in this life is this moment in time. To change your life all you have to do is change your mind and take action!

Love, Light, and Blessings to You.

Lee Milteer
www.milteer.com

Personal Notes

Bibliography

Addington, Jack, and Cornelia Addington, *Your Needs Met.* Marina del Ray, CA: DeVorss and Company, 1999.

Allen, Marc, *Visionary Business: An Entrepreneur's Guide to Success.* Novato, CA: New World Library. 1995.

Anand, Margot, *The Art of Everyday Ecstasy: The Seven Tantric Keys for Bringing Passion, Spirit and Joy into Every Part of Your Life.* New York: Broadway Books, 1998.

Covey, Stephen, *The Seven Habits of Highly Effective People: Restoring the Character Ethic.* New York: Fireside Books, 1990.

Day, Laura, *Practical Intuition.* New York: Broadway Books, 1996.

DeMarco, Frank, *The Cosmic Internet.* Faber, VA: Rainbow Ridge Books, 2011.

Dyer, Wayne, *Dr. Wayne Dyer's 10 Secrets for Success and Inner Peace.* Carlsbad, CA: Hay House, 2001.

Green, Brian, *The Fabric of the Cosmos.* Nova, PBS, July, 2012.

Hill, Napoleon, *Think & Grow Rich.* New York: Ballantine, 1960.

Hilton, Conrad, *Be My Guest.* New York: Simon & Schuster, 1994.

Holmes, Ernest, *The Science of Mind, The Complete Edition.* New York: Tarcher, 2010.

Kennedy, Dan, *NO B.S. Business Success*. Irvine, CA: Entrepreneur Media, 2004.

Maltz, Maxwell, *Psycho-Cybernetics: A New Way to Get More Living out of Life*. Englewood Cliffs, NJ: Prentice-Hall, 1960.

Nicklaus, Jack, *Golf My Way*. New York: Simon & Schuster, 1974.

Owen, Amanda, *Born to Receive: Seven Powerful Steps Women Can Take Today to Reclaim Their Half of the Universe*. New York: Penguin, 2014.

Peck, M. Scott, *The Road Less Traveled: A New Psychology of Love, Traditional Values, and Spiritual Growth*. New York: Simon & Schuster, 2002.

Roman, Sanaya, *Personal Power Through Awareness: A Guidebook for Sensitive People*. Tiburon, CA: H.J. Kramer, 1986.

Rowan, Roy, *The Intuitive Manager*. Boston: Little Brown and Company, 1986.

Ruiz, Don Miguel, *The Four Agreements: A Practical Guide to Personal Freedom*. San Rafael, CA: Amber-Allen, 1997.

Tolle, Eckhart, *A New Earth: Awakening to Your Life's Purpose*. New York: Penguin, 2005.

Wilde, Stuart, *Sixth Sense: Including the Secrets of the Etheric Subtle Body*. Carlsbad, CA: Hay House, 2000.

Williamson, Marianne, *A Return to Love: Reflections on the Principles of "A Course in Miracles."* New York: Harper Collins, 1992.

About Lee Milteer

Lee Milteer is an intuitive business coach, best-selling author, blogger, award-winning professional speaker, and TV personality. She is the founder of the Millionaire Smarts® Coaching Program, and runs the Peak Performers—Implementation Coaching Program for entrepreneurs from all over the world. Lee hosts the America's Premier Experts TV show, which is aired on NBC, CBS, ABC, and Fox Affiliates. Lee also hosts Untamed Success: Positive TV, a monthly web-based TV show. Lee speaks all over North America and Europe at conventions, private companies, and entrepreneurial and niche market events.

As president of Lee Milteer, Inc., Career Development Strategists, she has counseled and trained over a million people with her speeches. Her presentations are so effective that organizations such as Walt Disney, AT&T, XEROX, IBM, Ford Motor Co., NASA, Federal Express, 3M, Sales & Marketing Executive International, plus hundreds of government agencies and scores of conventions, associations meetings, and niche market events repeatedly retain her to inspire and motivate their audiences.

In her career, Lee Milteer has shared the platform with many well-known and famous personalities, such as Dr. Phil, Tony Robbins, Deepak Chopra, Dan Kennedy, Bill Glazer, Stephen Covey, Brian Tracy, the late Zig Ziglar, the late Dr. Norman Vincent Peale, the late Og Mandino, Jack Canfield, Mark Victor Hansen from the *Chicken Soup* book fame, Robert Cialdini,

T. Harv Eker, Coach Mike Ditka, Les Brown, Wally "Famous" Amos, Larry Winget, Gene Simmons from KISS, George Ross (Donald Trump's chief negotiator who appeared on the TV show *The Apprentice*), country western star and TV show *Apprentice* winner John Rich, reality TV star Ivanka Trump, news anchor Ted Koppel, movie star Lynn Redgrave, Marlo Thomas, TV Superman Dean Cain, former two-time World Heavyweight Champion and Olympic gold medalist George Foreman, British singer-songwriter Sade, the late comedian Joan Rivers, and Adam West from the Batman TV series, to mention a few.

Lee has created and hosted educational programs airing on PBS and other cable networks throughout the U.S. and Canada. Her video seminars are distributed through the Mind Extension Universe (MEU) Network, reaching 350 of the top FORTUNE 500 companies and major universities. She has developed training films for Bell Telephone, the U.S. Navy, Dun & Bradstreet, the U.S. Air Force, and many private companies, as well as hosting infomercials and TV commercials.

Lee is a recognized award-winning, best-selling audio and video author, whose products have been endorsed by Nightingale Conant, SyberVision, CareerTrack, and GKIC. Lee has written and co-authored 11 books: *Success Is An Inside Job*, *Spiritual Power Tools for Successful Selling*, *Reach Your Career Dreams*, *Walking with the Wise for Entrepreneurs*, *The Secrets of Peak Performers One and Two*, *The Phenomenon: Achieve More in the Next 12 Months than the Previous 12 Years*, *Ultimate Entrepreneur Success Secrets*, *Walking with The Wise Overcoming Obstacles*, and-*Women who Mean Business*. Lee has been featured in Woman Millionaires, and her programs and articles are translated into Japanese, Russian, Dutch, and Spanish, among other languages.

Lee has been an expert guest on more than 700 TV and radio shows on national and international TV and radio. She has been interviewed in newspapers, magazines, and trade journals all over the world, including *U.S.A. TODAY, Wall Street Journal,* and was featured in *INC.* magazine and The Huffington Post.

Lee hosted and produced her own cable television show, "Lee Milteer's Lifestyles," and had her own advice segment on Canada's #1 rated daytime talk show, "The Dini Petty Show."

A Reiki Master Healer and Metaphysician, Lee runs the Lee Milteer School of Wisdom which offers Metaphysical Mystery School and Mastermind Coaching for spiritually-minded business people.

Lee is not only a successful businesswoman, she is also a talented artist, writer, photographer, and painter who has shown and sold her work in galleries and art shows.

Lee lives on the beach in Virginia Beach, Virginia on the Chesapeake Bay and Atlantic Ocean with her dog "Angel," cat "Midnight," and her husband Clifton Williams. Her hobbies are painting, photography, reading, walking on the beach, and adventure traveling. Her favorite charities are the SPCA and animal rescue organizations. She owns her own office building where her publishing company, Lee Milteer Publishing, is located in Virginia Beach, Virginia.

Lee's background includes extensive experience in sales and marketing and commercial real estate. She was the owner and president of an electronics equipment sales and leasing company. Lee also traveled all over the world as a professional photographer. In addition, she has been a rock and roll disc jockey for WNOR-FM in Norfolk, Virginia and a former national catalog model.

In recognition of her achievements, Lee Milteer was awarded the title of Dame of the Order of the Imperial and Charitable Order of Constantine the Great and Saint Helen, which is one of the oldest Orders of Knighthood in the world. Lady Lee Milteer was honored for her contribution to mankind, human values, and quality of character.

Lee received an Honorary Doctorate in Motivational Theory from Commonwealth College. She attained top honors as "Highest Rated Speaker," presenting public seminars in over 100 cities annually while with CareerTrack, North America's premier seminar and training company. She was awarded the "Rising Star Award" by General Cassette Corporation, named "Most Outstanding Young Woman" by the Jaycees and "Most Professional Woman in Hampton Roads." She also received "Entrepreneurial Woman of the Year" from the National Association of Women Business Owners for the Southeastern Chapter, and "The Best of Virginia Beach in Training and Services." Lee's latest awards are: The Inside Business Women in Business Award, and the Inside Business & Regent University Entrepreneurial Excellence Award.

Lee has worked with the SPCA, horse rescue organizations, WVEC, WTKR, WHRO, and WAVY TV stations as an on-air personality for charities such as Easter Seals and more. Lee has donated time to the NSA chapters of Virginia for Speakers, spoken for many nonprofit organizations to help them raise funds for their projects, plus countless high schools and colleges to assist students. Lee also works for the Charitable Order of Constantine The Great and Saint Helen to raise money for needy children.

Special Free Gift Exclusive to the Readers of This Book!

Love getting free stuff?

Because I believe in providing value and teaching others to get the most from their lives, I'd like to offer you an additional *free* Program called *Deliberate Creators: Strategies for Manifesting the Life You Want.*

Deliberate Creators: Strategies for Manifesting the Life You Want is the perfect companion to *Reclaim the Magic* to help improve the quality of your life. My *Deliberate Creators* program will give you a specific set of strategies and exercises that you can enact today. You'll gain a laser beam focus to define and create exactly what you want in your life. *Deliberate Creators* provides you with guided exercises that will allow you to play and envision the life you truly want to live. Your thoughts determine exactly what you experience in your life, so why not live big?

This program includes a 68-page Play Book and Audio CD. Normally $129, *Deliberate Creators* is yours for FREE. You just pay shipping.

Here's how to get your free copy: Simply go to *www.milteer.com/creator* to order *Deliberate Creators.* At checkout, enter the coupon code: MAGICBOOK and simply pay shipping.

Related Titles

If you enjoyed *Reclaim the Magic,* you may also enjoy other Rainbow Ridge titles. Read more about them at *www.rainbowridgebooks.com.*

Conversations with Jesus: An Intimate Journey
by Alexis Eldridge

Dance of the Electric Hummingbird
by Patricia Walker

Coming Full Circle: Ancient Teachings for a Modern World
by Lynn Andrews

Consciousness: Bridging the Gap Between Conventional Science and the New Super Science of Quantum Mechanics
by Eva Herr

Jesusgate: A History of Concealment Unraveled
by Ernie Bringas

Messiah's Handbook: Reminders for the Advanced Soul
by Richard Bach

Blue Sky, White Clouds
by Eliezer Sobel

Inner Vegas: Creating Miracles, Abundance, and Health
by Joe Gallenberger

When the Horses Whisper
by Rosalyn Berne

Channeling Harrison, Book 1
by David Young

Lessons in Courage
by Bonnie Glass-Coffin and don Oscar Miro-Quesada

Dying to Know You: Proof of God in the Near-Death Experience
by P.M.H. Atwater

The Cosmic Internet: Explanations from the Other Side
by Frank DeMarco

Afterlife Conversations with Hemingway: A Dialogue on His Life, His Work and the Myth
by Frank DeMarco

God's Message to the World: You've Got Me All Wrong
by Neale Donald Walsch

Rainbow Ridge Books publishes spiritual, metaphysical, and self-help titles, and is distributed by Square One Publishers in Garden City Park, New York.

To contact authors and editors, peruse our titles, and see submission guidelines, please visit our website at *www.rainbowridgebooks.com.*